"This book is a desperately needed examination into the extensive impact that our food system has on our planet."

Randy Hayes, Founder of Rainforest Action Network

"Every food that we eat has an impact on our planet and our society. *The Avocado Debate* is a timely consideration of the journey of one fruit."

Vicki Hird, author of Rebugging the Planet

"*The Avocado Debate* is a much-needed examination of the far-ranging impact that one food can have on our society and our planet."

Rob Percival, author of The Meat Paradox

"Honor Eldridge's exploration of questions around global food trade and sustainability is both needed and timely."

Patrick Holden, Founder of the Sustainable Food Trust

THE AVOCADO DEBATE

Whether smashed on toast or hailed as a superfood, the avocado has taken the world by storm, but what are the environmental and social impacts of this trendy fruit?

This book does not seek to demonise the avocado and its many enthusiasts. Instead, it will illuminate consumers on the often unseen impacts of foods. A staple of cafes, restaurants, homes, and social media channels, demand for the avocado has grown exponentially over the past thirty years. From an everyday crop in South and Central America to a global phenomenon, this drastic change in demand has many consequences for people and the planet. As demand grows, so does the need for more land, with land clearances threatening habitats and biodiversity. As production grows, so does global distribution and the impacts that air and sea travel have on the environment. The shift from a local to a global product disturbs the local food system, raising serious questions around food sovereignty and food justice and the importance of establishing an agricultural system that is both environmentally and socially just. While focusing here on the avocado, this book allows readers to gain a better understanding of the food system as a whole. In doing so, it empowers us all to think carefully and critically about the environmental and ethical implications of our food choices more broadly. We shouldn't feel guilty about eating avocados, we should simply understand the impact of doing so.

This book is essential reading for all who are interested in learning more about the food system, sustainable diets, and the relationship between farming and the environment.

Honor May Eldridge has worked on sustainable food policy for the past decade in both the USA and the UK. During this time, she has focused on the environmental and social impact of agricultural systems and produced a wealth of reports and briefings for political and civil society audiences. She has worked both in and out of government, including for the Food Standards Agency, Sustainable Food Trust, the Soil Association, and the Center for Food Safety.

Changing Planet

Changing Planet publishes books addressing some of the most critical and controversial issues of our time relating to the environment and sustainable living. The series covers a broad spectrum of topics, from climate change, conservation, and food, to waste, energy, and policy, speaking to the varied and pressing issues that both human and non-human animals face on our planet today.

The Avocado Debate
Honor May Eldridge

For more information about this series, please visit: www.routledge.com/ Changing-Planet/book-series/CPL

THE AVOCADO DEBATE

HONOR MAY ELDRIDGE

Routledge
Taylor & Francis Group

LONDON AND NEW YORK

Designed cover image: © Getty Images

First published 2024
by Routledge
4 Park Square, Milton Park, Abingdon, Oxon OX14 4RN

and by Routledge
605 Third Avenue, New York, NY 10158

Routledge is an imprint of the Taylor & Francis Group, an informa business

British Library Cataloguing-in-Publication Data
A catalogue record for this book is available from the British Library

Library of Congress Cataloging-in-Publication Data
Names: Eldridge, Honor May, author.
Title: The avocado debate / Honor May Eldridge.
Description: New York, NY: Routledge, 2024 |
Includes bibliographical references and index.
Identifiers: LCCN 2023015669 (print) | LCCN 2023015670 (ebook) |
ISBN 9781032443935 (hardback) | ISBN 9781032443898 (paperback) |
ISBN 9781003371915 (ebook)
Subjects: LCSH: Avocado industry. | Avocado—Environmental aspects. |
Environmental ethics.
Classification: LCC HD9259.A95 E44 2024 (print) |
LCC HD9259.A95 (ebook) | DDC 338.1/74653—dc23/eng/20230707
LC record available at https://lccn.loc.gov/2023015669
LC ebook record available at https://lccn.loc.gov/2023015670

ISBN: 978-1-032-44393-5 (hbk)
ISBN: 978-1-032-44389-8 (pbk)
ISBN: 978-1-003-37191-5 (ebk)

DOI: 10.4324/9781003371915

Typeset in Joanna
by codeMantra

With thanks to:
My wonderful editors at Routledge for their support
My incredible research assistant, Lachlan McKessar
Rebecca Marcone and Maeve Pierson for their hard work
My patient husband, Simon
and our guac-a-bye baby, Coretta

CONTENTS

PROLOGUE

We should not demonise the avocado. It has done nothing wrong. Yet public discourse has made it into a green gremlin.

There has always been controversy around it, but today, there is a fresh crop of criticism that comes at it from all angles. Newspaper articles claim that it is stealing water from local communities. Swathes of Central and South America are going thirsty because of the unending demand for avocados with orchards draining the aquifers underneath so that rivers run dry. TV shows detail the fruit's complicity in the violence and corruption of drug cartels. The tone is so overblown that it almost implies that there is blood on the hands of anyone who has ever dipped a chip into a dish of guacamole. Pundits claim it's the reason why Millennials cannot buy houses due to their insatiable addiction to avocado toast. Apparently an entire generation would opt for brunch over home ownership because they are unable to resist the creamy, delicious taste of smashed avocados.

On the other side, it is also presented as the greatest food of all time. The avocado is exalted as a superfood. Hyperbolic claims are made about its nutritional value: it can cure cancer, reduce the risk of heart attack, and remedy inflammation. Women's health magazine and beauty blogs talk about its incredible powers as if the avocado is itself the fountain of eternal youth. Just by eating one, you can become a slim, tanned, beach goddess. It immediately evokes visions of surfer cool – of Bondi Beach or Malibu. It promises not only sex appeal but also sexual desire – an aphrodisiac to rival oysters, chocolate, or lobster.

This public attention has given the avocado cult-like status; the fruit that launched a million GIFs and memes. People seem obsessed! A quick

Google presents options to purchase avocado pyjamas, sketch books, mugs, pillow covers, necklaces, phone covers, cuddly toys, and socks. Cute little eyes peeking out over a round little pot-bellied pith – two million years of evolution reduced down to an emoji. The fruit has come to represent an entire generation. Something that no other food stuff can claim. Anyone born between 1981 and 1996 is immediately assumed to adore the fruit and be borderline addicted. Building on the association with the Millennial generation, the avocado has become a symbol of the polarisation between generations. In the growing war between the Millennial and the Boomer, the avocado has become a battleground.

But the avocado is neither good nor bad. It is more a question of how it was grown. It is the method of production that creates the knock-on impacts – some intentional, some accidental. Grown in an organic system, the price of a single avocado will be prohibitively expensive, denying low-income communities a healthy, delicious food. Mass produced in a high-yield, high-intensity system, the environment will suffer from biodiversity loss and ecosystem damage. But the avocado is not unique in this – it is true of almost any food.

The goal of this book is to explore and expose the complexity of our modern food system through the avocado. No longer a food of indigenous peoples, it has become a global commodity crop. What historical forces caused this to happen? From its beginnings in the highlands of Puebla, Mexico, it is now cultivated and consumed the world over. This has not happened accidently. It has happened through careful and deliberative action that transformed the fruit's cultivation and reputation reputation. A transformation that has taken decades (and considerable investment) to achieve, but yet has been imperceptible to the average person.

The fruit's impact becomes all the more complicated in our globalised world. What does it mean to grow fruit halfway around the world and ship it thousands of miles to reach a consumer? Does that bring wealth and prosperity into an agrarian community that would otherwise have limited opportunity? Or does it take natural resources away from an impoverished Global South held hostage by free market capitalism? Are food miles inherently bad? Is it better to buy local? Have 21st-century consumers become accustomed to having access to food regardless of the season? This book aims to consider those tensions.

As said by Tim Lang, professor of Food Policy at City University in London, avocados are the perfect example of what happens when "an exotic food becomes normalised with no thinking through of the consequences."[1]

Each chapter in this book aims to present and weigh the different effects of avocado production and consumption, with the intention of guiding the reader to make their own assessment. As citizens, we need to consider how our choices impact the world around us and shape the future. Increasingly mindful of the power of their purse, consumers want to know the impact of their plate. This book considers the impact our love of avocado truly has. Avocados, just like everything you put into your shopping basket, have consequences both to communities and to ecosystems.

The Avocado Debate discusses just one food, demonstrating the huge nuance within a single everyday product. You can produce avocados in a more sustainable or less sustainable way. The same is true of a pint of milk, a ribeye steak, a cup of coffee, or a tomato. Nothing is produced or consumed without consequence. No food is "good." No food is "bad." The debate needs to recognise that. The hope is that this book's in-depth consideration will help the reader peel back the incredible intricacy of our food system and get to the heart that so often goes unacknowledged.

NOTE

1 Finney, Clare, "End of the avocado: Why chefs are ditching the unsustainable fruit." *The Guardian*, 2021, November 1.

1

THE AMERICAN PEAR

THE HISTORY OF THE AVOCADO

INTRODUCTION

Today, avocados sit on market stalls and supermarket shelves in every corner of the world due to the globalisation of the fruit that was brought about by the colonial period. While the fruit had held a critical role for early Central Americans and was revered by the local communities, its consumption and social role shifted dramatically with the arrival of the Conquistadors and the European occupation of the region. From then on, the avocado bridged high- and low-wealth consumers, becoming a staple food of enslaved people and also gracing the best tables of the aristocracy. It was through the acquisition of the fruit by the colonial system that it transformed and brought it to the precipice of its modern history, a history written in California at the dawn of the 20th century. Reviewing the fruit's journey to California and how it was slowly co-opted by Europeans will help to understand its place in society today.

THE BEGINNINGS OF THE FRUIT

The formal Latin name of the avocado is the Persea americana – a member of the flowering plant family, Lauraceae, more commonly known as the laurel. As its name indicates, the avocado sits within the Persea genus, which contains 200–240 species of small to large evergreen trees. Persea plants are found mostly in eastern Asia and Central and South America,

DOI: 10.4324/9781003371915-1

with a few species in eastern North America and one in the Azores. That said, the genus is mainly confined to tropical and warm temperate regions, although extending as far north as Japan and South Korea. This desire for warmth is very much the case for avocados. They are a temperamental tree, and often react badly to the cold – to which anyone who has tried to coddle an avocado plant through an English winter can probably testify – and is ideally suited to the climate of moderately warm temperatures (15°C–30°C) with moderate humidity, although can withstand up to −2°C with minimal damage once established. A climate that is found in what is now south-central Mexico, where the species originates from.

The fruit is a remnant of an era long past. The clue to this history is provided by the defining stone at its centre. As with most plants, avocado trees need their seeds to be dispersed naturally to spread its genetic material and move into new areas. Clearly, no bird or small mammal is going to digest that stone and pass it through its intestinal system without noticing. In fact, it would likely kill them if the pip was accidently swallowed. Its method of seed dispersal comes instead, according to Connie Barlow's The Ghosts of Evolution,[1] from the megafauna of the Pleistocene, also known as the Age of the Great Mammals. The Pleistocene lasted from 2.58 million to 11,700 years ago, and during this period, megafauna weighing over 100 lbs roamed the land. The avocado evolved to attract these mammals, who would consume the green fruit in a single bite and then wander miles before defecating the seed out, surrounded by a nice mound of natural fertiliser, helping the avocado spread far and wide.[2]

However, these great mammals disappeared about 13,000 years ago in the Western Hemisphere when the planet moved into the Holocene era, which lasts to the present day. This is sometimes referred to as the "Sixth Extinction." During this period, North America lost 68% of its megafauna, and South America lost 80%.[3] As Barlow said, "The Age of Great Mammals may be over, but the plants have not yet caught on." Without larger mammals, like the ground sloth, to carry the seed far distances, the avocado fruit would fall directly underneath the parent tree and therefore had to compete with the parent tree for light and growth. Like many of us, the avocado did not do well growing up in its parent's shadow. Without enough space and denied the required nutrients to fully develop, the trees that sprouted underneath their parents never reached their greatest potential. And so, the avocado managed to continue in the wild decline of the megafauna through odd moments of luck when jaguar might swallow it or it was moved by water. As Barlow wrote,

> An avocado sitting in a bin at the grocery store is thus biology in a time warp. It is suited for a world that no longer exists. The fruit of the avocado is an ecological anachronism. Its missing partners are the ghosts of evolution.

MESOAMERICAN AVOCADOS

Simultaneously, to the decline of the megafauna, humans were evolving. When Homo sapiens reached the point where we began to cultivate land, the fruit had the chance to thrive again. Early farming systems provided a new method of spreading the avocado's genetic material beyond the immediate vicinity. It is believed that it became a crop domesticated by the locals approximately 5,000 years ago in the region of Mexico that is now known as Puebla, to which we will return in Chapter 6. The Coxcatlan caves contain remnants of avocados that Mesoamericans gathered from nearby trees in the Tehuacan Valley.[4] These caves held a community of approximately 25, who prepped for periods of scarcity by storing food in the caves when it was abundant. Avocado was one crop that they tried to store for the winter.

Outside the confines of the caves, the avocado became intrinsic to the culture of the region's indigenous people of Central and South America. The 14th month in the classic Mayan calendar is represented by the avocado glyph, pronounced K'ank'in, and the few surviving books (codices) of the Maya and Aztec cultures, as well as oral histories from their descendants, indicate that avocados held strong spiritual significance in some Mesoamerican cultures.[5] In fact, the Popul Vah, the Quiche Maya holy book, mentions the avocado within the creation myth. Other Mayan people might have had similar creation myths (including ones that featured avocados), which would explain the illustrations of avocado trees that decorate the sarcophagus of the Maya ruler Pacal at Palenque and the avocado remains that were buried in the ceremonial mounds at Huaca Prieta. However, many of these myths were lost through the subsequent Spanish colonialism and Christian conversion of the region so that today, much of it is guesswork about the role that avocados played within these communities.

AVOCADOS IN THE COLONIAL CONTEXT

When the Spanish arrived, everything changed. The conquistadores permanently altered the culture and economy of the Aztecs and Mayans through their colonial control. The avocado did not escape this seismic cultural shift and was increasingly subsumed into the colonial economy. Avocado was first mentioned in the Suma de Geographia by Martin Fernandez de Enciso, published in Spain in 1519.[6] Fernandez was originally from Seville but travelled to the "New World," and recorded his travels in the first Spanish language account of the territory. It also included a description of the avocado saying,

> Yaharo is a good port, with good lands, and here are groves of many different sorts of edible fruits, among others is one which looks like an orange, and when it is ready for eating it turns yellowish; that which it contains is like butter and is of marvellous flavour, so good and pleasing to the palate that it is a marvellous thing.

A more extensive description of avocado was written by Gonzalo Fernandez de Oviedo, a historian travelling with Hernando Cortez. In his writing, he introduced Europeans to the hammock, pineapple, and tobacco, in addition to the avocado. His Summario de la Natural Historia de las Indias was published in 1526.[7] De Oviedo described the avocado saying,

> They are large trees, with broad leaves similar to those of the laurel, but larger and more green. They bear pears weighing a pound and even more, though some weigh less, and the color and shape is that of true pears, and the rind somewhat thicker, but softer, and in the center of the fruit is a seed like a peeled chestnut…and between this and the rind is the part which is eaten, which is abundant and is a paste similar to butter and of very good eating and of good taste, and such that those who have these fruits guard them and esteem them highly and the trees are wild as are the others which I have mentioned, for the chief gardener is God, and Indians apply no work whatever to them. The pears are excellent when eaten with cheese, and they are gathered before they are ripe and stored, and when treated thus they ripen perfectly for eating but after they have reached this stage they spoil quickly if allowed to stand.

A Spanish missionary, Padre Bernabe Cobo, recognising their potential value, was the first to take the time to categorise the different varieties of avocado.

During his missions to South and Central America, he studied the local botany. From 1596 through to his death in 1657, he travelled through the region. More famous for his writings on quinine, he identified three different types of avocado within his *Historia del nuevo mondo*.[8] These were the Guatemalan, Mexican, and West Indian avocado, known in Spanish as avocatl, quilavocatl, and tlacacolavotl respectfully. Mexican avocados are small with an almost spherical seeds and a skin that are covered by a thin, purple-black skin. Guatemalan avocados are similar in shape and size to the Mexican but have an egg-shaped seed and have a thick, tough skin. The West Indian avocado, despite its name, is not from the West Indies at all, but rather were developed in the Maya lowlands of Central America.[9] They are the largest of the avocado varieties and tolerant of high levels of salt and chlorosis (plant nutrient deficiencies). The West Indian avocado fruit is rounder with a smooth easy-to-peel light green skin and abundant flesh with a slightly sweet taste. According to historian Jeff Miller, it is likely that the West Indian line a product of early attempts to breed avocados for cultivation. However, others argue that it only crossed from Central America to the islands when the Spanish arrived and began their colonialisation. Consequently, there is some debate as to whether the West Indian variety deserves its own category or whether it is a sub-variety of the Guatemalan line.[10] The famous Hass variety that we will consider in a later chapter is a mix of both the Guatemalan and the Mexican lines.

Consequently, one can consider the prominence of the avocado as following the expansion of exploitation and the colonialisation of land. While the Spanish were the first Europeans to discover the avocado during their conquest of Central America, they were not alone. The English followed hard behind them. Having navigated the Caribbean, English had their eyes on bigger prizes. One particular fortune hunter was William Dapier. In 1675, he had established himself in the Bay of Campeche in Mexico where he harvested logwood and documented the local flora and fauna, sending back notes of his discoveries to London.[11] Today, the Oxford English Dictionary credits him with introducing the word "avocado" into the English language.[12]

Having discovered the fruit, there was a new role that the colonialists envisioned for the fruit – one that was central to their economic interests. As the motivations of the Europeans moved from exploration to colonisation, the avocado took on a new role. According to Jeff Miller, "avocados were frequently used as food for enslaved people working the sugar plantations in the Caribbean" since the Spanish had quickly discovered that the fruit was full of fat and highly nutritious, without requiring much space to grow.[13] As Miller continues, a food that was energy-rich and easy to grow would have been attractive to colonial overlords looking for cheap, non-meat foods to feed the populations of their colonies. Avocado trees could be grown on the fringes of sugar plantations to feed the enslaved people working the cane fields, without competing for real estate with the highly profitable sugar cane crop.

The fruit therefore became a central component of the diet of enslaved people across the Caribbean, Central and South America, and as the colonial plantation model spread to places like Indonesia and the Philippines, slaveholders brought them along to feed the workers. Consequently, the fruit's spread across the globe mirrors the colonial expansion. The fruit reached Spain in 1601, Indonesia in 1750, Mauritius in 1780, Brazil in 1809, and (if somewhat surprisingly late) the United States in 1825. There is little direct evidence of how enslaved people grew and ate avocados across the colonial world. Enslaved people were denied the ability to read and write, and consequently, the majority of sources come from white European writers, making them susceptible to the biases of the period and vulnerable to inaccuracies.

It was within this context of slavery and sugar that many white Americans and Europeans first encountered avocados. George Washington, the future president of the United States, first came across the fruit when he visited the sugar plantations of Barbados in 1751, noting that he had tried an "agovago pair." It was the only trip outside the American mainland that he ever took. After their six-week journey to the island, he and his half-brother stayed for almost three months. In addition to exploring the island, the Washingtons socialised regularly with Bridgetown society, many of whom owned or ran sugar plantations that relied on the labour of enslaved people. According to a 1748 census, the population comprised 15,252 white colonists and 47,132 slaves, meaning free white colonists accounted for just under a quarter of the total population.[14] George's diary is heavy with entries of the two brothers attending parties and dinners and encountering many foods that he had not encountered before.[15] In addition to guava and passion fruit, he tried an avocado and noted in his diary that the fruit "is generally admired tho none pleases my taste as do the pine[apple]."

Similarly, the Irish naturalist and doctor, Sir Hans Sloane, encountered avocados during a trip to Jamaica. While working as the personal physician to the 2nd Duke of Albemarle, Hans used his free time on the island to study the local plants and gathered more than 1000 specimens. Sloane's visit to Jamaica came at the height of the transatlantic slave trade, which resulted in the enslavement of between 10 and 12 million African people between the 1600s and 1900s.[16] As Sloane crisscrossed the island conducting his research into the local plants, he was accompanied by enslaved men who shared their knowledge of the local plants. Just as was the case with de Enciso, Cobo, and Washington, enslaved people assisted Sloane in acquiring his specimens and their knowledge and skills proved essential to Sloane's discoveries. Without their service, he might ever have encountered the fruit. In fact, the UK's Natural History Museum (where his collection remains) highlights that the slave trade itself was intrinsic to the botanical discoveries of the period, saying that, "It is clear that trade, in both commodities and human lives, provided the infrastructure that allowed Sloane and his contemporaries to build their collections of natural history objects."

Following his return to England after his 15-month work trip, Sloane wrote up his studies and observations into two volumes. In the second volume, Hans details the "the Albecato Pear-Tree, Abacado, Avocado." This was the first reference to avocado (with the modern spelling) in England. He describes it saying,

> This Tree has a Trunc as thick as one's Middle, with a light brown or grey ash-coloured Bark, having deep Furrows or Sulci in it, rifing to twenty of thirty Foot high; the Ends of the Branches have a great many Leaves, standing without any Order on yellowish half Inch long Footstalks, they are three Inches long, and one and a half broad in the middle, where broadest very smooth and of a deep green Colour, with an Eye of yellow in it, having one Rib in the Middle and feveral transverse ones branch'd from it. Among the leaves come out a short half Inch long stalk, to which are fasten'd by short petioli from near the Bottom, Flowers of a yellowish green Colour, to which follows a Fruit shaped like a Pear, as big as one's two Fists, greenish on the outside, having a smooth Skin and a Pulp under it of an Inch in Tickness, which is green, soft, almost insipid to the Taste, and very nourishing. Within this lies a naked great Kernal bigger than a Walnut, having many Tubercles and Sulci on its Surface, divisible into two great Lobes, between which lies the young Sprout or Germen. It is planted and grows every where in this island. This is accounted one of the wholesomest Fruits of these Countries, not only by Way of Disert, being eat

with Juice of Lemons and Sugar to give it a Piquancy, but likewise for supporting Life itself. It is useful not only on these Accounts to Men, but likewise to all Manner of Beasts.[17]

While central to their diet, the fruit was not limited to the meals of enslaved people. The Spanish also developed a taste but in a particularly different way. Missing the tartness of their beloved olive back home, they sliced immature hard avocados and brined them to mimic the taste. Other colonial chefs also served it with vinegar and pepper or with salt and roasted plantain. Increasingly, it graced the tables of the most illustrious individuals across the region, and when they returned home to Europe, they took the taste with them. Soon, avocados were being seen of the plates of the great and the good across the Old World, including royalty.[18]

AVOCADOS ARRIVE IN AMERICA

Despite its success in Europe and spread to the enslaved regions of the colonial empires, the fruit took quite a while to arrive in the United States, despite the proximity to Central America and the Caribbean. It was due to one individual that the avocado came to the United States: Henry Perrine. Henry had been the US consul in Campeche, Mexico, on the Gulf Coast in the 1830s and a dedicated (if amateur) horticulturalist. His employers approved of his leisure activities, keen to learn from their overseas diplomats what local plants could be commercially grown in the US. Perrine quickly came to believe that two specific plants might thrive back in the southern states of the US: the avocado and a small variety of lime that would subsequently come to be known as the Key Lime. After corresponding with officials in the Floridian Keys, he was convinced that both fruit could be successfully introduced to the Sunshine State, given the similar climate. Setting up his home in Indian Key in south Florida, he developed a new technique for grafting the single avocado he brought to create an orchard and a plant introduction station. His introduction of the avocado (and the key lime) to Florida changed the future of the fruit.

However, despite Perrine's initial attempts, the avocado did not become widely popular, it took a long time for the fruit to take off in the US. It was not until the 1900s that avocados began spreading across Florida with saplings brought from Cuba and gathered a bit of success. However, while Floridian orchards would play a few roles in developing the US market for the fruit, another state would play a greater role in the avocado's future. The earliest arrival of the avocado into California was in 1856 when Dr. Thomas White planted one on his farm on San Gabriel, according to the California State Agricultural Society Report in 1856.[19] One sapling he planted was from Nicaragua and was likely a West Indian variety, but ultimately failed in the dry climate of California and died. A few years later, in 1871, another Californian, Judge R.B. Ord, planted a pair of Mexican trees in Santa Barbara. These proved heartier than those used in Dr. White's attempt. With the successful introduction of the avocado into California, the stage was set for the most transformative act in the avocado's history.

CONCLUSION

The fruit arrived in California as the new century dawned, and the avocado was poised for its next transformation. It had already undergone significant evolutions since it was first grown (and revered) by early communities in Central America where it was a staple of their food culture. When discovered by the colonialists, the new European arrivals had increasingly taken ownership of the fruit, using it to further their economic exploitation of the regions that they occupied and the people that they enslaved. Its role as a food for enslaved people meant that the fruit was transferred around the world to all the areas under colonial control and became globalised. Yet, perhaps unusually, despite its association with enslaved people, the fruit was still considered to be exclusive enough for the best of society to consume it – a luxury of the exotic new world that they had conquered. This balance of global recognition and its combined role in the diets of both the wealthiest and poorest in society positioned it perfectly for its next chapter.

NOTES

1   Barlow, Connie, *The Ghosts of Evolution Nonsensical Fruit, Missing Partners, And Other Ecological Anachronisms.* Perseus Books Group, 2002.

2   Smith, Annabelle, "Why the avocado should have gone the way of the dodo." *Smithsonian Magazine*, 2013.

3   Ibid.

4   Smith, Bruce D., Reassessing Coxcatlan Cave and the early history of domesticated plants in Mesoamerica, *Smithsonian Institution*, Vol. 102, Issue 27, 9438–9445, 2005.

5   Minster, Christopher, "The Maya Calendar," *ThoughtCo.*, 2017, December 2.

6   Fernández de Enciso, Martin, *Suma de geographia: que trata de todas las partidas e prouincias del mundo, en especial de las indias e...del arte del marear..., con la espera en romance, con el regimieto del sol y del norte*, Seuilla: po lua[n] Cromberger, 1530.

7 Fernández de Oviedo, Gonzalo, *Sumario de la natural historia de las Indias*, 1526. https://bvearmb.do/handle/123456789/1213.

8 Bandelier, Adolph Francis, "Bernabé Cobo," *The Catholic Encyclopedia*, Vol. 4. New York: Robert Appleton Company, 1908.

9 Hirst, Kris, "Maya lowlands." *ThoughtCo.*, 2019, December 14.

10 Galindo-Tovar, María Elena & Amaury Martín Arzate, West Indian avocado: Where did it originate, *International Journal of Experimental Botany*, 2010, December. https://www.researchgate.net/publication/266476678_West_Indian_avocado_where_did_it_originate.

11 Cordingly, David, *Under the Black Flag*. Random House Trade, 2006.

12 Thompson, Keith, *Born to be Hanged: The Epic Story of the Gentlemen Pirates Who Raided the South Seas, Rescued a Princess, and Stole a Fortune*. Little, Brown and Company, 2022.

13 Miller, Jeff, *Avocado: A Global History*. Reaktion Books, 2020.

14 *The Papers of George Washington Digital Edition*. Charlottesville: University of Virginia Press, Rotunda, 2008. https://rotunda.upress.virginia.edu/founders/GEWN.html.

15 Ibid.

16 Slavery and The Natural World, *Natural History Museum*, 2006. https://www.nhm.ac.uk/discover/slavery-and-the-natural-world.html.

17 Sloane. Hans & Gucht, Michael van der, *Voy. Isl. Madera, Barbados, Nieves, S. Christophers and Jamaica*. London: Printed by B.M. for the author, 1707–1725.

18 Ibid.

19 Guest Contribution, "The history and origins of avocado oil." *History Cooperative*, 2019, January 10. https://historycooperative.org/history-of-avocado-oil/.

KEY READINGS

• Bandelier, Adolph Francis, "Bernabé Cobo," *The Catholic Encyclopedia*, Vol. 4. New York: Robert Appleton Company, 1908.

• Fernández de Enciso, Martin, Cromberger, *Suma de geographia: que trata de todas las partidas e prouincias del mundo, en especial de las indias e...del arte del marear..., con la espera en romance, con el regimieto del sol y del norte*. Seuilla: po lua[n] Cromberger, 1530.

• Fernández de Oviedo, Gonzalo, "Sumario de la natural historia de las Indias," 1526.

• Sloane, Hans & Gucht, Michael van der, *Voy. Isl. Madera, Barbados, Nieves, S. Christophers and Jamaica*, London: Printed by B.M. for the author, 1707–1725.

• Smith, Annabelle, "Why the avocado should have gone the way of the Dodo." *Smithsonian Magazine*, 2013.

• *The Papers of George Washington Digital Edition*. Charlottesville: University of Virginia Press, Rotunda, 2008.

2

COMMERCIALLY VIABLE

THE CREATION OF THE HASS AVOCADO

INTRODUCTION

With the avocado's arrival to California at the turn of the 20th century, a new era for the fruit dawned. Rapidly, the fruit moved from an ornamental curiosity when horticulturalists saw its commercial potential. Growers in California were keen to turn an amateur avocado industry into a professional exercise and to challenge the dominance of Floridian avocados. California was already an agricultural powerhouse with the Central Valley producing huge quantities of fruit and vegetables. It seemed logical that an avocado industry could find success in the state too. However, they knew that they needed to identify a more resilient variety of avocado that could be better commericalised. The vulnerability of the fruit to temperature fluctuations had meant that almost all the trees in Southern California had been wiped out following the 1913 winter when a freak polar vortex descended on Southern California. Starting on January 5th, the temperatures plunged with overnight lows between −5 and −10°C, with much colder conditions in some isolated locations.[1] The search was therefore for a variety that was suited to the Californian climate and future incidences of extreme weather.

The other side of increasing the Californian avocado market was expanding the consumer base. The California Avocado Association (CAA) was founded by a group of horticulturalists in 1915 (although renamed the California Avocado Society in 1941) with the goal of popularising the fruit.[2] Among them was Dr. Coit, a Professor of Citriculture at UC Berkeley and a

DOI: 10.4324/9781003371915-2

farm advisor. In addition to his founding role with the CAA, he helped orga-
nise the California Avocado Growers Association (now Calavo) and served
as director until 1944. The 1939 Yearbook of the organisation would later
say that:

> Dr. J. Eliot Coit is truly "The Father of the California Avocado Indus-
> try." From its babyhood or the time when growing avocados was a
> hobby, through adolescence or the transitional period into maturity
> as a fully-fledged industry Dr. Coit has been its able and watchful par-
> ent. Long after his name will have been forgotten, consumers in New
> York as well as growers in California will unknowingly feel Dr. Coit's
> influence.[3]

Allowing for a little hyperbole from the publication that he edited for over
a decade, Coit certainly deserves credit for significantly expanding the avocado sector in California and increasing its influence through organisation.
Another CAA founder was Herbert Webber, who was a leading plant breeder
with the US Department of Agriculture and Dean of the University of California's Graduate School of Tropical Agriculture who was keen to increase
the reach of California's produce. Together with the others, Coit and Webber
set out to expand avocado production in California and to professionalise
the industry.

THE FUERTE

To meet the growing demand, CAA breeders started searching for a more
commercial offering. By the beginning of the 20th century, there were a few
avocado breeders in California. The most famous was West India Gardens
in Altadena in the northern reaches of Los Angeles, which was run by Wilson Popenoe and his father, Fred. In 1911, Fred sent a young agricultural
student, Carl Schmidt, to Mexico to track down new, more robust commercially viable avocado varieties. Schmidt travelled through the country sending back budwood to propagate. Eventually, he arrived at the home of Señor
Alexander Le Blanc, where Schmidt spotted an avocado tree in the backyard,
next to the kitchen. Marking its resilience, Schmidt took cuttings from the
particular tree in the garden and named the varietal, Fuerte (the Spanish
word for strong), which were successfully propagated in Altadena. A few
years later, Wilson would accompany Schmidt back to Le Blanc's home out

of curiosity to see the Fuerte parent tree that Wilson described as "the Mecca of California avocado growers."[4] In his diary, Wilson wrote,

> This tree Le Blanc possesses something of unusual character, as well as merit, and he knows it. The family is so fond of the fruit that they always keep the entire crop for their own use. Not only do they consider the flavor unusually rich, but they say that the seed is exceptionally small, leaving an abundance of meat. In addition, the tree is peculiar in that it ripens its fruits over a much longer period than any other known to them. They call it "ahuacate verde" because it remains green in color when ripe. They know when the fruit is ready to be picked by the yellowish tinge which it assumes on one side.[5]

Fuerte was so resilient that it went from strength to strength and proved a commercial success across the state. The Californian growers were in such awe of the new variety that the CAA Yearbook exclaimed,

> It seems to us that the Fuerte avocado growers are under a lasting obligation to Senor and Senora LeBlanc, and to Mr. C. B. Schmidt who obtained the buds from the parent tree that Mr. Popenoe propagated in his West India Gardens at Altadena. So far as we know the parent Fuerte tree is the most interesting commercial parent avocado tree to Southern California growers, yet discovered, and as about 75% of the avocado trees that now grow in southern California are of that variety, it is probably the most important avocado tree to this district known at the present time.[6]

The Fuerte won a famous fan who helped increase its popularity. The railway magnet. Henry E. Huntington had an estate in San Marino, California, close to Pasadena. Huntington had hired William Hertrich in 1908 to transform the old peach orchard into a magnificent garden, featuring an avocado grove. Hertrich had initially planted a range of different local avocado varieties in the orchard. However, all had been wiped out in the 1913 Freeze. When Huntington tasked him with replanting, Hertrich switched to Fuertes exclusively. Such a vote of confidence in the new variety did not pass unnoticed. A large-scale grower, John Whedon, bought a number of these trees off the Popenoe's family and planted them on his Yorba Linda ranch, becoming the first commercial grove of Fuertes in California. This small orchard proved profitable. The Californian historian, John Shepard, said of the venture,

> When his orchard came into production, he had standing orders from hotels in Los Angeles and San Francisco who were willing to take all he could ship, paying as much as $12.00 per dozen. Because of the Fuerte's cold resistance and high quality fruit, the buds from his trees were in great demand, and in some years, he realized as much as $6,000 from buds alone.[7]

Popenoe must have been delighted at his success and the avocado industry in California started to take off. However, the growers in California had little idea that the dominance of the Fuerte would be fleeting and that a new variety would break onto the scene. The year 1925 saw the arrival of the Hass.

THE HASS

The Mother Tree was planted in 1925 in La Habra Heights, California. Back then, La Habra Heights was a very different place. Today, it is essentially part of greater Los Angeles, absorbed into the spread of the city. Back then, La Habra Heights offered newly married couples a rural idyll, surrounded by orchards, nurtured by the balmy Californian climate. The town was created in 1919 by Edwin G. Hart, who purchased and developed an area of land, turning it into 1 acre lots and building single family homes.[8] This was the time to do it: California was booming. According to the US Census, from a population in 1900 of almost 1.5 million people in the entire state, by the end of the 1920s, there were 5,677,251 people living in California.[9] Rudolph Hass and his wife, Elizabeth, were two of those new arrivals. They moved to California from Wisconsin in 1923. The couple settled in Pasadena initially, where he began his lifelong career as a mailman. However, after two years there, the couple decided to purchase one of the new homes developed by Edwin G. Hart and relocated to 426 West Street in La Habra Heights. Part of the appeal was the property's garden. The lot already had a number of established avocado trees, growing on it. Hass family legend holds that Rudolph saw a magazine article with an illustration of an avocado tree with dollar bills hanging from its branches, in place of leaves, and decided that his future was in the fruit business.[10]

While he had a dream of being an avocado grower, he didn't have much of the knowledge of how to do it. Therefore, he turned to A.R. Rideout. While Rideout owned and ran a commercial nursery, known as "Rideout Heights," he saw himself more as a botanist than a businessman. He had a passion for avocados and wanted to encourage more amateurs into the industry – he travelled around the state, attending agricultural fairs to promote the fruit. Determined to breed the best avocado, he began planting any seeds he could get his hands on. He searched continuously, including the garbage from restaurants, planting seeds on marginal land to see what varieties they might produce. He was happy to play the mentor to Hass. Rideout gave Hass avocado seeds that he had collected from the bins of an LA eatery. He advised Hass to plant the seeds in a cluster and then pull up the two weakest seedlings and graft the strongest. Hass rolled up his sleeves and planted the seeds as instructed. According to Hass's granddaughter, Rudolph "planted the rest of the grove on 12 foot centers with three seeds in each hole."[11] Once the saplings had grown, it was time to graft them. Given his limited knowledge of tree cultivation and horticulture, Hass hired a professional grafter named Mr. Caulkins, to graft cuttings from existing Lyon avocado trees onto the strongest of the three trees from each hole.

Grafting is a common practice in orchards, particularly for highly heterozygous species like the avocado. Heterozygous means that the organism has two sets of chromosomes, and, as a result, makes it difficult for breeders to predict what genes are going to be expressed in the offspring since it could express genes from either of those chromosomes. Similar to homo sapiens, which are also heterozygous species, an avocado plant could express the genes from either strand of their genetic makeup. For us, that means we could have the blue eyes of our mother or the brown eyes of our father. For avocados, that means it could have thick skin or smooth. Consequently, heterozygosity makes it challenging to know exactly how the plant will mature. To avoid this complication, avocado breeders almost always propagated through grafting, in order to ensure that the tree reflects desirable traits.

The process of grafting is simple enough. A tree is selected for the rootstock, and the seeds are planted and encouraged to grow. Varieties of rootstock are often selected for its disease resistance, particularly to soil-borne diseases and pests. Once the rootstock has reached a decent size (approximately four to five months for an avocado), then the tree can be grafted. The grower will select another tree that has already been shown to bear good-quality fruit or have other advantageous attributes like a high yield. A small section (known as a scion) from the extremity of this second tree will be cut to attach to the rootstock. The stem of the scion is cut into a point, while a v is cut into the trunk of the rootstock so that they fit seamlessly together. The junction is then bandaged together, and after four to six weeks of healing, the tree will be fully grafted. This technique of grafting avocados was first developed by Henry Perrine in Florida, who's contribution to avocado history was discussed previously.

Caulkins attempted to graft Lyon avocados onto the rootstock that grew from Rideout's seeds. Caulkins' grafts succeeded and Hass's orchard began to thrive. However, three of the seeds rejected the graft. So, a year later, Caulkins tried again with one of the trees and re-grafted a Lyon scion onto the now larger rootstock. But again, it didn't take. Hass's granddaughter remembered the frustration and annoyance of her grandfather and said that Hass "was ready to give up and chop the tree down."[12] Caulkins cautioned against such a drastic action, saying that the fact that the rootstock kept rejecting the scion meant that it was a strong tree. He advised Hass to "just let it grow and see what happens."[13] The tree that grew had significant benefits. It produced fruit quickly. When it was only 14″ tall, it already had three walnut-sized fruit on it. Unlike the skin (known as the exocarp) of the Fuerte avocado, this new variety had a thicker and bumpier skin. This made it more resistant to disease and insects since it was better protected from the environment. Ultimately, this also made it more commercially attractive since it was easy to ship and store without being bruised and damaged and had a longer shelf life since it ripened at a slower rate. Also helpful from a commercial perspective, the tree grew straight up and didn't spread out as much as the Fuerte trees, increasing the number of trees per acre. While the Fuerte variety had gained popularity for its resistance to cold, Hass's new variety was even more resilient to temperature fluctuations.

Given the ignoble origin of the seeds – plucked from the trash – it was impossible to know the genealogy of the new tree at the time. The avocado experts at the time suggested that it was likely to have been from Guatemalan line of avocados since these are associated with thick or woody exocarps (ideal for protecting the fruit when shipping), while Mexican landrace avocados tend to have much thinner skins (such as the Fuerte).[14] In 2019, the genome of the Hass was finally mapped at the US's National Science Foundation and revealed that the Hass avocado inherited about 61% of its DNA from Mexican varieties and about 39% from Guatemalan ones. None of the genetic history was known to Hass at the time. All he knew was that people also seemed to prefer the taste (tests now demonstrate that the Hass has a higher fat content, which creates a richer and creamier taste).[15] He first sold the fruit to his neighbours and then through the Model Grocery Store to wealthy Californians. The market sold the fruit for $1 a pop, equivalent to $16.21 today.[16]

But Hass was mindful that selling the fruit was not the only way he could benefit financially from his discovery. In 1935, he patented the tree.[17] This gave him the legal rights over the variety for 17 years. With the patent in his pocket, he approached Harold Brokaw, who owned a local nursery. The Brokaw Nursery still exists today, run by the great-nephew of Harold. Brokaw offered to grow and sell grafted trees propagated from Hass's cuttings and to split the profits 75:25 (with Rudolph getting the smaller share). With the deal signed, the nursery marketed the Hass saplings price was $5.00 per tree, considerably higher than Fuerte saplings that ranged in price from $1.25 to $3.50.[18] The tree proved popular and soon word got out. Growers from all over California wanted a Hass sapling. Soon, avocado orchards in Florida wanted to order them. Slowly, the Hass spread and eventually took over the world, reaching all the way to Australia and New Zealand.

One might think that this worldwide sensation meant a huge windfall for Hass. However, Rudolph's plan to get rich backfired. Despite the huge success of the variety and the renowned of his name, Hass made a profit of less than $5,000 from the royalties before the patent expired in 1952.[19] This was because it was impossible to control what happened to his trees once they left Brokaw's nursery, and soon growers realised that a single Hass tree purchased from Brokaw could then be used to provide scions to graft onto other avocado rootstock and propagated whole orchards of Hass avocados.

While Hass passed away in 1952 without ever seeing a fortune from his tree, the original tree itself continued to thrive until, eventually, in 1992, it was diagnosed with phytophthora, also known as root rot. For a decade, it clung on under the expert care of Hank Brokaw, whose uncle had sold the first Hass trees professionally. Hank nursed the mother tree, trying to save her from the fungus, but eventually on September 11th 2002, the tree was cut down. Determined that the monumental shift that the Mother Tree had generated in the avocado industry should not go unacknowledged, the CAA unveiled a plaque at 426 West Road to mark the location. The plaque read, "Through its progeny this tree, planted in 1926 by Rudolph G. Hass, has played an important role in the development of the California avocado industry."

IN CONCLUSION...

Hass's inadvertent discovery of a new variety was perfectly timed to coincide with the increase in demand for the fruit. This increase was due to the efforts of Californian growers to professionalise the industry. They had taken the first step with the cultivation of the Fuerte, but Hass gave them a perfect product that was more resilient and more commercial than the Fuerte had ever been. Without the Hass, it's unlikely that the fruit would have been able to achieve such dominance. Today, 80% of the annual 8.2 million metric tonnes of global avocados bear the Hass name.[20,21] Not bad for a seed that got thrown away in the trash.

NOTES

1 Coats, Daniel, "In 1913, Southern California was under the polar vortex. It transformed the region's economy, helped found a UC campus and gave rise to a U.S. President," Explore Southern California, 2021, May 10.

2 California Avocado Society, "History of CAS." 2023.

3 California Avocado Society, "Coit: The father of the avocado industry." Yearbook 48, 1964.

4 Popenoe, Wilson, "The parent fuerte tree at Atlixco, Mexico." California Avocado Society Yearbook 10, 1925–1926.

5 Ibid.

6 Shamel, A.D. "The parent Fuerte avocado tree." California Avocado Association Yearbook 21, 1936.

7 Shepherd, John & Bender, Gary, "The history of the avocado industry in California." California Avocado Society Yearbook, Vol. 85, pp. 29–50, 2001.

8 La Habra Heights Improvement Association, "Edwin G. Hart-Vision for La Habra Heights." 2015.

9 Demographia, "US population by state from 1900." 2004.

10 Cayotetale, "History of Hass avocados." 2007, August 19.

11 Denny, "History of the Hass." Social Network Access, 2012, March 1. http://www.avocado.socialnetworkaccess.com/history-of-the-hass-rimes-with-pass/.

12 Ibid.

13 Ibid.

14 Storey, W.B. "What kind of fruit is and avocado?" University of California Agriculture & Natural Resources, California Avocado Society Yearbook, 1973–1974.

15 Collins, Karen, "Nutritional value of different types of avocados." *American Institute for Cancer Research*, 2013, February 9.

16 Rager, Gregory, "Avocado varieties and cultural practices of Southern California." *South Coast Research and Extension Center*, 2001.

17 Denny, "History of the Hass."

18 *California Avocado Society*, "Mother Hass tree." 2023.

19 Denny, "History of the Hass."

20 Handwerk, Brian, "Holy Guacamole: How the Hass avocado conquered the world." *Smithsonian Magazine*, 2017, July 28.

21 Shahbandeh, M., "Avocado production worldwide from 2000 to 2021." *Statista*, 2023, January 19.

KEY READINGS

- *California Avocado Society*, "History of CAS." 2023.
- Handwerk, Brian, "Holy Guacamole: How the hass avocado conquered the world." *Smithsonian Magazine*, 2017, July 28.
- Shepherd, John & Bender, Gary, "The history of the avocado industry in California." *California Avocado Society Yearbook*, Vol. 85, pp. 29–50, 2001.

3

SUPERFOOD

THE NUTRITIONAL VALUE OF AVOCADOS

INTRODUCTION

Most people, if asked, would confidently say that the avocado is a healthy option. When sat next to a Snickers, it would certainly seem better for you – it is after all, a fruit. Some might go as far as to say that it's a superfood, given its particularly high levels of nutrients that support health. However, while the fruit does have lots of vitamins and minerals, this reputation has been carefully cultivated through the years to connect with the consumer's desire for better health. As the desire for wellness and clean eating has increased, so has the popularity of the avocado.

NUTRITIONAL BENEFITS

The avocado clearly has a lot going for it in the nutritional sense. While they might not have understood the science behind it, the early hunter gatherers in Mexico discerned that it provided a filling and calorie-rich food and benefitted from its nutritional value, just as the giant sloths and the other megafauna had before. The fruit is filling and rich – enough to satiate a hungry belly. But, in addition to the calories, there are also high levels of vitamins and minerals that benefit the consumer. Through nutritional analysis, we now know that the fruit has high levels of antioxidants, such as folic acid, Omega 3, magnesium, potassium, lutein, and fibre. It is also rich in vitamins A, C, D, E, and K and a range of the B group vitamins too.

DOI: 10.4324/9781003371915-3

According to the United States Department of Agriculture (USDA),[1] half an avocado will provide:

- Calories: 160
- Fat: 14.7 g
- Sodium: 7 mg
- Carbohydrates: 8.5 g
- Fibre: 6.7 g
- Sugars: 0.7 g
- Protein: 2 g
- Magnesium: 29 mg
- Potassium: 485 mg
- Vitamin C: 10 mg
- Vitamin E: 2.1 mg
- Vitamin K: 21 μg

That said, it is quite fatty with oily flesh, which makes it a more appealing taste for humans who particularly enjoy the sensation in the mouth.[2] A whole avocado contains roughly 4.2 g of saturated fat, almost 20 g of monounsaturated fat, and 3.6 g of polyunsaturated fat. So, while most of the calories in an avocado come from fat, it is primarily healthier monounsaturated fat – fat molecules that have one unsaturated carbon bond in the molecule (also called a double bond). Monounsaturated fatty acids are considered healthier fats because they can help reduce bad cholesterol levels in your blood, which ultimately can lower the risk of heart disease and stroke. They also provide nutrients to help develop and maintain your body's cells, and vitamin E, which is good for skin and tissue health.

ANTI-FAT AGENDA

However, for a number of years, the avocado was demonised – teased for being too fat. In the late 1980s and early 1990s, dietary advice steered many consumers away from products with high fat levels – regardless of whether they were monounsaturated or not.[3] Motivated by rapidly rising obesity rates in America, the medical profession decided it was time to encourage people to diet.[4] The low-fat craze saw consumers in the Global North actively encouraged to shun high-fat foods. For the most part, this meant avoiding cheese and other dairy products, but, due to its high fat content, the avocado also slipped into the list of "foods to avoid." According to renowned academic, Marion Nestle,

> In the late 1980s, there were two major reports that came out, identifying dietary fat as the single most important change that needed to be made in order to improve diet and health ... The idea was to reduce saturated fat, but the assumption was that it was too complicated to explain all that, and that if people just reduced their fat content, the fat content of their diet, they would be improving it.[5]

Despite the fact that avocado fat is monounsaturated, nutritionists at the time focused on reducing the intake of all fats and did not differentiate between the different types. As a consequence, the popularity of the avocado plummeted and sales dropped. "I can remember seeing a fact-sheet that came from a doctor my husband went to years ago," said Jan DeLyser, vice president of marketing with the California Avocado Commission (CAC).[6] "It was a heart-health type message. It said, 'Do not consume avocados.'" However, while the objective was noble, it did not have the desired outcome that the health community aimed for. The low- or anti-fat guidance led to many food brands reformulating and substituting sugar for the demonised fat. Nestle gives the example of Snackwell cookies that were advertised as no-fat cookies but had almost the same number of calories, so while they were lower in fat, they were higher in carbohydrates and sugar.[7] According to Walter Willett, the Chair of the Nutrition Department at the Harvard School of Public Health,

> This campaign to reduce fat in the diet has had some pretty disastrous consequences... One of the most unfortunate unintended consequences of the fat-free crusade was the idea that if it wasn't fat, it wouldn't make you fat... The reality is that during this campaign for fat-free and reduced-fat products, actual fat consumption did go down, but Americans got much fatter during this period of time.

The medical community had to change tack, and began to offer more nuanced dietary advice. This shift was simultaneous to the publication of several trials that clearly indicated that some types of fatty acids (monounsaturated fats), in particular the omega-3 fatty acids, can actually reduce heart arrhythmias – the exact fatty acids that people were eliminating from their diet with the goal of being healthier. Given the history of trade organisations commissioning and sponsoring studies to advance their product, the avocado industry, specifically the CAC, began to commission studies that focused on the health benefits of the fruit to challenge the anti-fat narrative. According to Hoy Carman's history of the period, in 1997, the CAC began to fund nutritional and diet research and to proactively communicate the nutritional and health benefits of avocados to consumers.[8] Eventually, the public narrative caught up as nutritionists started to actively distinguish between "good" fat and "bad" fat. As nutritional science has adopted an increasingly nuanced approach to dietary fats, avocado was once again restored to its pedestal as a superfood.

That said, despite the rehabilitated reputation of the healthy avocado, the legacy of the low-fat diet craze remains a powerful force. As a consequence, companies still find success in marketing products as low fat or fat free, especially given the rise of the wellness and clean eating trend that will be discussed shortly. This was therefore the motivation behind the launch of Isla Bonita's new range of "Avocado Light," an avocado that had been bred to have a lower calorie count with 30% lower levels of fat, and the Slimcado, a Guatemalan varietal with lower calories.[9] The reaction to the launch of these two products was quick. In an interview with USA Today, health expert, Joy Bauer said, "Being that fresh avocados are pretty much a perfect, creamy, dreamy, and delicious produce pick, I'm a tad sceptical about fussing with something that's not broken," while Keri Glassman added, "This sounds like an awful idea to me! It reminds me of low-fat peanut butter, which I say is about as good as eating vitamin-free vegetables!"[10]

SUPERFOODS

Setting aside the fat debate, because of all of the goodness contained within the little green fruit, many have labelled it as superfood. But what is a superfood? A superfood is defined by the Merriam-Webster Dictionary as "a food (such as salmon, broccoli, or blueberries) that is rich in compounds (such as antioxidants, fibre, or fatty acids) considered beneficial to a person's health."[11] However, the idea has no basis in science. While some fruits might offer high levels of desirable nutrients, linked to promoting personal health and wellness or preventing disease and sickness, they are not "super."

The term "superfood," which has been so frequently applied to the avocado, is a marketing ploy. The first appearance of the term was in a Canadian newspaper, the Lethbridge Herald, in 1949 when referring to the supposed nutritional qualities of a muffin as "a superfood that contained all the known vitamins and some that had not been discovered."[12] But it was the United Fruit Company that popularised it. The company used the term to market bananas in the early part of the 20th century, saying that they had high nutrient levels and provided a daily source of cheap, easily digestible nutrition. It published informational pamphlets including Points About Bananas and the Food Value of the Banana – all of which stressed the "super" nature of the banana.[13] The rise of this term drew inspiration from the comic book superheroes that were gaining popularity at the time, implying that these foods could come to humanity's rescue, and connected with a public that were emerging out of rationing and food insecurity caused by the Second World War.[14] The term caught on and was soon being applied to anything and everything from pomegranates to acai.

While some of these "superfoods" (avocados included) do have well-proven health benefits, and good levels of vitamins and minerals, sceptics argue that the term is merely a marketing device that quickly reaches the point of misrepresentation. Despite the claims on social media or in magazines, goji berries cannot cure cancer, and dragon fruit will not reverse heart disease. However, they can be part of a healthy diet and support wider nutritional goals. According to UC Davis, "it is clear the term [superfood] is more useful for its marketing value than providing ultimate nutrition" – and its marketing value seems to be going from strength to strength.[15] According to a 2016 Mintel study, between the period of 2011 and 2015, there was a 202% increase in the number of new food and drink products launched around the world containing the terms "superfood," "superfruit," or "supergrain."[16] As a marketing ploy, the concept of superfoods is effective because it taps into a deep trend towards healthy living. According to an article published by The University of California Davis, consumers are looking for "functional foods that provide benefits that can either reduce their risk of disease and/or promote good health."[17]

However, the term can be disingenuous and risks deceiving the consumer who might be manipulated into thinking that the "superfruit" avocado was the elixir of the gods and a panacea for all ailments. Mindful of this risk, the European Union prohibited the use of the term in advertising and marketing materials in 2007, unless accompanied by a specific authorised health claim supported by credible scientific research. This reflects a wider commitment by regulators across the world in the past few years to clamp down on spurious claims that have little meaning.[18] Terms such as all-natural, heart-healthy, or environmentally friendly are increasingly regulated to ensure that they are not used to deceive the public. Despite pressure from civil society and consumer groups, the US government has not yet acted similarly.

CLEAN EATING CLAIMS

Another contentious term that is connected to the idea of superfoods and healthy eating is the concept of "clean eating." The term was first introduced in 2007 by a Canadian fitness coach who stressed the importance of avoiding processed foods. Currently, there is no clear or regulated definition of clean eating. Aware of the ambiguous nature of the term, the Food Insight conducted a 2021 study that found that nearly half of consumers consider themselves to be "clean" eaters.[19] When asked what that meant, one in five – 21%, ranked "eating foods that aren't highly processed" as their top definition of the term. Another 14% of self-described clean eaters defined it as eating foods found in the fresh produce section, 13% as eating organic foods, and 11% as eating foods with simple ingredients lists.

This trend within the Global North towards healthy foods and "clean eating" has been growing for the last decade – a trend likely to increase following the Covid-19 pandemic – and avocados have been central to that story. Those consumers with higher levels of disposable incomes are willing to pay a premium for health benefits.[20] Given that avocados can retail for $2 a pop at some Whole Food stores, avocados certainly sit in the premium category. Interestingly, foods already perceived as healthy that also carry a health claim show the greatest sales, since it reinforced the existing knowledge of the consumer.[21] However, there are dangerous extremes arising from the fascination with healthy clean eating. A new type of disorder, orthorexia, causes a fixation on proper or healthful eating. Individuals struggling with orthorexia may experience a fixation on "pure" eating so strong that it harms their physical and psychological status. While not yet been officially classified as an eating disorder by the *Diagnostic and Statistical Manual of Mental Disorders* (DSM), it is a serious condition according to the National Eating Disorders Association.[22]

Ironically, however, those in the Global North in high-enough income bracket to afford the "superfoods," and have enough time on their hands to worry about "wellness," already have the highest health outcomes within the global society. Disease and illness disproportionately harm people living in poverty.[23] In America, Black and Latinx people, and people who live in rural and urban areas without adequate medical resources, face higher levels of ill health and are more financially impacted by illness. In the UK, Black and minority ethnic (BME) individuals generally have less access to high-quality care and ensure poorer overall health and worse health outcomes than the wider population. BME communities are also more likely to have co-morbidities, i.e. a combination of long-term health conditions such as diabetes, hypertension, COPD, etc.[24] The link between poverty and ill-health is even more apparent in the Global South. While life expectancies have improved and poverty rates have decreased globally in recent decades, concerns about "wellness" still remain a far way away from the concerns of most in the Global South who just want to be able to have enough food to avoid hunger.

For those who can afford to focus on wellness and clean eating, one individual brand, and one person within that brand, has become synonymous with the trend: Gwyneth Paltrow's Goop. The Oscar-winning actress launched her website in 2008 firstly with recipes, recommendations, and reviews, but it quickly expanded into an e-commerce platform. The brand oozes health and wellness and markets the breezy Californian glow of its founder. Courted or not, controversy has followed the brand, most infamously for its unscientific claims about vaginal eggs. However, Gwyneth's love of the super healthy avocado has also come in for mocking when she had the audacity to include a recipe for avocado toast in her cookbook – which many found a bit comical in its inanity since it doesn't take a step-by-step guide to decipher how to smash an avocado and spread it on toasted bread.

More recently, with the rise of body positivity and anti-fat movements, there have been more specific challenges against the concept of marketing wellness. Goop has once again proved a lightning rod for that criticism. The Atlantic's Amanda Mull wrote:

Instead of questioning long-standing assumptions about women's bodies, as Goop often claims is its goal, the company's products embrace one of America's oldest health myths: that physical beauty is proof not only of a person's health but of her essential righteousness. If the outside is perfect, the inside must be too. It's a retrograde vision of womanhood for a company that so frequently deploys the word *empowerment*...Wellness companies can feel predatory, even those not making Gwyneth Paltrow richer. It's a largely unregulated industry, and it operates in an environment of open desperation.[25]

AVOCADOS AND VEGANISM

Another rising dietary trend has contributed to the popularity of the avocado. Veganism and flexitarianism has increased considerably in the last decade. In May 2016, the Vegan Society commissioned Ipsos Mori to poll 10,000 people on their dietary habits and found that Britain's vegan population had increased from 150,000 to 542,000 in the space of a decade (alongside a vegetarian population of 1.14 million).[26] Of those, 63% were female and, significantly for veganism's future growth, almost half were in the 15–34 age category. In part, this has been driven by a series of successful documentaries (Cowspiracy and The Game Changers) and public figures (such as Tom Brady, Natalie Portman, Ariana Grande, among others) discussing the need to reduce meat consumption. There has also been a connected rise in flexitarianism, also known as casual vegetarianism or plant-based diets. Again, Goop and Gwyneth have been central to the rising popularity. In the States, 36% of consumers identify themselves as flexitarian, consuming meat or poultry as well as vegan or vegetarian meals. Consumers have been looking to decrease their meat consumption, and they have been searching for alternative ingredients to provide filling calories.[27] Given its fat content and oily texture, the avocado has proven itself an ideal candidate and is now a staple of many plant-based dishes. Similarly, the fruit has been used as a substitute for some dairy products since it has a creamy consistency. Recipes for ice-cream, brownies, and pies that exchange mashed avocado for cream or butter are common in vegan dessert recipes. However, this is not a new tradition. As discussed in Chapter 1, Gonzalo Fernandez de Oviedo observed in 1526 that the fruit has a similar viscosity to butter and that it was often spread by local communities. In fact, early Spanish arrivals in Mexico called the avocado "mantequilla del pobre," which translates as butter of the poor. The buttery smoothness of the fruit is intrinsic to the 21st-century dish that is possibly most associated with the fruit – the infamous avocado toast. However, we will dive into that phenomenon in the next chapter.

THE SEXY FRUIT

However, the reputation of the avocado is not limited to nutrition. Since its early history, the fruit was thought to be an aphrodisiac, which still continues to this day. In 2001, the CAC conducted a survey and found that

63% of those polled believed in this seductive fruit's reputation as a food of romance.[28] This association has deep roots. The Aztecs considered it a symbol of love and fertility, particularly because of its shape, which they thought resembled testicles. In fact, the Aztecs thought that the fruit looked so much like men's genitals, that they named the fruit ahuacatl – the Aztec word for testicles. Noble women were said to not have been allowed outside during the harvest season since the aroma might drive them mad with desire and cause them to do all sorts of salacious things, and the five-day festival in the northern region of what is now Peru to help the avocados ripen and become flavourful saw men gather together "stark naked in an open space among the orchards, and [run] from there to a distant hill," which sounds fairly Bacchic.[29] Perhaps then, the residents of the Maya city of Pusilha in Belize were particularly rambunctious since avocados are part of the name glyph of the city and it was known as the "Kingdom of the Avocado"? There is potentially some truth to the suggestion that they increase libido since avocados are extremely high in phytonutrients, which helps dilate blood vessels required for sexual arousal, including beta carotene, zinc, magnesium, and vitamin E. This reputation in Central and South America proved problematic when Wilson Popenoe (the aforementioned nurseryman who popularised the Fuerte) attempted to live solely on a diet of avocados and was evicted from his accommodation since the landlady thought he was a risk to her unmarried daughters.[30]

This reputation for the fruit improving virility and sexual prowess spread far and wide and encouraged the European adoption of the fruit. According to The Aphrodisiac Encyclopaedia, the Sun King (Louis XIV) nicknamed the avocado, "la bonne poire" (the good pear) because he believed it restored his lagging libido.[31] Louis was rapacious and famed for his sexual exploits in the French Court of Versailles. No doubt the King's endorsement of the avocado would have helped strengthen its reputation among his fawning courtiers. In a society that was desperate to win favour with the King, he was the ultimate influencer. While some the rakes and cads of history might have searched out the exotic fruit in the hope that it increased their libido and sexual stamina, others saw this sexy reputation as a reason to avoid the fruit. Some suggest that the reason that avocado production did not take off in California until the 20th century was that, prior to that, much of the agricultural land was managed by priests who ran the missions along the length of California. These Catholic establishments, along the rough and rocky coast, ran from 1769 to approximately 1833 with the goal of converting (sometimes forcefully) the Native Americans in the region to Christianity and defending the land from other potential settlers. The Franciscan priests that ran them were fearful of introducing any lusty elements into their midst that might create temptation. Consequently, the fruit did not make a significant appearance in the orchards of the California missions. However, the less pious growers in Florida did not have such issues – or perhaps the Floridians welcomed the idea of an aphrodisiac fruit?

IN CONCLUSION...

The fruit clearly has nutritional attributes that help in a balanced diet, and its reputation as a "superfood" has developed over the generations. Producers of avocados have played on this reputation to appeal to consumers. These perceptions of the fruit for its health benefits and its "other" properties, whether to vegans or to those searching for a bit of oomph in the bedroom, arose over generations. Whether these were true or not, the reputation proved essential for those looking to promote the fruit. As we will consider in Chapter 4, marketers leveraged the reputation to capture the attention of the public and get them to shift consumption and make avocados popular.

NOTES

1 *U.S Department of Agriculture*, "Avocados, raw, all commercial varieties." 2019, April 1.

2 Rolls E.T. "Neural representation of fat texture in the mouth." In Montmayeur J.P., & le Coutre, J., editors. *Fat Detection: Taste, Texture, and Post Ingestive Effects.* Boca Raton, FL: CRC Press/Taylor & Francis, 2010. Chapter 8.

3 Liu, A.G., Ford, N.A., Hu, F.B., Zelman, K.M., Mozaffarian, D., & Kris-Etherton, P.M., A healthy approach to dietary fats: understanding the science and taking action to reduce consumer confusion. *Nutrition Journal*, Vol. 16, Issue 1, p. 53, 2017, August 30.

4 Freedman, D.S. "Obesity—United States 1988-2008." *Centers for Disease Control and Prevention*, 2011, January 14.

5 Shafer, Jessie, "The big FAT question." *Delicious Living*, 2016, January 22.

6 Khazan, Olga, "The selling of the avocado." *The Atlantic*, 2015, January 31.

7 Shafer, Jessie, "The big FAT question." *Delicious Living*, 2016, January 22.

8 Carman, Hoy, "The story behind avocados' rise to prominence." *Giannini Foundation for Agricultural Economic at The University of California*, 2019.

9 Walansky, Aly, "Diet avocados are now a thing ... but are they actually good for you?" *Today*, 2017, October 12.

10 Ibid.

11 "Superfood." *Merriam-Webster.com Dictionary*, Merriam-Webster, https://www.merriam-webster.com/dictionary/superfood.

12 Wilson, Bee, "What's so super about super foods?" *The Economist*, 2019, September 4.

13 "Food value of the banana; opinion of leading medical and scientific authorities." *United Fruit Company*, 1917.

14 Wilson, Bee, "What's so super about super foods?"

15 Davis, U.C., "What makes superfood so super?" 2021, March 9.

16 Mintel, "Super growth for 'super' foods: New product development shoots up 202% globally over the past five years." 2016, May 5.

17 Davis, "What makes superfood so super?"

18 Reed & Phartiyal, "Transparency in food labeling." *Center for Science and Democracy at the Union of Concerned Scientists*, 2016, July 19. https://www.ucsusa.org/resources/transparency-food-labeling.

19 *International Food Information Council*, From "Chemical-sounding to "Clean": Consumer Perspectives on Food Ingredients." 2021, June.

20 *Nielson, I.Q.*, "An inside look into the global consumer health and wellness revolution." 2021, October 28.

21 Ibid.

22 *National Eating Disorder Association*, "Orthorexia." 2022. https://www.nationaleatingdisorders.org/learn/by-eating-disorder/other/orthorexia.

23 Cunningham, Peter, "Why even healthy low-income people have greater health risks than higher-income people." *The Common Wealth Fund*, 2018, September 27.

24 Oluwatosin, Ajayi, A perspective on health inequalities in BAME communities and how to improve access to primary care. *Future Healthcare Journal*, Vol. 8, 2021.

25 Mull, Amanda, "I gooped myself." *The Atlantic*, 2019, August 26.

26 The Vegan Society, "Find out how many vegans there are in Great Britain." 2016, May 17.

27 Malochleb, Margaret, "Flexitarianism on the rise; transparency tops 2021 trends." *Food Technology Magazine*, 2020, December 1.

28 Reiley, Amy, "Is avocado an aphrodisiac? Discover the benefits of avocado sexually." *Amy Reiley's Eat Something Sexy*, 2022, January.

29 Frazer, James George, *The Golden Bough: A Study in Religion and Magic*. Dover Publications, 2003, March 28.

30 Rosengarten, Frederic, *Wilson Popenoe: Agricultural Explorer, Educator, and Friend of Latin America*. Allen Press, 1994, January 1.

31 Hill, Mark Douglas, *The Aphrodisiac Encyclopaedia*. Random House, 2012, April 24.

KEY READINGS

- Carman, Hoy, "The story behind avocados' rise to prominence." *Giannini Foundation for Agricultural Economic at The University of California*, 2019.
- Khazan, Olga, "The selling of the avocado." *The Atlantic*, 31 January, 2015.
- Mull, Amanda, "I gooped myself." *The Atlantic*, 26 August, 2019.
- Wilson, Bee, "What's so super about super foods?" *The Economist*, September 4, 2019.

4

AVOCADO TOAST

SOCIAL MEDIA, MARKETING, AND INFLUENCE

INTRODUCTION

The fact that the Californian centre of the avocado industry was Los Angeles was fortuitous. In the 1920s, Hollywood was booming as people followed their dreams of stardom to California. The city was full of people who knew how to craft perceptions and create an image. The studio executives at MGM and Warner Brothers had carefully turned Clara Bow, Gloria Swanson, and Louise Brooks into celebrities known from coast to coast. The Dream Factory was about to work its magic on the avocado.

As was discussed previously, the California Avocado Association (CAA) was determined to commercialise the fruit. The first step had been to identify a commercial variety. Second was to increase demand. This required crafting a new reputation for the fruit. When they gathered together in 1927, they were aware that they needed to change the public's perception. The first stage of achieving this was to remove the fruit's nickname "alligator pear." The name reflected the knobbly skin of the fruit, although some suggest that it is a bastardisation of "aguacate." Either way, the CAA thought the name made the fruit unappealing – who would want to eat a scaly, reptilian, green, slimy fruit? In a statement released following their meeting, they firmly stated, "That the avocado, an exalted member of the laurel family, should be called an alligator pear is beyond all understanding."[1] Many starlets have been encouraged to adopt a more appealing stage name, so altering the fruit's name seemed a reasonable proposition. Just like Rock Hudson,

DOI: 10.4324/9781003371915-4

Marilyn Monroe, and Judy Garland, the alligator pear discovered that the right name change can help to open doors in Hollywood. So, the fruit underwent a makeover, and the name "avocado" was successfully adopted.

ANTI-LATINX SENTIMENT

Furthermore, the CAA wanted to remove the association with Latinx cuisine and culture. The early part of the 1920s had seen a surge of anti-immigrant and racist sensibilities. While today, California is seen as a progressive state that is diverse and welcoming to Latinx migrants, that was not always the case. Mexican and other Latinx immigrants have continually faced racism and hostilities. Mexican immigration in the 20th century came in three surges. The first surge began in the 1900s, following the revolution in Mexico. Not long after came a second wave – between 1910 and 1930, the number of Mexican immigrants counted by the US census tripled from 200,000 to 600,000.[2] The actual number was probably far greater. Estimates suggest that every year during the 1920s, approximately 100,000 Mexican workers illegally entered the United States, driven by economic opportunities north of the border.[3] This quick expansion of Latinx communities was met by hostility and resentment, which reached fever pitch in the 1930s when the country faced high unemployment and the Depression. During the 1930s and into the 1940s, up to two million Mexicans and Mexican-Americans were deported or expelled from cities and towns across the United States and shipped to Mexico.[4] Given the growing anti-immigrant sentiment, it was clear to the completely white board of the CAA in 1927 that foods associated with Latinx communities were unlikely to appeal to the affluent Anglo-Saxon consumer. As Jeffrey Charles, a professor of food history at California State University at San Marcos, explained, "they could not imagine (nor could the American food consumer) the 'Mexicanized' tastes of society."[5] To alter this, CAA worked to shift the reputation of the avocado so that it was not intrinsically linked to Latinx culture. Essentially, they aimed to "whitewash" the fruit. To achieve this, they argued against the use of the Spanish term "aguacate" and insisted on the more anglophone "avocado."

That said, some Latinx connotations did seem acceptable. The silent-screen superstar Ramon Novarro was asked to contribute his guacamole recipe to the 1929 Photoplay Cookbook: 150 Favorite Recipes of the Stars.[6] Novarro's unusual recipe calls for grapes to be added into the guac. Novarro (who's proper name was José Ramón Gil Samaniego) was a Mexican-born American actor who MGM billed as a "Latin lover" and became known as a sex symbol after the death of the legendary Rudolph Valentino. His hunky reputation was unusual for the period that tended to see studios minimise the sex appeal of Latino stars so that the white audience would not be offended. He was one of the few Latino actors who managed to get cast as a leading man in 1920s Hollywood and played the role of the romantic lead in many a Hollywood movie during his career. However, his support for Communism, his alcoholism, and closeted homosexuality ultimately curtailed his film career and saw the film roles dry up. His life finished tragically in 1968 when he was murdered by two men who he had hired for sex.

NOT SO SEXY

The association with a Hollywood heartthrob raises again the question of the avocado's reputation as being an aphrodisiac. As was discussed in Chapter 3, the reputation of the avocado as improving sexual performance had a long history that dated back to the Pre-Columbian period that had continued to be reinforced. However, this lusty association was proving problematic for the CAA when they wanted to increase the popularity of the fruit in the US market. Just as the priests of the Californian missions rejected the avocado, the white Anglo-Saxon protestants in the United States (with their legacy of Puritanism) found the sexiness unappealing. One can easily imagine that the housewives of 1920s America might not feel comfortable stacking their shopping basket with an aphrodisiac, especially if it might incur some side-eye from their neighbours. While the CAA were happy with the endorsement of Novarro as a Hollywood star, they decided it was necessary to debunk the provocative reputation. To that end, the CAA sponsored a promotional advertising campaign to explicitly deny that the avocado had powers to improve libido.[7] However, some more cynically suggest that it was all a smart marketing ploy. By stressing that there was absolutely no scientific proof that the fruit was an aphrodisiac, consumers thought it might be. Under this more cynical interpretation, the hope was that consumers would be tempted to indulge in the forbidden fruit.

While the CAA wanted to (at least superficially) downplay the aphrodisiac qualities of the fruit, in order to make it more socially acceptable to Anglo-Saxon consumers, the association with a famed Hollywood star in Novarro was a boon. The CAA wanted to shift the avocado market to appeal to affluent (white) consumers and convert it into a luxury. They wanted to make it an aspirational food, not something commonplace. So that it would appeal to middle- and upper-income consumers across America. To do this, they employed the same techniques as they would with a new starlet. While downplaying its overt sexuality, they aligned it with a famous actor. They put it in all the right places to make it look super fashionable. They commissioned writers to come up with recipes that positioned the fruit at the heart of haute cuisine, such as serving it in salad with grapefruit and lobster.[8] It was seen in the best restaurants up and down the Californian Coast and in New York. It graced the pages of *Vogue* and *The New Yorker*, branded as the "aristocrat of salad fruits."[9] Their efforts quickly paid off and avocados soon started to appear on the tables of more affluent Americans.

HEALTHY CLAIMS

As had been discussed in the last chapter, the fruit had long been associated with health and nutrition. The CAA decided to leverage this reputation and make the avocado the paragon of health. Their pamphlet on Advertising and Publicity in their relation to the avocado industry said,

> Still looking ahead a bit we can anticipate the discovery of certain wonderful qualities in the avocado, making it perhaps a veritable "fountain of youth." Perhaps we can find in the avocado a quality which will clear an aging face of wrinkles or restore hair to the bald spot of the middle-aged man... Seriously, we know that the avocado possesses important medicinal properties.[10]

This was particularly timely. The interwar years saw a growing fixation on fitness and physical health. People started engaging in gymnastics and athletics. Children were required to do exercise drills in school. Part of improving your physical fitness and becoming the best version of yourself was improving your diet. Suddenly, raw vegetables were in vogue. A study of the diet of Smith College students in the 1920s, quoted a campus warden who noticed that consumption of potatoes had diminished, while students were eating more celery, tomatoes, and lettuce. The CAA jumped on this trend and pitched the avocado as "the fountain of youth." It is necessary to highlight that much of this obsession with health and fitness was simultaneous and connected to the growing societal fascination with concepts of eugenics, the perception of the superiority of certain races over others, and the desire to create ideal "breeding stock."

However, there was another factor, beyond health, that motivated the girls of Smith College to switch from fries to fresh fruit. There had been a sharp shift in fashion. Gone were the voluptuous curves of the past. Instead, the girls wanted to emulate the flapper, which was the rage in the 1920s. This look was androgynous, angular, and thin. Coco Chanel, Louise Brooks, and Clara Bow exemplified the figure of a svelte and bony woman with a long cigarette and a form-fitted black dress with a dropped waist. "Though the flapper image minimized breasts and hips, it radiated sensuality," writes historian Margaret A. Lowe.[11] The slender silhouette seemed modern. Female curves seemed old-fashioned. The women who wanted to emulate these new icons and be at the height of fashion were increasingly worried about their weight. This anxiety was not helped by the invention of the bathroom scale in 1916, which soon made it into homes across America, to the torment of women ever since.

The new flapper look was deeply connected to Hollywood and the actresses that embodied it. As a result, a new fad diet gained popularity with the promise of making the doughy housewives of middle America look more like the stars of the silver screen. The Hollywood 18-Day Diet promised to deliver that svelte flapper body. The diet limited the woman to 500 calories a day. Given that the recommended calorie intake for adult women ranges from 1,600 calories per day to 2,400 calories per day, according to the 2020–2025 Dietary Guidelines for Americans, 500 isn't very many at all. Fans wrote to local fashion magazines to extoll its success. One acolyte wrote,

> In order to follow the diet at luncheons, I had to resign from the Rotary Club, but it was worth it. In 18 days, I not only lost a dozen pounds, but missed three after-dinner speeches.[12]

Who created the diet is unknown, but rumour has it that the actress Ethel Barrymore had the diet designed to get her quickly into shape for a role.[13] It generally consists of eating one grapefruit at each meal, along with meat, eggs, and other foods that are rich in fat and protein. The marketing campaign of the CAA pushed hard to have the avocado considered to be one of the few acceptable foodstuffs under the diet's strict rules. Given its links to California and to Los Angeles, in particular, it didn't seem like a difficult sell. Ultimately, the 18-Day Diet lost popularity. A famous Viennese actress Marietta Millner died having contracted tuberculosis following a voluntary starvation diet that had been deemed necessary to get her beneath the weight ceiling established by her studio contract.[14] While Millner's death may not have been specifically linked to the 18-Day Diet, it did open the door to criticism. "The 18-Day Diet is the worst fad this country has ever known," exclaimed Dr. J.J. Carter to the *Los Angeles Evening Post*.[15] "People who follow the diet are dying. The diet brings on tuberculosis and heart trouble as well." However, while the popularity of the diet declined, the popularity of the fruit continued to grow, helped by the association with Hollywood and health.

1980S CONSUMERISM

The avocados popularity seemed to grow steadily from the 1920s onwards. The one hiccup that they faced was the low-fat fad that was discussed in Chapter 3. With sales declining under the misconception that the avocado was fatty and unhealthy, drastic action needed to be taken to bolster the market. In addition to actively trying to promote the fruit as a "healthy fat," the avocado producers reverted to the standby of sex appeal and Hollywood to connect with their consumers. In 1981, Angie Dickinson, the actress and supermodel, was recruited to do TV ads to promote the fruit. In the clip, the actress Angie Dickinson lies seductively on the ground in a white leotard and gold stilettos.[16] She eats half an avocado with a silver spoon while asking the viewer softly, "Would this body lie to you?" The campaign continued by claiming that there were only 17 calories in a slice of avocado and that California avocados contained quantities of vitamins A, B1, C, and E, plus potassium. However, the National Advertising Division (NAD) of the Council of Better Business Bureaus didn't agree with this assessment and asserted that the size portion that would justify the vitamin claim is half a fruit, which actually contains 132 calories.[17] The NAD therefore required a copy change that was duly made. However, for the majority who saw the advert, most didn't see much beyond the provocative figure of Ms. Dickinson.

Seeing some evidence of the success of the campaign, the California Avocado Commission (the renamed CAA) decided to continue with the marketing campaign. They hired Hill & Knowlton, a marketing firm, to increase sales of the fruit across America. Hill & Knowlton came up with a mascot. Known as Mr. Ripe Guy, he would appear at various events as an avocado cheerleader of sorts. A popular and jovial figure, the novelty connected with consumers. However, key to any successful marketing campaign is keeping the content fresh. Consequently, in 1995, the Commission announced that Mr. Ripe Guy was feeling lonely; they would commence a nationwide search for "Ms. Ripe."[18] Contestants (for clarity, real women, as opposed to fruit) who "exemplified the California lifestyle of good health and healthy eating" were asked to apply.[19] Once again, the image of healthy lifestyles and Southern Californian chic was central to the avocado's image. And if that connection was not sufficiently rammed home enough with the advertisement's copy, the winner received a walk-on role on the TV show *Baywatch Nights* – the ultimate in California beach cool.

Next, the firm decided to link guacamole to sports. Nachos were already becoming a popular option at the concession stands, and so the firm aimed to make guacamole the key snack to eat while watching the NFL Super Bowl. The 1992 Super Bowl featured an ad for avocados (the first ever Super Bowl ad for fruit) that cost $4.5 million, and has been a staple each year since. In addition, the PR people set up camp in stadium press boxes and doled out guac samples to sports reporters. They peppered newspaper editors with avocado factoids to include in their copy. They concocted the idea of a "Guacamole Bowl" by soliciting recipes from NFL players with the public voting for the best recipe. A 1992 Philadelphia Eagles version, for example, recommended four ripe avocados, lemon juice, garlic, tomato, onion, cumin, pepper sauce, and "Pasadena red rose petals for garnish (optional)." This ploy was a huge success. Today, 26 million avocados were consumed on Super Bowl Sunday across America.[20] "No other single American event impacts the sale of avocados like the Super Bowl" said former Commission president Mark Affleck.[21] However, this high demand for guacamole for Super Bowl Sunday creates challenges for production. The game tends to be held in late January. This is fairly early in the growing season of the avocados in Michoacán. Most aren't yet ripe. The pressure to cash in on the unique Super Bowl opportunity has caused huge pressure on farmers to bring forward the harvest to accommodate the high demand.

AVOCADOS TOAST

As successful as the marketing of avocados for the Super Bowl was in expanding the market, it was nothing in comparison to the explosion caused by the creation of one specific dish. Ubiquitous to brunch menus from South

Korea to Spain, Oakland to Osaka, avocado toast has become a staple of Millennial diners. The success of avocado toast was deeply connected with both the rise of Instagram and wider social media and with the trend for "clean eating" that was discussed in Chapter 4. The dish photographed well and looked appealing – especially with a Clarendon filter. The New Yorker magazine is quick to highlight these overlapping trends, saying that the avocado toast has gained popularity,

> because it overlaps with another potent trend: "clean living" … it's healthy yet indulgent: "good fat," on the one hand, carbs on the other. It's incredibly easy to make. Most important, it looks great on Instagram, thereby making whoever posts photos of it look great.[22]

The myth goes that the first avocado toast was served up at Bill Granger's restaurant in Brisbane, Australia, in 1993. It exuded Aussie surfer cool – comparable with the Californian surfer chic with which avocados had long been associated. Granger himself said that his goal was to celebrate "the blue skies, the surf culture, the outdoors" with his food.[23] Australia's Gold Coast shares many of the same cultural trends as California: beaches, sun, and a vibrant surfer culture. The Australian dish taps into the same iconography and amplifies the connections that the CAA build between the fruit and the easy sunshine glamour and good health. The dish was an overnight success, and the chef launched a global brand on the back of its success.

However, much of the myth of the Brisbane birth of avocado toast proves exactly that, with little basis in fact. Avocado toast had been commonly served in San Francisco since at least 1885 when a recipe was published in a local newspaper,[24] and by 1915, the CAA itself recommended serving small squares of avocado toast as an hors d'oeuvre, possibly with a spot of caviar to accompany it.[25] References popped up through the decades, including in The New Yorker in 1937[26] and The New York Times in 1962,[27] long before it appeared on Granger's menu. Yet, despite that American history, Cafe Gitane in Manhattan (and now with a second location in the trendy Brooklyn) claimed to be New York's first avocado toast after consultant chef, Chloe Osbourne, added the dish to the menu in 1998. She used to eat the dish in Australia. Osbourne said "The thing of putting things on toast is very Australian, it stems from the British breakfast. Fresh tomatoes on toast has been an Australian breakfast for a long time."[28] The fact that a cafe in NoLita was the first US location for the dish represented something deeper about how it's perceived by society. *The New Yorker* writer, Nathan Heller, for whom the dish "remains a cultural cipher," wrote in his treatise, *A Grand Unified Theory of Avocado Toast,*

> The ascent began, say, in NoLita and SoHo, a district filled with well-travelled, fashion-adjacent people who could spread the good news. Avocado toast, in turn, was a fashion-friendly food: small, nourishing, refined, easy to share, customizable. It could be eaten in prim fashion, with a fork and knife. It could be consumed with the hands, without drippings or squirts. Carbohydrate-phobic diners could eat the avocado off the bread without looking demented. The toast stays simple enough to be calorie-countable, or to be ordered by special request in unknown lands. And, avocados being what they are, it's guaranteed fresh: an avocado mash laid to rest for an hour is visibly the worse for wear. In this respect, it is the ultimate cosmopolitan food, a dish for familiar pursuits in unfamiliar settings. That it seems to have arrived in the U.S. from a kindred nation only makes its urban transfer, all along the long-haul air routes of the world, apt.

GREEN MILLENNIALS

The pinnacle of the hundred year campaign to manipulate the image of the avocado as an affluent food that embodied surfer cool and wellness has resulted in the dish (and, by extension, the fruit itself) becoming synonymous with an entire generation. A Google search of avocado prompts the suggestion of "what is it with millennials and avocados?" Millennials are those born between 1980 and 1996 and came of age as the internet took hold. According to avocado historian, Jeff Miller, "Avocado consumption expresses [the] aspirations and assumptions for a millennial generation."[29] No other generation is epitomised by a fruit but yet somehow, Millennials have become inextricably associated with the fruit. Celebrities, such as Shawn Mendes, Miranda Kerr, and Chrissy Teigen, have exclaimed their love of the fruit. Miley Cyrus even has a tattoo of the fruit on her arm, while Kourtney Kardashian has talked[30] of the fruit as a hair mask. And the connection exists offline too. For example, Virgin Trains UK featured a promotion where Millennial travellers (and only Millennial travellers) could qualify for a discount if they presented an avocado when they purchased their railcard.[31]

Of even greater renowned is the scandal caused when Australian real estate mogul Tim Gurner suggested that Millennials were unable to purchase their own home because they wasted their money on avocado toast.[32] Speaking on the TV show, 60 Minutes in Australia, in 2017, he said, "When I was trying to buy my first home, I wasn't buying smashed avocado for $19 and four coffees at $4 each."[33] Asked if he believes young people will never own a home, he responded: "Absolutely, when you're spending $40 a day on smashed avocados and coffees and not working. Of course." The comment echoed those of another Australian, Bernard Salt, a demographer who wrote in the Australian in 2016,

> I have seen young people order smashed avocado with crumbled feta on five-grain toasted bread at $22 a pop and more. I can afford to eat this for lunch because I am middle aged and have raised my family. But how can young people afford to eat like this? Shouldn't they be economising by eating at home? How often are they eating out? Twenty-two dollars several times a week could go towards a deposit on a house.[34]

The pushback against both inflammatory and ill-conceived comments was fast and visceral. Some Millennials argued that avocado toast represents experiential spending. Well aware that they can't afford their own home, they find smaller pleasure spending on daily experiences. Others responded with a simpler response of "okay, boomer," highlighting the hypocrisy of the claim. The Guardian's Rhiannon Lucy Cosslett wrote back in response,

> Brunch has become a convenient scapegoat for structural inequality. Instead of truly examining the social and economic forces that lock young people out of the property market, why not focus on our expenditure? Never mind that, for most young people, it would take over a century of skipping their luxurious monthly brunch in order to get a mortgage for a poky starter home. Never mind that older generations had access to free or heavily discounted education, cheap property prices and stable, unionised employment, or the fact that their breakfast options were severely limited.[35]

However, the fact that avocados were selected as the symbol of the generation deserves deeper consideration. Vice News has referred to "the humble avocado, which has become an unwitting mascot in an intergenerational war, a proxy for the spendthrift ways of the youth."[36] For social commentator, Ash Sarkar, the avocado acts as a shortcut for a deeper generational tension between Millennial and Baby Boomer. Speaking on BBC Radio4, she said,

> This speaks to a deeper cultural narrative and that cultural narrative is about Millennials and Zoomers [also known as GenZ, born between 1997–2012) who tend to have more progressive views saying, "well you hold all these lofty opinions but look at you. You're hypocrites! You're buying this [fruit] but yet you're making me feel bad for driving an SUV and having three holiday homes in the South of France". What that's about is trying to discredit the social, cultural, political disposition of young people by pointing out hypocrisy. Now if you wanted to hold up a symbole of clueless entitlement and privilege, you could talk about Chateauneuf-du-Pape but nobody does because that's what Telegraph comment writers drink.[37]

Essentially, Sarkar's argument is that Baby Boomers use the avocado as a way of demonstrating the hypocrisy in the Millennial generation. It provides a method by which Baby Boomers can critique the Millennial generation by saying that for all their talk of "wokeness" and progressive political ideals, they still purchase and consume a product that is ethically and environmentally damaging. This was certainly the undertone of the 2019 *Daily Mail* headline on Meghan Markle, Duchess of Sussex, attacking her for serving avocado toast at a Kensington Palace high tea, titled, "How Meghan's favourite avocado snack – beloved of all millennials – is fuelling human rights abuses, drought and murder."[38] The article raised legitimate questions about the production of the fruit (all of which will be discussed in later chapters), but the tone was hardly academic and dispassionate. The article fixated on the hypocrisy of her eating avocado toast while campaigning for a more progressive politics, saying, "The campaigning duchess may be passionate when it comes to racial equality and female empowerment, but for someone who wants to save the planet, she's committed something of a faux pas with avocados." Implicit to the story was the shared Californian connection of the dish and the former Hollywood actress, turned Duchess, lending it even more resonance. By just serving avocado toast (admittedly on a not so egalitarian silver platter), she had provided a perfect symbol for the right-wing media to critique her liberal progressivism.

IN CONCLUSION...

Ultimately, the marketing campaign launched by the CAA in the 1920s to increase American consumption of the fruit has been an unmitigated success. They transformed the image of the fruit from something that only Central Americans ate into something that was consumed in every corner of the world, in particularly by affluent, White consumers. They did this by consistently altering the image from an aphrodisiac into a clean eating phenomenon that evoked the laid-back beach cool of Southern California. From novelty food of the elites, it is now a common sight on supermarket shelves across the Global North. This explosion of demand for avocado – whether smashed on toast or for Superbowl nachos – has led to ramped-up production of the fruit around the world.

NOTES

1 "Avocado growers see ruin in name 'alligator pears'." *The New York Times*, 1927, February 10.

2 "Immigration and relocation in U.S. history." *The Library of Congress*.

3 Ngai, Mae, *Impossible Subjects: Illegal Aliens and the Making of Modern America*. Princeton University Press, 2004. https://press.princeton.edu/books/paperback/9780691160825/impossible-subjects.

4 Florido, Adrian, "Mass Deportation may sound unlikely, but it's happened before." *National Public Radio*, 2015, September 8.

5 Khazan, Olga, "The selling of the avocado." *The Atlantic*, 2015, January 31.

6 "Cooking with the (Silent) stars: Ramon Novarro's Guacamole." *Movies Silently*, 2017, November 2.

7 Root, Waverly, & Rochemont, Richard, "Eating in America." *PerfectBound*, 1999, May 24.

8 Calder, "Lobster and grapefruit salad." *Cooking Channel*. https://www.cookingchanneltv.com/recipes/laura-calder/lobster-and-grapefruit-salad-2119775#.

9 Khazan, Olga, "The selling of the avocado." *The Atlantic*, 2015, January 31.

10 Knollin, J.C. "Advertising and Publicity in their relation to the avocado industry." *California Avocado Society*, 1920–1921.

11 Ewbank, Anne, "Looking like a flapper meant a diet of celery and cigarettes." *Atlas Obscura*, 2018, April 20.

12 Douglass, Ian, "The golden age hollywood diet that starved its famous starlets – And then America." *Bunk*, 2022, March 31.

13 Addison, Heather, *Hollywood and the Rise of Physical Culture*. Routledge, 2015, April 23.

14 "Marietta Millner." *Wikipedia*, 2023, January 19.

15 Douglass, Ian, "The golden age Hollywood diet that starved its famous starlets—And then America." *Bunk*, 2022, March 31.

16 "California Avocados w/ Angie Dickinson," *YouTube*, 17 July, 2007.

17 Dougherty, Philip, "Advertising; The truth about avocados." *The New York Times*, 1981, February 17.

18 Klein, Charles, & Rao, Vivek. "The Rice Thresher (Houston, Tex.)," Vol. 82, issue 25, Ed. 1 Friday, 1995, April 7, newspaper, 1995, April 7; Houston, Texas.

19 Ibid.

20 "Super bowl consumption by the numbers." *Bleacher Report*, 2008, February 1.

21 Khazan, Olga, "The selling of the avocado." *The Atlantic*, 2015, January 31.

22 Goldfield, Hannah, "The trend is toast." *The New Yorker*, 2014, May 2.

23 Parker, Pamela, Ishikawa, Juntaro, Nagao, Futa & Ishitani, Yoko, "Bill Granger: 'Godfather' of avocado toast." *BBC News*, 2019, February 26.

24 Daily Alta California, General notes, *California Digital Newspaper Collection*, Vol. 39, Issue 13019, 1885, November 5.

25 "The California avocado association is issuing in folder form the following suggestions for preparing the avocado for the table," *California Avocado Association*, 1915.

26 Perelman, S.J., "Avocado, or the future of eating," *The New Yorker*, 1937, April 23.

27 Oyler, Lauren, "My fruitful search for the origins of avocado toast," *Vice*, 2016, September 13.

28 Orenstein, Jayne, "How the Internet became ridiculously obsessed with avocado toast." *The Washington Post*, 2016, May 6.

29 Miller, Jeff, *Avocado: A Global History*. Reaktion Books, 2020.

30 Campbell, Deena, "Kourtney Kardashian says an avocado smoothie is the secret to getting shiny hair." *Allure*, 2016, November 28.

31 Coulter, Martin, "Millennials left baffled by Virgin Trains bizarre avocado offer." *Evening Standard*, 2018, March 13.

32 Levin, Sam, "Millionaire tells millennials: If you want a house, stop buying avocado toast." *The Guardian*, 2017, May 15.

33 Ibid.

34 Ibid.

35 Cosslett, Rhiannon Lucy, "Stop spending money on avocados? Good idea, I'll have a house deposit by 2117." *The Guardian*, 2017, May 16.

36 Vice, "Millennials and their avocado toast." *YouTube*, 2019, January 15.

37 Kazim, Leyla, "Avoiding the avocado." *BBC Audio*, 2022, November 7.

38 Leonard, Tom, "How Meghan's favourite avocado snack - beloved of all millennials - is fuelling human rights abuses, drought and murder." *Daily Mail*, 2019, January 22.

KEY READINGS

- "Avocado growers see ruin in name 'Alligator Pears'." *The New York Times*, 1927, February 10.
- Cosslett, Rhiannon Lucy, "Stop spending money on avocados? Good idea, I'll have a house deposit by 2117." *The Guardian*, 2017, May 16.
- Khazan, Olga, "The selling of the avocado." *The Atlantic*, 2015, January 31.
- Knollin, J.C., "Advertising and publicity in their relation to the avocado industry." *California Avocado Society*, 1920–1921.
- Oyler, Lauren, "My Fruitful search for the origins of avocado toast." *Vice*, 2016, September 13.

5

GREEN GOLD

THE CREATION OF NAFTA AND
THE RESISTANCE OF US PRODUCERS

INTRODUCTION

The North American Free Trade Agreement (NAFTA) sparked the transformation of the production of avocados in North America. The Agreement meant that avocados from Mexico could be sold in the United States for the first time, which ultimately meant that Mexican avocados came to dominate the US market. Opening up the US market was hard won since US avocado producers fought bitterly to protect their interests. Prior to NAFTA, domestic avocados had an advantage over imported ones since there were protectionist policies in place. But, with the signing of NAFTA and the move towards free trade, those protections started to be eroded, and eventually, the Mexicans were granted tariff- and barrier-free access. Once the protections had been removed, US producers could not compete and Mexican avocados came to dominate the US market, which could never have been achieved without NAFTA. Ultimately, the Agreement enabled the fruit to move from a traditional, local fruit into a global commodity crop.

BACKGROUND

Based on theories put forward by the 18th-century economists, Adam Smith and David Ricardo, the desire for free and open trade gathered pace in the 20th century. In the Post-War period, there was an increased global desire to

DOI: 10.4324/9781003371915-5

integrate markets to allow goods and services to flow across borders seam-lessly as US prosperity and global influence grew. The first step in this pro-cess was the Bretton Woods Agreement in 1944 and the General Agreement on Tariffs and Trade (GATT). As the Cold War came to an end, there were more and more leaders who were pushing for free trade and open markets, believing that it would bring increased prosperity. Around the globe, there was a growing desire for nations with closely aligned interests (i.e. geo-graphic proximity) to deepen trade relations and strengthen regional eco-nomic alignment. Bilateral – or multilateral – free trade agreements (FTAs) occur when two nations (or more in the case of multilateral FTAs) agree a set of trade terms to govern the exchange between their two economies and create a free flow of goods and services.

The vision behind NAFTA was to create a free trade zone across Mex-ico, the United States and Canada so that goods (including avocados) could move across the borders without barriers. The 1994 agreement was first conceptualised by President Reagan who made it core to his elec-tion campaign in 1980, promising that a free trade zone within North America would bring economic growth and opportunity to America.[1] To this end, the United States signed an FTA with Canada in the last year of Reagan's tenure, which was known as the Canada–US Free Trade Agree-ment (CUSFTA) of 1988. A year later, Reagan's Vice-President George H. Bush had replaced Reagan in the Oval Office and now-President Bush started the negotiations to create a new FTA with its southern neighbour. However, Canada was concerned that they could lose the advantage they had achieved with CUSFTA if a new bilateral arrangement between the United States and Mexico went ahead. So, despite their pre-existing FTA, they petitioned to join the discussion and make it a trilateral FTA. While its main objective was to alter the trade dynamics between the three North American nations, its importance in the wider global economy cannot be understated. According to Hufbauer and Schott in their book, NAFTA Revisited, NAFTA played a role in facilitating the liberalisation of world trade at the multilateral level.[2] The agreement helped provide the final push to the completion of the Uruguay Round of the WTO and has become a template for the subsequent FTAs that have come to dominate trade policy in recent years. After 14 months of hard slog, the negotia-tions concluded in 1992 with a text to which each of the three nations were willing to sign up.

SHIFTING IDEOLOGY

The growing adoption of free market economics from the end of WWII to the 1990s was quite a shift in economic history of the United States. Prior to that, there had not been such a fixation of free trade nor on the perceived benefit of globalisation. The United States had historically has a strong focus on protecting and nurturing domestic industries. This had been achieved by an array of policy levers – some more obvious than others. Bans on imports of specific goods or from specific countries were easy to spot, such as the ban on all imports from Cuba. Others were achieved through tariffs that made domestic goods more competitive by forcing imported products to be sold at higher prices to recoup the additional border charge. This was the motivation behind the Smoot-Hawley Tariff Act, which was enacted in June 1930.[3] This Act raised import duties on foreign agricultural products (and manufactured goods) by 20% with the goal of restoring the failing US farming sector. However, the sneakier approach, which is the one taken to protect the US avocado industry, related to the use of sanitary and phytosanitary (SPS) measures. On the surface, these regulations ensure the protection of public health, allowing a nation to block the import of food (or other products) considered to be potentially damaging or dangerous. These are not considered to be barriers to trade, provided that they meet certain standards.

- Not arbitrarily discriminate among like goods,
- Based on scientific principles and would be repealed if that scientific basis changed,
- Based on an appropriate risk assessment,
- Applied only to an extent necessary to protect the public,
- Not based on a bad-faith attempt to distort the free market.

However, these measures often provide cover for protectionist action. Such was the case with avocados. The United States enacted a ban on the import of Mexican avocados on February 27, 1914, when the USDA imposed a quarantine on avocados grown in Mexico and Central America to prevent the introduction of seed weevils, stem borers and other pests.[4] The USDA argument rested on the SPS threat of invasive species and pests being able to enter the States through the imported fruit, which could destroy the orchards in Florida and in California. However, while the weevils did pose some degree of threat to the trees in the US orchards, in reality, the ban enabled a fledgling industry to grow without competition from abroad. According to John Shepard and Gary Bender in their article on the history of the avocado industry in California, "it allowed the young California industry to nurture and grow without excessive competition."[5] The 1914 ban remained in place and was still active when NAFTA negotiations began.

NAFTA OPPOSITION

Presidents Reagan and Bush were both enthusiastic supporters of NAFTA. However, just because US leaders had moved their ideology towards globalisation and were on board with a push towards free trade, it did not mean that everyone saw it as a positive step. From the right wing to the left wing of America, community leaders and power brokers raised their voices in protest of the Agreement's push for free trade. Their objections were wide-ranging – they argued that it would do everything from destroying jobs in the United States, undermining communities, to threatening the environment. In the United States, the agriculture sector was massively divided over it. For example, the American Farm Bureau Federation was for NAFTA, while the National Farmers Union was against it; the National Corn Growers Association was pro-NAFTA, while the American Corn Growers Association was anti-NAFTA. The opposition saw the threat of the protections that they had previously enjoyed disappearing and were scared that cheaper goods from abroad would undercut their market. Those in favour thought that they would be able to benefit from being able to sell into the two other countries.

The US opposition to NAFTA campaigned against President George H. Bush as he sought re-election. Instead, they favoured a candidate that they thought would be more receptive to their concerns over the deal. Despite the different ideology to his predecessor, President Clinton was still generally in favour of NAFTA and was keen to enact it into law, but with a few caveats. He argued for the creation of two side agreements: the North American Agreement on Labor Cooperation[6] (NAALC) and the North American Agreement on Environmental Cooperation[7] (NAAEC) that protected workers and the environment, respectively – both of which impacted the avocado sector. Clinton's demand for these concessions were enough to win him the support of many of those who had opposed President Bush and gave the Agreement enough political support to pass through Congress. Surrounded by an array of flags and with adequate pomp and circumstance, President Clinton signed the NAFTA into law on December 8th, 1993.[8] Less than a month later, the world's largest free trading bloc came into being.

NAFTA AND AGRICULTURE

By signing up to the Agreement, all three nations committed to removing any barriers to free trade in all sectors of their economy. To achieve free trade and meet the objectives laid out in NAFTA, agricultural tariffs and price controls within US food and farming had to be removed. Given the fact that the US farming industry had been so reliant on them, there was some trepidation of removing them in one fell swoop, in case it disrupted the sector. In addition, industry groups lobbied hard to ensure they continued to receive agricultural subsidies. To avoid rocking the sector, the removal of barriers was done slowly and some tariff-rate quotas were allowed to remain for specific goods. However, some controversial farm subsidies were allowed to remain more permanently, something that has continued to cause dispute. Most notably, US farmers have kept access to subsidies via the US Farm Bill. Since 1994, Mexican and Canadian producers have repeatedly pointed to these as trade distorting, claiming that they give US producers an unfair advantage since farm businesses are propped up and subsidized by the US government. For example, between 1998 and 2000, the average agricultural subsidy received by a US producer was $20,803, while the average support payment to a Mexican producer was $720.[9] But despite protests over these differences, these US subsidies remain in place.

AVOCADO-SPECIFIC NEGOTIATIONS

What did NAFTA mean for avocados? The saga of the Mexican vs. US avocado battle of market access was protracted and convoluted. However, ultimately, it led to the commodification and globalisation of the fruit. As Nathan Heller wrote in his *New Yorker* article, *A Grand Unified Theory of Avocado Toast,*

> a politics of avocadoism is intrinsic to this history.[10] If you worry about the eclipse of American agriculture—or the market effects of cheap, distance-shipped produce—you'd be right to regard this international trade with disgust... If, on the other hand, you celebrate competitive international trade and cosmopolitan access, the avocado is a fruit of heroism.

Despite NAFTA's stated goal of market access and free trade, throughout the negotiations, the US avocado industry pressured the US government to safeguard their industry from Mexican competition. The industry wanted to see the 1914 ban remain in place. US growers used their political heft to lobby the USDA to maintain the ban. To achieve this, the Floridian avocado growers joined forces with the Californian growers to fight side by side. First, they created an emotive narrative – one based in fear. Using similar scare tactics, incendiary language, and political proficiency that had proved successful in getting the ban enacted in the 1910s, the growers stoked fears about the threat of Mexican imports. Their language echoed the narrative that surrounded the original ban and was racist in tone, with suggestions that Mexican produce was dirty and dangerous and should not be allowed to contaminate America by being allowed to cross the border. Second, they used Florida's electoral importance. Given that Florida was a critical swing state in US elections, the growers knew that they would be able to exert more pressure on the Clinton Administration with the promise to deliver Floridian votes. Promising to help canvas for Clinton, the Florida Fruit and Vegetable Association successfully applied pressure to get the concessions they wanted on avocados, and the USDA upheld the ban.

However, their victory was not secure for long. By the mid-1990s, American growers could not keep up with the demand for avocados in the United States. Growers in California and Florida could sell their entire crop without issue – and there would still be a clammer for more. US supermarkets were desperate to give the consumer fruit consistently available across the entire year. This meant looking across the border since the avocado orchards in California and Florida could only fill the shelves during the summer season when the fruit was ripe. The climate south of the border enabled year-round avocado production and the retailers started lobbying the USDA to relax the ban. The USDA was receptive to this message. As Tom Bellmore, the Senior VP and Corporate Counsel of the California Avocado Commission, acknowledged; "maintaining an exclusion policy [had] become an untenable position for the US government.[11] The consequence of maintaining the exclusion goal in the face of a NAFTA-changed arena are legal challenges founded on claims that the US is not complying with NAFTA provisions." The risk of Mexico bringing a case against America for breaking the terms of NAFTA was undesirable to the US government to say the least. And so, as 1995 began, the USDA started to look at how to lift the ban.

The Florida Fruit and Vegetable Association was not going to give up without a fight. But they increasingly had other problems to contend with. Instead of Mexican farmers looking to cut into their market share, developers were trying to convince Floridian farmers to sell their land for housing from the mid-1990s onwards. The farmland in Florida became highly desirable. A report by the American Farmland Trust (AFT) describes Florida as "one of the top 12 most threatened states in the nation due to the loss of farmland to poorly planned real estate development."[12] This prompted an exodus from the agricultural sector in Florida and weakened the lobbying power that their trade organisation had once had. By 1995, the political power of the state's agricultural sector had waned enough that they could no longer keep the protections in place. However, the Californians were standing by to take up the cause and continued to insist that the risk of disease spreading to their fruit from Mexico was still too high to be acceptable. Yet, their argument was meeting more and more resistance within the Clinton Administration and the USDA that were increasingly in favour of opening the market to competition.

The USDA published an initial notice in the *Federal Register* that proposed allowing avocados from orchards in Mexico that were inspected and met the USDA standards to be shipped to the United States.[13] The USDA amended the proposed rule so that imports would only be allowed into 19 northeastern US states.[14] The Californian growers still objected, asserting that Americans "might buy the Mexican avocados in New York and still bring them to California," spreading pests and disease in their wake.[15] Keen to keep some advantage over the Mexican producers, even when the tide was moving against them, the US growers managed to have the proposed USDA rule amended. The USDA agreed to the Californian proposal that Mexican avocados could only be shipped between November and February to avoid direct competition with Californian avocado producers that couldn't supply in the winter months and insisted that the trucks carrying the Mexican fruit would not pass through California, with the aspiration of minimising the chance of diseases or pests from Mexican orchards travelling to Californian trees.[16] Furthermore, still under the auspices of SPS criteria, the Californian growers insisted that Mexican avocado producers would have to pay to have the USDA monitor the presence of pests in Mexican orchards if they wanted to gain access to the US market.[17] With all these stipulations agreed, the USDA published the Final Rule allowing for the shipment of Mexican avocados that met the conditions outlined from March 1997 onwards.[18] Only one state in Mexico could meet these SPS requirements: Michoacán. They were posed and ready to go when the USDA finally allowed Mexican avocados to cross the border. We will look at the impact and subsequent impacts in the next chapter.

USMCA

While the fate of the US avocado industry was sealed in 1997, the saga of NAFTA was not over, and its role in partisan American politics was far from finished. Tension over free trade vs. American production has continued to be a contentious subject. No more so than in recent years under President Trump. Who made opposition to free trade and his goal to put "American First" a core part of his 2016 campaign and administration. NAFTA won particular ire. In one of the debates against Hilary Clinton, he bluntly stated that "NAFTA is the worst trade deal maybe ever signed anywhere, but certainly ever signed in this country."[19] It was not lost that it was her husband, Bill, who signed NAFTA into law during his presidency. This opposition to NAFTA fit within Trump's wider anti-Mexican agenda that centred around immigration and his desire to halt illegal access to the United States by building a wall along the southern border, launching his campaign saying "They are not our friend, believe me… They're bringing drugs. They're bringing crime. They're rapists. And some, I assume, are good people."[20] Once in office, he started the process of renegotiating NAFTA. These negotiations resulted in the new USMCA (US–Mexico–Canada FTA) trade deal that was signed and ratified by the US Congress in January 2020.[21]

While the rejection of NAFTA as unfair and un-American has become closely associated with President Trump in recent years, the Democrats in reality have a much longer history of fighting against the Agreement. It was Republican Presidents Reagan and Bush who started the push for a North American FTA while the Democrats were the ones that were more hesitant to free trade historically. Trump's 2016 rhetoric was oddly reminiscent of (Bill, not Hillary) Clinton's language in the 1994 campaign. Then, Clinton criticised the Republicans saying, "If I had negotiated that treaty, it would be better"[22]. John Edwards (who's political career ultimately unravelled in a spectacularly sordid manner) similarly pitched himself against the deal in 2004, saying "trade policies are killing your jobs,"[23] while, at the same time, John Kerry, who became Secretary of State under President Obama, critiqued the deal in his 2004 Presidential run saying that it should be renegotiated.[24] Yet, as of 2023, it is former President Trump and the Republican Party that dominate the anti-trade, anti-NAFTA agenda.

IN CONCLUSION...

The NAFTA was one of the foundational FTAs and has set the standard for subsequent FTAs around the world. The negotiation was a hard-fought political battle with entrenched parties on both sides. Ultimately, it changed the economic dynamics of all three countries and ushered in a new era of integration. While the Agreement (and the disagreements) was broader than avocados and agriculture, the impacts felt by American farmers specifically growing the fruit were sizable and changed the market forever. Now, Mexican orchards, instead of growing avocados for local communities, could grow for the United States, priming the avocado industry to move from subsistence to commodity crop. We will look at this shift in more detail in the next chapter.

NOTES

1 Wilson, M., "The North American free trade agreement: Ronald Reagan's vision realized." *The Heritage Foundation*, 1993, November 23.
2 Hufbauer, Gary, & Schott, Jeffrey, assisted by Grieco & Wong, *NAFTA Revisited: Achievements and Challenges*. Peterson Institute for International Economics, 2005, October.
3 *United States Senate*, "The Senate passes the Smoot-Hawley Tariff." 1930, June 13.
4 Groves, Martha, & Sheridan, Mary Beth, "U.S lifts ban on avocados from Mexico." *Los Angeles Times*, 1997, February 1.
5 Arpaia, M. L., Bender, G. S., Francis, L., Menge,. J. A., Shepherd, J. S. & Smothers, V. W., *Avocado Production in California: A Cultural Handbook for Growers*. The University of California Cooperative Extension & The California Avocado Society, 2004.
6 U.S. Department of Labor, "North American agreement on labor cooperation: A guide." 2005, October.
7 *Wikipedia*, "North American agreement on environmental cooperation." 2021, November 13.
8 Amadeo, Kimberley, "The history of NAFTA and its purpose." *The Balance*, 2022, March 18.
9 Sarmiento, Sergio, "Mexico alert: NAFTA and Mexico's agriculture." *Center for Strategic and International Studies*, 2003, March 3.
10 Heller, Nathan, "A Grand unified theory of avocado toast." *The New Yorker*, 2017, July 13.
11 Bellamore, Tom, "Mexican avocados: History...The full story." *California Avocado Society, Yearbook 86*, 2002.
12 Farms Under Threat, "The state of the states." *American Farmland Trust*, 2020.

13 King, "Importation of fresh hass avocado fruit grown in Michoacan, Mexico." *Federal Register* Vol. 60, Issue 127, 1995, July 3.

14 Groves & Sheridan, "U.S lifts ban on avocados from Mexico."

15 Bellamore, "Mexican avocados: History…The full story."

16 USDA, "Importation of fresh Hass avocado fruit grown in Michoacan, Mexico." *Federal Register,* Vol. 60, Issue 127, 1995, July 3.

17 Osoyo, Ariel, "Avocado annual." *United States Department of Agriculture,* 2020, September 10.

18 APHIS, "Importation of fresh Hass avocado fruit grown in Michoacan, Mexico." *"Federal Register,* Vol. 62, Issue 24, 1997, February 5.

19 Gillespie, Patrick, "Trump Hammers America's 'worst trade deal'." *CNN Business,* 2016, September 27.

20 Phillips, Amber, "'They're rapists.' President Trump's campaign launch speech two years later, annotated." *The Washington Post,* 2017, June 16.

21 Swanson, Ana, & Tankersley, Jim, "Trump just signed the U.S.M.C.A. here's what's in the new NAFTA." *The New York Times,* 2020, January 29.

22 Auerbach, Stuart, "Mexico's President hedges on trade pact deals." *Washington Post,* 1992, October 10.

23 Witcover, Jules, "In Ohio, trade talk resonates." *The Baltimore Sun,* 2004, February 25.

24 Nagourney, Adam, "Edwards says NAFTA is important, but in need of change." *The New York Times,* 2004, February 24.

KEY READINGS

- Arpaia, M.L., Bender, G.S., Francis, L., Menge,. J.A., Shepherd, J.S. & Smothers, V.W., *Avocado Production in California: A Cultural Handbook for Growers.* The University of California Cooperative Extension & The California Avocado Society, 2004.

- Bellamore, Tom, "Mexican avocados: History…the full story." *California Avocado Society Yearbook* 86, 2002.

- Heller, Nathan, "A grand unified theory of avocado toast." *The New Yorker,* 13 July, 2017.

- Hufbauer, Gary, & Schott, Jeffrey, assisted by Grieco & Wong, *NAFTA Revisited: Achievements and Challenges.* Peterson Institute for International Economics, October 2005.

6

HOLY GUACAMOLE

IMPACT OF NAFTA ON MEXICAN FOOD SYSTEMS

INTRODUCTION

Just like the political leaders in the United States, President Carlos Salinas de
Gortari promised Mexicans that the NAFTA Agreement would bring wealth
and opportunity to Mexico. Mexico had a young and rapidly expanding
population that needed jobs and economic opportunities. The leading political party, Institutional Revolutionary Party (PRI), had governed Mexico for
decades and believed that increased integration with the US market would
create that much-needed growth in Mexico by stimulating the economy.
He was positive about the potential outcome and pushed for signing the
agreement. According to Hufbauer and Schott, "NAFTA was an economic
opportunity to capitalise on a growing export market to the south and…
NAFTA reforms promised to open new doors for US exporters."[1]

However, the immediate aftermath from NAFTA wasn't as positive as
President de Gortari might have hoped. Firstly, Zapatista rebels in Chiapas
Mexico launched an uprising to coincide with the signing of the Agreement.
This destabilised the region and called into question the democratic underpinning of the PRI. However, that was not the biggest shock. Mexico experienced a huge economic crisis after the signing of NAFTA. In 1994, with the
current account deficit widening, the Mexican government suddenly deval-
ued the peso, which caused panic. The run on the Mexican banks prompted
a massive recession as foreign investment fled.[2] The gross domestic product
(GDP) declined by 6.2% in one year,[3] causing prices in Mexico to rise by

DOI: 10.4324/9781003371915-6

24%[4] over a four-month period and total inflation for the year reaching 52%.[5] As a result, extreme poverty skyrocketed, real wages plummeted, and unemployment nearly doubled. Hufbauer and Schott highlight that

> to opponents, the temporal connection between NAFTA ratification and Mexico's economic collapse was too powerful to be mere coincidence.[6] To supporters, the peso crisis was rooted in macroeconomic policy mistakes, far removed from the trade and investment bargain struck within NAFTA

Such a mistake would include the lax regulations and corruption within the Mexican banking sector. The reality is probably a blend of the two.

Eventually, in Jan 1995, the United States stepped in to secure a loan package to rescue the Mexican economy from further collapse.[7] The package totalled $20 billion in immediate assistance and $30 billion from other sources (e.g. IMF) with restrictions of fiscal constraint, tight money supply, and currency devaluation.[8] The intervention saved the Mexican economy – even if the medicine was tough to take – and it is quite possible that the United States would never have acted to intervene were it not for the economic ties that NAFTA had created. The ties also provided for an export-led recovery to take off. American companies moved into Mexico since the economy made it an attractive proposition, especially with wages depressed. Mean manufacturing wages fell by 21% over the 1994–1996 period following the peso crisis, which was enticing for US employers who could get a good deal south of the border.[9]

LONG-TERM ECONOMIC INTEGRATION

Once the Peso Crisis subsided, the Mexican economy did start to benefit from the Agreement with exports to the US rising and money coming in from the North. Trade between the NAFTA countries grew considerable in the decade following the treaty. From 1993 to 2000, Mexico's trade with NAFTA partners increased from 25% of Mexico's GDP to 51%, and, overall, NAFTA helped to create jobs and alleviate poverty in Mexico.[10] Evidence shows that average salaries in foreign-funded companies (i.e. the American ones that relocated to Mexico after NAFTA) are 48% higher than the national average. With these better paying jobs came prosperity for many families. According to the World Bank, the share of the Mexican population living below $2 a day declined from 42.5% in 1995 to 26.3% in 2000.[11] It is likely that this economic growth in Mexico since 1994 would have occurred without the free trade agreement (FTA) due to the trend towards globalisation and increased international trade, coupled with the new technologies available. However, NAFTA sped up this process.

However, this increase was not felt equally across the country. In rural Mexico where 65% of the country's extreme poor live, inequality has worsened.[12] This is, in part, due to the realities of the rural job market. Rural agricultural labourers work under much harsher conditions and earn far less pay than urban workers, especially those in the manufacturing sector, encouraging a migration to cities. This isn't helped by the fact that the industrialisation of agriculture reduces the need for workers since more and more can be automated. For example, a large harvester requires a single driver vs. scything, which requires a team of labourers. Since 1994, the share of agricultural employment in Mexico fell from 26% of total employment to 18% in 2001,[13] dropping from 8.1 million pre-NAFTA[14] to 6.8 million in 2003.[15] Many of the small rural businesses (such as small farms or small processing plants) have been forced to shutter also, unable to compete with the large international firms. This had been an identified risk before NAFTA was signed (at the time, it was estimated that NAFTA would displace 1.4 million rural Mexicans) but the powers that be thought that the benefit to the wider Mexican economy would be worth it.[16]

MICHOACÁN'S AVOCADO OPPORTUNITY

Michoacán is located west of Mexico City. The region's mountainous landscape is perfectly suited for avocados since it is situated within the Trans-Mexican Volcanic Belt. The ash from these volcanoes supplies the surrounding land with nutrients, creating a particularly fertile landscape. In addition to the rich volcanic soil, there is enough sunlight and rainfall throughout the year for the fruit to grow.[17] Uruapan, where most avocado orchards in Michoacán are located, receives around 64 in. of precipitation annually. Therefore, historically, growers did not need irrigation to maintain their orchards. Nature provided a perfect location for avocados to grow in huge quantities.[18]

By the time NAFTA was signed, the region had already undergone a transition towards large-scale growing. From the 1950s onwards, a new farming dynamic had emerged and taken hold in Michoacán.[19] Academics,

Dela Cerda Gastélum and Núñez de la Peña, referred to this model as the "empresario model" which saw one individual run the daily operations, while a separate entrepreneur assumed the financial risk and owned the land. This model, coupled with its landscape, made the region's agriculture sector more efficient and allowed it to adopt the large-scale, export-based horticulture required to make a success of the opportunities that NAFTA presented. The region also commercialised the varieties that they were growing, just as the Californian growers had done in the 1920s and 1930s. In the early 1950s, several entrepreneurs, notably none native to Michoacán, established nurseries in Uruapan, bringing in budwood from Poblano Fuertes. As the decade progressed, these local nursery owners began to import Fuerte and Hass budwood from California, making the harvest more consistent and commercially viable. As the Hass increasingly took over, the indigenous landrace avocados were cut down or grafted with Hass scions, and mixed farming in the region progressively switched to monoculture plantations. This large-scale, more commercial production meant that wages in the avocado plantations of Michoacán are also considerably higher than for other low-skilled jobs in the region.[20] Avocado plantation worker can earn $60 per day, well more than the $5 minimum wage in Mexico, making the work very attractive.

As discussed in the last chapter, the United States maintained a ban on avocado imports from Mexico on the basis of the poor phytosanitary standards in Mexican orchards but eventually relented and allowed exports from states that met the USDA standard and covered the cost for the inspections. Only Michoacán could meet these requirements. Because of the earlier transition to more industrialised farming under "the empresario model," they were already geared up by 1997 with the required infrastructure (pack houses, refrigeration, roads and rail) and business model to adopt the USDA standards and companies that had the economic ability to meet the additional inspection costs. Consequently, as the US avocado market slowly and incrementally opened up, the Michoacán farmers were ready to seize the opportunity and began exporting their fruit into the United States.

Seize it they did. Soon Michoacán's avocados were making their way north. Within a few years of the ban being lifted, the region dominated as the largest producer of avocados in Mexico.[21] However, the United States still limited the states that could accept Mexican fruit and the months in which it could be sold. Before too long, the region's growers grew frustrated with the lack of access. Just as the Floridian and Californian growers had lobbied their government, so did the Michoacán farmers push Mexico City[22] to challenge the restrictions. President Ernesto Zedillo made a formal request to the US government to increase access to the American market and lift the remaining restrictions.[23] On November 1st, 2001, USDA/APHIS (Animal and Plant Health Inspection Service) published in the US *Federal Register* the "Mexican Avocado Import Final Rule" that meant Mexican avocados could be sold on supermarket shelves in 31 states and lengthened the time of the shipping season through April 15 of each year.[24] The Californian growers fought back, filing a lawsuit in federal court asking that the rule be declared invalid based on phytosanitary issues. Superficially, they claimed to still be scared of those pesky Mexican avocados bringing in disease. They lost when the judge saw through their weak argument, to the delight of Mexican exporters. On November 30th, 2004, USDA issued a Final Rule that allowed Mexican avocados to be shipped to all 50 states for all 12 months of the year. After a decade of fighting, the American avocado industry had finally lost and could no longer stop the flow of Mexican fruit.[25]

By then, Michoacán dominated the Mexican avocado industry, accounting for 80% of the avocados produced in the country. Its professionalised production system and impressive supply chain infrastructure had put all other avocado-producing regions in Mexico to shame.[26] But the complete removal of all restrictions gave Michoacán's orchards another boost. The yields (and associated profit) went stratospheric. Today, it produces 5.5 billion pounds[27] of the fruit a year from 42,000 avocado orchards.[28] It is the heart of the global avocado market and its economy is thriving. Through determination to push the United States to open the industry, endurance to weather the storm of the economic crisis, and dumb luck of location, Michoacán was able to emerge from NAFTA victorious.

PUEBLA'S AVOCADO DECLINE

However, while Michoacán benefitted from the avocado market that NAFTA created, the story was quite different in other states in Mexico. The state of Puebla sits on the other side of Mexico City from Michoacán. It's always been a forested area; well suited to pines across its higher elevations. Even today, 22% of the state is covered in trees.[29] For generations, this region had been at the heart of avocado production in Mexico with indigenous communities living in harmony with the land. Farmers here grew landrace varieties to feed themselves and their families, before selling the surplus avocados. In fact, some maintain that the avocado originated in Puebla.[30] Recognising this history, the Mexican Tourism Board now promotes the

Poblano route from Atlixco to Acatlán de Osorio as the 'ruta del aguacate', the "avocado route."[31]

Life in Puebla was transformed after NAFTA. Without any history of commercial agriculture, and with the avocado ban still in place, there was little move to expand any of the growing businesses in the region. Unlike Michoacán, Puebla had not experienced a transition to more industrialised forms of agriculture in the 1950s and 1960s and was still dominated by indigenous subsistence farmers. This was because the topography of the rural highlands had long made it challenging to establish the necessary infrastructure required to switch to large-scale agriculture. The lack of irrigation systems and deficit of supply chain infrastructure has ensured that farming had remained at a subsistence level. This had, in turn, limited the potential for commercialisation, making it unattractive for large-scale production. Consequently, they were not able to meet the USDA standards set for avocado export in the way that Michoacán was. In fact, Alyshia Galvaz said in her book *Eating Nafta: Trade, Food Policies and the Destruction of Mexico*, "these [USDA protections] almost single-handedly decimated the avocado export industry in many states in Mexico," such as Puebla.[32] The region's growers could not export their products to the United States due to the ban, but they were also undercut in the domestic market.

However, while the agriculture sector struggled, manufacturing in the state boomed. Post-NAFTA, when the Mexican economy crashed, saw US manufacturing companies swoop into the region, looking to benefit from the lack of tariffs with the United States and the cheap labour. Puebla lowlands became home to large-scale manufacturing plants that produce cars and fabrics for the American market, so that today, Puebla is one of the most industrialised states in Mexico.[33] That same surge of foreign investment did not happen in the horticultural highlands, and the agricultural sector of Puebla never recovered from the shock of Mexico entering NAFTA and the associated Peso Crisis. With the economic crisis hitting hard, a huge number of farmers in Puebla had sold up. Some Poblano farmers chose to migrate internally to work on the new production lines, building American cars. However, many others choose to leave and travel to the States, pulled by the desire to start a new life and to earn money to send back to Mexico.[34] They sold their land to whomever would buy it and travelled to America in the hope of finding a better life. This was a new phenomenon. The Central Region of Mexico (which includes Puebla) had not previously experienced high levels of migration since people tended to remain there – close to their family. Following NAFTA, there was a huge exodus from the countryside of Puebla into the north-eastern area of the United States. One US state proved particularly appealing for Poblanos: New York City. Many of those migrants from the 1990s remain in New York today, in a community that continues to grow as those first arrivals encourage others to follow them.[35] In an interview, Sebastian Benitez, a consultant at Mi Casa Es Puebla NY, a non-profit that helps New York's Poblanos adapt to life in the tri-state area, said,

> Poblanos leave everything behind, to come to a place that is completely stranger to them, that completely disregards them, isolates them, only to bring money to send back so that they can live in peace, and with some sort of comfort.[36]

TODAY'S MARKET

Over the subsequent years post-NAFTA, the avocado industry in Mexico grew and expanded to become the giant of avocado production it is today. Mexico became a powerhouse for avocado export, and Mexican orchards expanded from 57,490 ha in 1990 to around 100,000 ha in 1998 as a direct result of the Agreement.[37] The popularity of the fruit in the United States was so substantial and the export profits so lucrative that other Mexican states started to switch over to avocado production by building the necessary infrastructure and investing in the USDA certification requirements. Jalisco was approved to export into the United States by the USDA in 2021. The state hopes to dramatically increase production as more orchards come online in the coming years. Yet, this expansion of the export-based avocado industry beyond Michoacán happened too late for the avocado farmers for Puebla. By that point, they had sold off their land, forced to move into different jobs with no option to return.

FAST FOOD IN MEXICO AND NAFTA

NAFTA opened the door for Michoacán avocados to head north to the United States and initiated a transformation of avocados from a local subsistence crop into an export-based commodity crop, increasingly separated from local food culture. However, NAFTA also catalysed another shift in food that furthered the separation of avocados from Mexican communities. The creation of an FTA meant that, just as Mexican goods started flowing north,

American goods started flowing south. Without any restrictions to trade, the floodgates opened to American ultra-processed food in Mexico. These foods were no longer subject to the import tariffs that they once had been, making them less expensive for regular Mexicans to purchase. If the cheap price wasn't appealing enough, still bathing in the glow of America's soft power, they were also considered desirable and associated with wealth and status. People wanted to be seen purchasing a Mountain Dew or eating a Snickers. After 1993, traditional Mexican foods and snacks declined dramatically, including those from avocados. The ultra-processed foods imported from the United States were sold at a cheaper price, undercutting Mexican alternatives. Some Mexican growers managed to initially stick out the bleak years of economic downturn after the influx of American foods, following the signing of NAFTA. However, they eventually saw their sales decline as people turned away from traditional foods towards American imports. As a result of increased availability, cheaper prices, and American glamour, obesity rates rose significantly in Mexico with the rise in consumption of sugary beverages.[38] In 1993, the obesity rate in Mexico was 15.4%, and by 2000, it stood at 19.10%.[39] This was not surprising – as Alyshia Galvez, professor of American and Latino Studies at Lehman College, points out: "Every major trade deal results in higher rates of obesity, diabetes, heart and kidney disease."[40]

This shift was not accidental or unintended. The American companies were keen to make the most of the opportunity that NAFTA afforded them and used marketing tools (such as advertising and product placement) to penetrate into the Mexican market. One example is Sidral Mundet, an apple-flavoured soda made by Coca-Cola that misrepresents itself as containing a high concentration of natural apple juice, when in reality it contains less than 1%. These American companies marketed themselves with portrayals of traditional family values, health, good jobs, and wealth. The long-running health campaigns by the Mexican government in the 1990s largely vilified the traditional street vendors, for both being unhygienic and selling unhealthy street food like tamales and tacos. In reality, many of the traditional Mexican street foods contain more fruit and vegetables than imported junk food, but the public perception has already been altered. Traditional Mexican food, like guacamole, through a combination of marketing and shifts in consumer behaviour and expectations, is often seen as unhygienic, old-fashioned, and associated with a lower social class.

If the marketing was not enough, the US food itself was chemically more desirable, almost addictive. Transnational food brand identify and market "supernormal stimuli," often referred to as hyperpalatable foods, designed to specifically evoke the natural cravings for sweet and high-fat and salt foods. The main culprit was high-fructose corn syrup (HFCS). HFCS is a common-type sweetener made from corn by-product that is 45% fructose and 55% glucose.[41] It is not sold to consumers in the grocery store – rather it is used commercially, often in ultra-processed goods, such as sodas. According to the Harvard Medical School definition,

> Ultra-processed foods are made mostly from substances extracted from foods, such as fats, starches, added sugars, and hydrogenated fats. They may also contain additives like artificial colors and flavors or stabilizers.[42]

As of 2020, 23.1% of the Mexican population's total dietary energy comes from ultra-processed foods, in particular sugary beverages, which Mexico was the highest global consumer of carbonated drinks.[43]

By 2019, 72.5% of Mexican adults (approximately 56 million people)[44] were considered obese or overweight, an increase of 42.2% over the previous 30 years.[45] This had the impact of rising non-communicable diseases (NCDs) and huge pressure on the healthcare service in Mexico. Obesity is closely linked to a range of comorbidities, including cardiovascular disease, type 2 diabetes, cancer, and joint-related disorders. In 2010, the estimated cost of these health issues on the Mexican healthcare system, resulting from obesity were $806 million, and based on projected increases in obesity rates, this could rise to $1.7 billion by 2050.[46] These increasingly widespread health issues put huge pressure on the Mexican economy; dietary risks accounted for more than 10% of disability adjusted life years (DALYs).[47] This means that of all the years of life lost prior to meeting average life expectancy, 10% are directly attributed to dietary risks. As a result of this crisis, the Mexican government declared an epidemiological emergency[48] in 2020 and introduced mandatory food labelling to indicate high fat or high sugar content in foods.[49] The design of the new labelling would require foods with a high content of fat, salt, sugar, or excess calories per 100 g to be given an on-package alert. They also implemented a 20% tax on HFCS.

OBJECTION AND REJECTION

However, the requirements under NAFTA (and its USMCA replacement) created a route for businesses impacted by the policy decision to challenge the public health interventions of the Mexican government. FTAs provide a legal route for big business to potentially challenge the labelling, creating a barrier to trade, known as Investor-State Dispute Settlements and the WTO allow for cases to be brought where a country can demonstrate unfair barriers to trade. Activists often object to the ISDS mechanism. According to Debbie Barker, International Coordinator at the International Coalition on Climate and Agriculture, "these mechanisms give too much power to companies and undercuts a national government's ability to intervene and impose policies to improve public health, as well as environmental and labour standards."

Firstly, the 20% HFCS tax was challenged. In Jan 2002, US Corn Products International filed a claim against the Mexican government's decision to impose a tax on HFCS. This was on the basis that Mexico had violated Article 1102 of NAFTA, which requires each state party to treat investors and investments of another nation any less favourably than their own investors and investments.[50] In this case, they argued that HFCS and sugar cane producers were comparable and that both 'sweeteners' were similarly used in a variety of food products.[51] They maintained that the tax was designed to favour the predominantly Mexican sugar cane producers and destroy the HFCS market, which was largely foreign owned.

The advertising ban and labelling requirement enacted by Mexico has been similarly challenged. Chile had originally tried to implement nutrition labels on all foods that exceeded 275 calories, 400 mg of sodium, 10 g of sugar, or 4 g of saturated fats per 100 g.[52] Under the Chilean law, products that featured the labels were not allowed to be advertised to children and could not be sold in or near schools. However, the US Trade Representative took Chile to the WTO claiming that the labels create an unfair barrier to trade, and the labels were removed. Transnational food businesses are already suggesting similar action in Mexico.[53] While the labels still remain on ultra-processed foods in Mexico that meet the prescribe criteria, there has been relatively little change in the consumption of sugary foods and drinks, encouraging calls to remove the labels from food producers. However, there are no signs yet of the Mexican government backing down.

IN CONCLUSION...

When NAFTA was signed, the transformation of the Mexican economy went into overdrive. Some, like the avocado growers in Michoacán were able to seize that opportunity. They had been transitioning towards an industrialised version of agriculture (in particular of avocado production) for decades and therefore were perfectly placed to take advantage of the opportunities that NAFTA presented. However, the farming communities of other states like Puebla that were still dominated by subsistence agriculture were decimated by the changes that NAFTA brought. In addition to the production size, NAFTA prompted a transformation in the consumption side of Mexican food systems. Ultra-processed food from US brands were able to flood the Mexican market at cheap prices and quickly became more desirable than traditional foods. This led to a rise in NCDs and obesity, and Mexico is still reckoning with today through public health policies and interventions.

NOTES

1 Hufbauer, Gary, & Schott, Jeffrey, assisted by Grieco & Wong, *NAFTA Revisited: Achievements and Challenges*. Peterson Institute for International Economics, 2005, October.

2 Lustig, Nora, "The Mexican peso crisis: The foreseeable and the surprise." *Brookings*, 1995, June 1.

3 Lederman, Daniel, Menédez, Ana Maria, Perry, Guillermo, & Stiglitz, Joseph E., "Mexico: Five years after the crisis," *The World Bank*, 2000, April 13.

4 Hufbauer & Schott, assisted by Grieco & Wong, *NAFTA Revisited: Achievements and Challenges*.

5 Ibid.

6 Hufbauer & Schott, assisted by Grieco & Wong, *NAFTA Revisited: Achievements and Challenges*.

7 Glass, Andrew, "Clinton bails out Mexico, Jan. 31, 1995." *Politico*, 2019, January 31.

8 Chandler, Clay, "Mexico, U.S. Sign $220 billion aid pact." *The Washington Post*, 1995, February 22.

9 McKenzie, David, *The Consumer Response to the Mexican Peso Crisis*. Department of Economics, Stanford University, 2003, May.

10 Kose, Ayhan M., Meredith, Guy, & Towe, Christopher, "How has NAFTA affected the Mexican economy? Review and evidence." *International Monetary Fund*, 2004, April.

11 Lederman, Daniel, Maloney, William, & Serven, Luis, "Lessons from NAFTA for Latin America and the Caribbean." *The World Bank*, 2004, November 15.

12 Social Panorama of Latin America, *United Nations Economic Commission for Latin America and the Caribbean*, 2002–2003.

13 Columbia and Mexico Country Management Unit, "Poverty in Mexico: An assessment of conditions, trends and government strategy." *The World Bank*, 2004, June.

14 "The World Bank world development report 2005: A better investment climate for everyone." *The World Bank*, 2004.

15 *The World Bank Development Report 1995: Workers in an Integrating World. The World Bank*, 1995.

16 Hinojosa-Ojeda, Raul, Robinson, Sherman, & De Paolis, Fernando, Regional integration among the unequal: A CGE model of NAFTA and the Central American republics. *The North American Journal of Economics and Finance*, Vol. 10, Issue 1, 1999.

17 *Avocado Institute of Mexico*, "The Magic of Michoacan's four blooms," 2020.

18 *Avocado Institute of Mexico*, "Why avocado orchards thrive in Michoacán," 2020.

19 Stanford, Lois, "Mexico's Empresario in export agriculture: Examining the avocado industry of Michoacan." Department of Sociology and Anthropology, 1998.

20 Echanove, Flavia, "Abriendo fronteras, El auge exportador del aguacate mexicano a Estados Unidos, Instituto de Geografía." *Universidad Nacional Autónoma de México*, 2003, January 16.

21 Comisión de Comercio Nacional e Internacional, "Situación de las expotaciones de eaguacate de Jalisco y Michoacán." *Consejo Mexicano Para el Desarrollo Rural Sustentable*, 2019, December 18.

22 Stanford, Lois, "Constructing "quality": The political economy of standards in Mexico's avocado industry." *Agriculture and Human Values*, 2002, December.

23 Bellamore, Tom, "Mexican avocados: History…the full story." *California Avocado Society Yearbook* 86, 2002.

24 Federal Register, "Mexican Hass Avocado Import Program; Final Rule." *Federal Register*, Vol. 66, Issue 212, 2001, November 1.

25 Federal Register, "Mexican Avocado Import Program." *USDA Animal and Plant Health Inspection Service*, 2004, November 11.

26 Curry, "Introduction—Oro verde, social change and environmental destruction." *Noria Research*, https://noria-research.com/violence-and-avocado-capitalism-in-mexico/.

27 Ayala, Manual Ochoa, "Avocado: The 'green gold' causing environmental havoc." *World Economic Forum*, 2020, February 24.

28 Descalsota, Marielle, "The US temporarily banned avocado imports from Mexico. Take a look inside the country's biggest avocado-producing region." *Insider*, 2022, February 18.

29 *Place and See*, "Puebla." 2021, July 30.

30 Galindo-Tovar, Maria Elena, Fernández, Amaury, Ogata-Aguilar, Nisao, & Landero-Torres, Ivonne, "The avocado (Persea Americana, Lauraceae) crop in Mesoamerica: 10,000 years of history." *Harvard Papers in Botany*, Vol. 12, Issue 2, 2007.

31 Graber, Karen Hursh, "Culinary travel in the Mixteca Poblana: The avocado route." 2009, October 16.

32 Gálvez, Alyshia, *Eating NAFTA: Trade, Food Policies, and the Destruction of Mexico*. University of California Press, 2018.

33 *Co-Production International*, "Puebla: Strategically located between Mexico City and the major container ports of Vera Cruz." https://www.rvo.nl/sites/default/files/2019/05/opportunities-for-port-development-and-maritime-sector-in-mexico.pdf.

34 Machuca, "Puebla, seventh undeveloped state: UN," *Milenio*, 2008, November 16.

35 Waters, Mary, & Kasinitz, Philip, Immigrants in New York City: Reaping the benefits of continuous immigration. *Daedalus Journal of the American Academy of Arts & Sciences*, 2013. https://www.amacad.org/publication/immigrants-new-york-city-reaping-benefits-continuous-immigration.

36 Orbach, Jon, "Despite pandemic, New York's Poblanos sent a record amount home in 2002." *Columbia News Service*, 2021, March 25.

37 Stanford Lois, "Mexico's Empresario in export agriculture: Examining the avocado industry of Michoacán." University of New Mexico State *Department of Sociology and Anthropology*, 1998.

38 Balcazar, Hector, & Lizaur, Ana Bertha Perez, "Sugar-Sweetened soda consumptionn in Mexico: The translation of accumulating evidence for an increasing diabetes risk in Mexican women." *The Journal of Nutrition*, Vol. 149, Issue 5, 2019, May.

39 Our World in Data, "Share of adults that are obese, 1975–2016." University of Oxford. https://ourworldindata.org/grapher/share-of-adults-defined-as-obese.

40 Gálvez, Alyshia, "What's more deadly to Mexicans than the drug war? Diabetes." George Washington University, 2018, November 18.

41 Sollid, Kris, "What is high fructose corn syrup," *Food Insight*, 2020, October 16.

42 McManus, Katherine, *What Are Ultra-Processed Foods and Are they Bad for Our Health?* Harvard Health Publishing, 2020, January 9.

43 Barquera, Simon, & Rivera, Juan, "Obesity in Mexico: Rapid epidemiological transition and food industry interference in health policies." *Lancet Diabetes Endocrinology*, 2020, August 18.

44 Spencer, Natasha, "Obesity levels in Mexico call for emergency action." *NutraIngredients*, 2019, September 26.

45 Barquera & Rivera, "Obesity in Mexico: rapid epidemiological transition and food industry interference in health policies."

46 DiBonaventura, Marco, Meincke, Henrik, Lay, Agathe, Fournier, Janine, Bakker, Erik, & Ehrenreich, Allison, *Obesity in Mexico: Prevalence, Comorbidities, Associations with Patient Outcomes, and Treatment Experiences.* Dove Medical Press Limited, 2017, December 22.

47 Barquera & Rivera, "Obesity in Mexico: rapid epidemiological transition and food industry interference in health policies."

48 Spencer, Natasha, "Obesity levels in Mexico call for emergency action." *NutraIngredients*, 2019, September 26.

49 Pan American Health Organization, "Front-of-package labeling advances in the Americas." *The World Health Organization*, 2020, September 29.

50 Foreign Trade Information System, "North American Free Trade Agreement." *Organization of American States*. http://www.sice.oas.org/default_f.asp.

51 Lowenfield, de la Vega, Greenwood, & Flores, Corn Products International, INC. and The United Mexican States, "Decision on responsibility," *International Centre for Settlement of Investment Disputes*, 2008, January 15.

52 Luxton, Emma, "Which countries consume the most sugary drinks?" *World Economic Forum*, 2015, December 3.

53 Treat, Sharon, "The bully inn the lunchroom: The U.S. moves to weaken Mexico's new junk food labeling law." *Institute for Agriculture & Trade Policy*, 2020, January 29.

KEY READINGS

- Bellamore, Tom, "Mexican avocados: History...the full story." *California Avocado Society Yearbook* 86, 2002.
- Gálvez, Alyshia, *Eating NAFTA: Trade, Food Policies, and the Destruction of Mexico.* University of California Press, 2018.
- Hufbauer, Gary, & Schott, Jeffrey, assisted by Grieco & Wong, *NAFTA Revisited: Achievements and Challenges.* Peterson Institute for International Economics, October 2005.
- Lederman, Daniel, Menédez, Ana Maria, Perry, Guillermo, & Stiglitz, Joseph E, "Mexico: Five years after the crisis." *The World Bank*, 2000, April 13.
- Stanford, Lois, "Mexico's Empresario in export agriculture: Examining the avocado industry of Michoacan." *New Mexico State University, Department of Sociology and Anthropology*, 1998.

7

NEW MARKETS

REGIONAL CHALLENGES TO MEXICO'S AVOCADO MONOPOLY

INTRODUCTION

Avocados now have a place on the table in every corner of the world. This is due to the marketing efforts of the Californians and the explosion of production in Mexico. However, witnessing the global demand for the fruit, other nations have stepped into the picture, hoping to break the hold that Mexico has on production and divert a little of the avocado gold into their own pockets. Due to the climate required for avocados to flourish, many of these nations are in the Global South, raising the same questions of equity and food sovereignty as were raised by the export-based production of the fruit in Mexico. However, as the climate changes, more nations in the Global North are investing in avocado farms too.

THE GLOBAL SOUTH

Swathes of agricultural land in the Global South are being cultivated to meet consumer demands for guacamole in the Global North. As land becomes more limited and costs of production rise in the Global North, more food is being grown in the Global South and shipped to the Global North. This keeps costs down and ensures easy access for affluent consumers who expect fresh produce to be available all year round since the climate in these countries are often well-suited to growing fruit across a longer growing season. This means they can supply a more consistent flow of the fruit across the year.

DOI: 10.4324/9781003371915-7

This supply is predicated on the globalised network of shipping that lets goods move around the world easily, which we will discuss in more depth in Chapter 8. Exporting countries are able to supply at a lower cost because of lower labour costs and economies of scale. This gives them a comparative advantage in production. Countries in the Global South often have more land to assign to farming. For example, according to the World Bank, 79.2% of South Africa's land is agricultural, versus 7.4% in Sweden. This abundance of land also increases the scope for crop specialisation (i.e. switching from the mixed cropping of traditional farming to monoculture), so producers can improve efficiencies with knock-on environmental consequences that we will discuss in Chapter 9. This switch to export-based agriculture has an immediate and direct impact on local food sovereignty (i.e. local and equitable control over one's own food). While this can bring jobs into the local economy, allowing families to lift themselves out of poverty, it also changes the local consumption patterns as the majority of local agricultural products are shipped out of the vicinity, and there are often concerns over whether it benefits wealthier individuals higher up the business over the local community. These concerns will be discussed in greater detail later.

In the case of avocados, it was logical for other Central and South American farmers to consider avocados once they saw the success in Mexico. Due to the geographic proximity to the United States, the cultural links to the fruit, and an appropriate climate, it was an easy switch for many. Additionally, many farmers in these countries have been forced to switch crops in recent years due to the shifting climate. These regions used to be major coffee producers but have seen Arabica yields decline due to climate change.[1] Coffee producers either have to shift to higher altitude regions to counteract the rising temperatures and inhospitable soil conditions or switch to Robusta, a less lucrative variety of coffee.[2] Avocados have proved to be better suited to the environment where the Arabica coffee plants used to thrive – at least for the time being – and, from an economic perspective, incomes from avocado are too tempting for low-income coffee producers in South and Central America who are facing economic hardship as coffee yields decline.

- **PERU**

    In 2021, Peru shipped 483,00 tons of avocados and an estimated 600,000 in 2022.[3] The majority of the fruit are grown in the Sierra, south of Lima, which is slightly cooler than the coastal regions and therefore well-suited to avocados. Farming in the Sierra region gives Peru an advantage in the global market because it allows it to harvest longer in the season and can now produce up to 11 months of the year. This also allows Peruvian fruit to supply the US market when the Michoacán fruit are not yet ripe. In Peru, less than 20% of avocado exports come directly from small farmers.[4] The rest is produced by large agribusinesses that control the market by virtue of their size. That said, small-scale farmers still dominate the acreage of avocados in Peru since out of the total 50,000 ha of this fruit, 23,000 belong to 7,500 small-scale farmers.[5] Europe is the largest market for Peruvian avocados (53%), followed by the US (16%) and Chile (14%), according to statistics from Peru's National Agriculture Health Service (SENASA).[6]

- **COLOMBIA**
  Colombia is probably more famous for producing cocaine that guacamole. It had a long history of growing coca, but many farmers switched from the narcotic to avocados in recent years, and much of the territory previously controlled by rebel groups and narcos is now prime plantation land. Plantations are centred around Antioquia near the towns of Sonson, Salamina, and Albermorral. The Colombian avocado market has grown by 600% in the last five years and 2020 exports reached a record 544,000 tons.[7] Currently, Colombia is the eighth-largest producer of Hass avocados in the world, but the government has grand plans to increase its position. Colombia has become a major exporter to Europe with exports to Europe growing by 41% between 2016 and 2021, equal to $193.6million worth.[8] The Colombian avocado industry is determined to continue growing so that they can become the world's second-largest producer, within the next decade. Additionally, they have been actively promoting the fruit in-country and established an Avocado Festival, in the city of El Carmen, located within the department of Santander to promote the fruit. However, due to the shift towards export-based agriculture, more and more Hass are planted, while many of the native varieties of Colombian avocados are being cut down or lost to disease. To combat this, a movement among non-profits and the government has been launched to educate growers on the importance of preserving the native fruits, and some growers are responding by promoting the importance of diversity and preservation of unique cultivars.

- **DOMINICAN REPUBLIC**
  Behind Mexico, the Dominican Republic (DR) in the Caribbean is currently the world's second-largest producer of avocados. According to the

International Institute for Cooperation on Agriculture, today around 21,875 ha of land in DR produce avocados, of which 32% are in the north region, 28% in the south-west, 26% in the central region, and 14% in the south region.[9] The most prolific period is the beginning of November, which is locally dubbed the "avocado escape." However, unlike Mexico, the typical avocado from DR is green-skinned, meaning that they are from the West Indian family of avocados – or West Indian × Guatemalan-type hybrids. Unlike elsewhere, the Hass does not dominate production with the Semil 34 variety proving the most popular. Since farmers cultivate different varieties that ripen at various points across the seasons, Dominican avocados are available year-round and are shipped to the United States. These green-skinned avocados are more commonly recognised in the United States where the avocado market is more developed, while in Europe, they remain still uncommon. The history of the avocado industry in DR can be traced to the 19th and 20th centuries, when avocado production transitioned from small subsistence farmers growing a few fruit trees on their land into a major agricultural endeavour, and DR avocados began being exported into the United States in the late 20th century when the US demand for the fruit grew. This was supported by various development banks, including the IFAD, to encourage poverty alleviation across the country by developing an export-based agricultural industry. To support the professionalisation, the Dominican Association of Exporters, or Adoexpo, was formed in 1972 to help facilitate the horticultural export process.

- **CHILE**

As of 2019, Chile was ranked the world's third-largest exporter of Avocados thanks to its abundant avocado plantations, located mainly in the arid Valparaiso region, to the north of the country's capital, Santiago.[10] According to the USDA, Chile was expected to produce 220,000 metric tons of avocados in the 2021/2022 marketing year.[11] Chile's Petorca province (which is located within Valparaiso) is responsible for the bulk of avocado farming – approximately 30%.[12] Most of Chile's avocados are exported to the Netherlands, Argentina, the United Kingdom, and the United States, with the Netherlands accounting for 50%[13] of all exports. Chile is currently facing a dangerous water shortage which some believe is in part due to the arrival of large commercial avocado farmers who arrived nearly a decade ago and are threatening the survival of small-scale producers who seek not to export the fruit. Water stress in Chile will be discussed in a subsequent chapter.[14]

AVOCADOS IN AFRICA

Just like nations in South America and the Caribbean, African nations have been expanding their export agricultural sectors to meet the demand of the Global North. Kenya, South Africa, and Senegal have expanded their horticultural sectors and have become major exporters of fruit and veg to the Global North, in particular into the European market. Kenya and South Africa now both have a significant share of the global avocado market – ranking 8th and 12th globally. Tanzania, Zimbabwe, and Mozambique also produce the fruit for export but in much lower quantities.[15]

- **KENYA**

  Kenya is a serious food exporter, with their agricultural sector accounting for a third of their national GDP and employing 80% of the population, with avocados becoming an increasingly popular export. Having a well-established cut-flower and green bean market, Kenyan expansion into avocados was a logical step. Data from the Horticulture Crops Directorate (HCD) at Kenya's Agriculture and Food Authority shows that avocado exports rose from 66 million tonnes in 2018 to 86 million tonnes in 2021.[16] Like in South America, many Kenyan tea and coffee farmers who were facing reduced harvests due to the changing climate have switched to avocado orchards. For example, according to Doris Maina of Jayashah General Supplies, "as a widespread drought was devastating crops in Kenya, our farmers in Muranga County decided to clear their half-acres of coffee production and plant Hass avocados instead."[17] To support this growth and lobby for the industry, the Avocado Society of Kenya was established and now has over 50,000 members from smallholders to large exporters. They estimate that the industry supports the livelihoods of 4 million people across the country.[18] Part of the appeal for retailers in the Global North is the cheap price of fruit grown in the Global South. This, as discussed, is because production costs are lower. Hass avocados can fetch up to $0.38 per fruit in the international market, but the Kenyan producers sell them for just about $0.04.[19] Part of this lower price is because the wages in Africa make the price of production a lot lower than it might be in other nations. The minimum wage for unskilled agricultural workers in Kenya is equivalent to $65 per month.[20] It is reported that many workers do not get paid this rate. Yet, Kenya's minimum wage is considered one of the highest in the region.

- **SOUTH AFRICA**

  About half of South Africa's avocado production is exported, mainly to Europe, with an annual production of between 80,000 and 120,000 tonnes.[21] Another 10–15% is processed for oil and pulp.[22] The majority of trees produce Hass avocados. While some green-skinned varieties have been planted, these are mainly for the local market. Production of avocados in South Africa is concentrated mainly in the humid, subtropical areas of the north-east. Regionally, Limpopo accounts for 59% and Mpumalanga 33%.[23] The avocado industry in South Africa expanded steadily from the early 1970s to 2003. Due to economic constraints, expansion slowed from 2003 to 2008 with little growth taking place. However, since 2009, total plantings have increased due to a growing consumer demand for avocados. In 2021, 15,439 ha of avocados were planted in South Africa, which was a 747 ha increase from 2020 to 2021.[24] South Africa has strong trade links with Europe, hence the largest share of export being sent to the EU and the United Kingdom. Currently, the phytosanitary requirements and the trading relationship between South Africa and the United States mean that it's challenging for producers to export there. This is also the case for exports to Japan and China, although some fruit are sent to Hong Kong.

AFFLUENT AVOCADOS: GROWING IN THE GLOBAL NORTH

While the fruit has long been considered tropical, the reality is that the changing climate has meant that more northern areas can cultivate the fruit now. With such growing demand for the fruit, European producers have been switching over to avocado production. Southern Europe increasingly features the topography and climate that the avocado prefers. Given the increased demand to support local producers, there is a potential for European-sourced avocados to increase market share. Spain, Portugal, and Greece are the main producers in Europe. Ironically, however, the largest exporter of avocados in Europe is the Netherlands since it acts as a horticultural hub and receives the majority of European shipments of avocados into the Rotterdam port before sending them out across Europe.[25] The largest consumers of avocados per capita in Europe are Denmark (2.81 kg per year), Norway (2.76 kg), and Switzerland (2.19 kg) with the United Kingdom in the eighth place. In comparison, as a reminder, the per capita consumption of the fruit in the United States is over 4 kg and is anticipated to rise.

- **SPAIN**

  Spain is the main producer of avocados in Europe with 99,000 tonnes in 2020 according to Eurostat and likely to increase in coming years.[26] There are large avocado plantations across the country, but growing is focused in Andalucía (97% of total production) and particularly in the province of Málaga (70%). The total cultivation acreage is around 19,000 ha.[27] However, Spain also acts as a conduit for avocados coming into Europe from the rest of the world. Acting as a middleman, Spanish fruit companies buy fruit from South America and Africa to re-export across Europe. This makes Spain Europe's second-largest exporter of avocados. In 2021, Spain imported 214,000 tonnes of avocados, 80% of which came from Peru and Mexico.[28] But there is also an increase in imports from Morocco (17,000 tonnes in 2020) that has a growing season that extends the Spanish production, and given its proximity to Spain, Moroccan fruit often is used to supplement Spanish supply.

- **PORTUGAL**

  Portugal is also a major European producer of avocados, second behind Spain. According to the latest data from the 2019 Agrarian Census by the National Statistics Institute (INE), there are about 2,000 ha of avocados planted in Portugal, and most of that acreage is located in the southern region.[29] Avocados are a new crop for Portuguese farmers and one driven by a demand for profit. Célia Vences, an avocado farmer in Portugal said:

  > My father was a farmer, but never had avocados. However, I did market research and at the time it was one of the most profitable and sustainable crops that I could get, that's why I decided to embrace this project.

  However, it isn't just small producers like Celia, larger companies are getting into avocado production. The company, Global Avocados was born from the merger of three companies devoted to the production and marketing of avocados from the Algarve area. By the end of 2022, they anticipated cultivating 850 ha, with the goal to eventually reach 1,000 to 1,200 ha, 95% of Global Avocados are Hass, and the remaining 5% are Bacon and Fuerte. However, they are considering the Maluma variety to try to extend the supply window. The company said that they want to become the leading supplier of Portuguese avocados, detailing that

"Our current production amounts to around 3 million kilos, but given that almost 50% of our plantations are young farms, we expect this to increase rapidly in the coming years. Next year we expect to harvest 4.5 million kilos, and in 3–4 years our production will exceed 10 million kilos."[30]

- **GREECE**

Greek avocado production is primarily in Chania, Crete, due to the climate and the soil. The market is just emerging but has potential to grow sizeably. In 2018, the total harvest was 6,633 tons, showing a 4.7% growth compared to 2017[31]. The first avocado crops in the region were established as early as the 1960s.

Lately, we are seeing a shift in Greek producers' cultivation preferences. The high prices of avocado combined with the low prices in citrus fruit and the various illnesses that have befallen them, have led to the planting of new avocado trees, disclosed Mr. Giorgos Kornarakis from the Citrus Fruit, Avocado Department of the Agricultural Cooperative of Chania. Unlike Spain and Portugal, the Cretan producers are much more focused on the domestic market than exporting across Europe. George Polychronakis, Special Adviser to the Greek Association of Export and Distribution of Fruits, Vegetables, and Juices, Incofruit Hellas wants to increase the domestic market for the fruit first and explains that consumption in Europe is relatively limited, especially in Greece where it amounts to 0.650 kg per person per year. Therefore, marketing efforts to promote consumption should focus on encouraging the emergence of a 'Greek avocado salad', as well as integrating it into the restaurant and hotel menus in tourism areas starting from Crete

That said, unusually Greek consumers do not like the Hass variety that dominates globally since they find the knobbly black skin unappealing. As a result, Cretan producers are focused on other green-skinned varieties.

LOOKING BEYOND THE WESTERN WORLD

Some Global North countries outside of Europe have become major avocado producers also. Israel has become a major exporter of the fruit. Avocado plantations in Israel total 7,000 ha and yield more than 115,000 tons of fruit.[32] The principal growing areas are along the Coastal Plain (70%) and in the Jordan and Eastern Valleys (30%), primarily within kibbutzim. The main export destinations are France, the United Kingdom, Germany, the Netherlands, and the Scandinavian countries.[33] Part of the success of the Israeli fruit in the European market is the proximity. From Israel, the fruit is transported to Europe within four to five days[34] in Europe, whereas it takes approximately 21 days for Peruvian avocados to reach the European market.[35]

However, the world's largest producer outside of the Central and South American region might not be immediately obvious. Indonesia produced over 660,000 metric tonnes of avocados in 2021 and ranked in the top five of global producers.[36] Due to the climate, Indonesian trees can bear fruit all year round, making them an attractive option for supermarkets looking for continuous supply. The plantations tend to be located in Java and in Western and Southern Sumatra. They are also commonly eaten in the country, particularly as the famed dessert known as el teler, and as a result, local varieties (like the Wina, Miki, and Pluwang) tend to thrive.

Despite Indonesia being a much larger producer, there is another nation in the Pacific region that is more frequently associated with avocados. More famous for the fruit than perhaps any other nation than Mexico is Australia that has become culturally linked to the fruit. Yet, Australia is only the 19th-largest world producer of the fruit, according to FAOSTAT.[37] Unusually, Australia produces for its own market, meeting domestic demand as the top priority. In 2021/2022, overall production was estimated at 124,000 tonnes with only 12,500 tonnes imported.[38] Production is still increasing. The forecasts predict that overall production will expand by 40% (equating to roughly 50,000 tonnes) in the next five years.[39] Thankfully, Australians cannot get enough of the fruit, and this oversupply was coupled with a 31.2% increase in avocado consumption in Australian households. However, if Australia's avocado plantations continue to grow, it will surely eventually surpass domestic consumption – there must be an actual limit to how much avocado toast Brisbanites can consume! At that point, Australian avocados will need an export outlet. Given Australia's relative isolation from the avocado consumers in Europe, they have looked to their neighbours in Asia. Australian avocados have been well received in Singapore and Hong Kong in particular, now accounting for 46% and 12% of the market share, respectively, and with Malaysia a keen importer of Australian avocados too.[40] However, the Australians will need to reach into other Asian nations if they want to continue to expand their avocado exports. This might prove tricky. Australia currently faces a number of trade barriers preventing them from exporting to China, Japan, and Korea – the three biggest avocado importers in Asia.

Of course, China is the most attractive market due to its growing affluence and demand. As with most goods, China is proving a growing market for avocados. A decade ago, avocados were virtually unknown in China. The country imported only two tons in 2010, but in 2018, it imported 43.86 kilotons, with an import value of USD 133.38 million.[41] This is due to rising income levels across China and a desire to emulate Western diets. The trend for the fruit accelerated in 2017 when KFC ran an ad campaign for its avocado wraps called "Green Is Going Red" (implying that the fruit was a hot commodity). It featured a pop star sporting an avocado moustache. The ad helped to make avocados cool for China's millennials. However, the fruit is still a novelty and not integrated into the food culture. Californian-based Mission Produce aims to change this. In partnership with Pagoda Stores that operate over 1800 fresh produce stores across China, Mission built China's first distribution centre (known as a "ripe center") in Shanghai 2017 with another to follow in Shenzhen.

While Mexico did initially supply China with the fruit, Chile has become the main exporter to China, with Peru targeting the market also. All three countries have a zero tariff trade agreement with China for avocados. This is distinctly different from Australia that is struggling to access the Chinese market, due to government posturing and bureaucracy. However, other countries have their eyes on the burgeoning Chinese avocado market too.[42] Given the recent investment that China has made across Africa, specifically for infrastructure projects such as roads and rail, there were pre-existing geopolitical relationships that made it logical for African nations to look to export to China. Kenya was the first to do this (after various rounds of trade negotiations) and has established an export route for their fruit into China – first with frozen and then with fresh fruit.[43] However, China is keen to achieve self-sufficiency where possible to reduce its trade deficit. Consequently, farmers within China are also considering whether there might be an opportunity for domestically produced fruit. With state backing, avocado plantations have emerged in the southern province of Guangxi, although it will take time for them to fruit.

IN CONCLUSION...

The explosion of demand for avocados by affluent consumers in the Global North has caused farmers across the world to switch over to avocado production. For many farming businesses, they saw the significant profit that they could make in exporting avocados at a time when other crops (like coffee) were declining in productivity due to climate change. The near monopoly that Mexico had for the export of the fruit is slipping away as more and more places get in on the avocado act. This is driven by price primarily since tariff-free trade deals, low wages, and an abundance of land allow for the fruit to be produced and shipped at cheaper prices. However, international trade relationships will never stay static. The climate will continue to change, bringing challenges and opportunities to different growers. The growth in the Chinese avocado market is likely to perpetuate another major shift – as will the changing trade partnerships across the world.

NOTES

1 Craparo, C.W., Van Asten, P.J.A., Läderach, P., Jassogne, L.T.P., & Grab, S.W., "Coffea arabica yields decline in Tanzania due to climate change: Global implications." *Agricultural and Forest Meteorology*, 2015.
2 Farah, Hibaq, "Regions growing coffee, cashews and avocados at risk amid global heating." *The Guardian*, 2022, January 26.
3 Ilyas, Sarah, "Agronometrics in Charts: Large swathes of Peru's avocado production poised to start." *Fresh Fruit Portal*, 2022, April 28. https://www.freshfruitportal.com/news/2022/04/28/agronometrics-in-charts-large-swathes-of-perus-avocado-production-poised-to-start/.
4 Haller, Vera & Regatão, Gisele, "Peru's avocado 'green-gold' rush loses some shine." *The World*, 2022, July 12.
5 Ilyas, Sarah, "Half of Peruvian avocado production under threat due to fertilizer shortages, says industry body." *Fresh Fruit Portal*, 2022, July 8.
6 Haller & Regatão, "Peru's avocado 'green-gold' rush loses some shine."
7 McInnes, Jon, "Columbia's hass avocado boom—Mining the new green gold." Columbia Travel Reporter: Off the Beaten Path. https://colombiatravelreporter.com/colombias-hass-avocado-boom-mining-the-new-green-gold/.
8 *Fresh Fruit Portal*, "Columbian avocado sales to Europe grow by 41%." 2022, August 2.
9 Pérez, Hector, "The avocado crop: Great potential for the Dominican Republic." *Instituto Interamericano de cooperación para la agricultura*, 2017.
10 Milne, Nicky, "Chile's booming avocado business blamed for water shortages." *Global Citizen*, 2019, June 3.
11 USDA, "Chile: Avocado annual." *Foreign Agriculture Service*, 2021, November 26.
12 Milne, "Chile's booming avocado business blamed for water shortages."
13 USDA, "Chile: Avocado annual." *Foreign Agriculture Service*, 2021, November 26.
14 Milne, "Chile's booming avocado business blamed for water shortages."

15 Atlas Big, "World avocado production by country." https://www.atlasbig.com/en-gb/countries-by-avocado-production.

16 Trade Map, "Export volume of avocados from Kenya between 2010 and 2020." *Statista*, 2021, November 24.

17 Joyce, Tom, "Kenyan avocados rise to the standard." Eurofruit, 2022, August 9.

18 Owino, Vincent, "Kenyan farmers have a new market for avocado: China." *The East African*, 2022, August 9.

19 Ibid.

20 Hairsine, Kate, "What Kenya's minimum wage rise means." *DeutscheWelle*, 2022, May 10.

21 Louw, Marinda, "Avocado production fruit farming in South Africa." *South Africa Online*. https://southafrica.co.za/avocados-south-africa.html.

22 Ibid.

23 Ibid.

24 Donkin, Derek, "SA avocado industry overview." *The South African Avocado Association*, 2022, April 26.

25 CBI Ministry of Foreign Affairs, "The Dutch market potential for fresh fruit and vegetables." *ICI Business*, 2022, March 8.

26 CBI Ministry of Foreign Affairs, "The European market potential for avocados." *ICI Business*, 2023, January 23.

27 Ministerie van Landbouw, Natuur en Voedselkwaliteit, "Spain: Avocado, the most fashionable fruit in Europe." *ABC*, 2019, June 13.

28 CBI Ministry of Foreign Affairs, "The European market potential for avocados."

29 Instituto Nacional de Estatística - Recenseamento Agrícola. Análise dos principais resultados: 2019. Lisboa: INE, 2021.

30 *Fresh Plaza*, "In 3 or 4 years, our Portuguese avocado production will exceed 10 million kilos." 2022, March 18.

31 Antonopoulou, Vana, "Greek avocado: 4.7% growth in one year." *Ambrosia Magazine*, 2019, December 3.

32 Dor, Reuven, "The Israeli Avocado Industry."

33 Ibid.

34 Dor, "The Israeli Avocado Industry."

35 McShane, Gill, "First hass avocados shipped to Europe." *La Dona Cooperate News*, 2020, June 23.

36 Statista, "Production of avocado in Indonesia, 2012–2021." 2022, March 7.

37 Food and Agriculture Organization of the United Nations, "Crops and livestock products." *United Nations*, 2022, December 23.

38 O'Callaghan, Liam, "Australian avocado industry face 'avolanche'." *Produce Plus*, 2022, July 25.

39 Ibid.

40 Ibid.

41 Research and Markets, "Research report on avocado imports in China 2020–2024." 2020, September.

42 Greber, Jacob, Tingle, Laura, & Grigg, Angus, "Almost one year after FTA, avocado trade with china still smashed." *Financial Review*, 2016, October 26.

43 Owino, Vincent, "Kenyan farmers have a new market for avocado: China." *The East African*, 2022, August 9.

KEY READINGS

- Farah, Hibaq, "Regions growing coffee, cashews and avocados at risk amid global heating." *The Guardian*, 2022, January 26.
- Ilyas, Sarah, "Agronometrics in Charts: Large swathes of Peru's avocado production poised to start." *Fresh Fruit Portal*, 2022, April 28.
- O'Callaghan, Liam, "Australian avocado industry face 'avolanche'." *Produce Plus*, 2022, July 25.
- Research and Markets, "Research report on avocado imports in China 2020–2024." 2020 September.

8

THE HIGH SEAS

THE GLOBAL AVOCADO TRADE AND SHIPPING

INTRODUCTION

Our globalised society is reliant on shipping; 95% of all manufactured goods in the world are transported via container ships, equivalent to $4 trillion dollars.[1] Over $1 trillion of this is agricultural goods – food, seed, and fertilisers.[2] More than 90% of the United Kingdom's food imports arrive by sea (as opposed to 1.5%[3] via more costly air freight), while WorldWatch estimates that the average American dinner plate will have travelled a total of 1500 miles.[4] Most of the time, this global shipping system works flawlessly and predominantly behind the scenes. Most consumers are happy not to think about the journey that the food took to reach their plate.

This includes avocados, which are shipped on vast container ships (as opposed to air freight as popular culture might suggest) that have been finely tuned to meet the logistics needs of the 21st-century consumer. To cope with the scale of the demand, today's vessels are vast. One ship alone would have the capacity to carry 740 million bananas – enough for one European each.[5] They have huge refrigeration capacity to keep food fresh. The speed and efficiency of shipping fresh produce has had a profound impact on the avocado industry, making it possible for the fruit to reach consumers in regions that would never be able to support their own production and bringing the price down so that it's affordable to many more consumers. It was revolutionary when M&S first brought avocados to the United Kingdom in 1959 – the little green fruit was alien to most consumers. Yet today, if you

DOI: 10.4324/9781003371915-8

pop into any supermarket in Manchester, and you can purchase avocados at any time in the year, regardless of season. This is what consumers want, and now expect – and not just for avocados. In 2020, the United Kingdom imported 46% of the food it consumed.[6]

This transportation needs to be done quickly. Avocados need to be fresh, and supermarkets don't want to have old stock sitting on the shelves, slowly rotting. They demand just-in-time readiness when products are delivered within a tight and responsive timeframe to avoid the fruit from building up, achieved by stacking more and more containers on ever larger ships and increasing refrigeration to keep produce fresh. And this is only likely to continue as demand for avocados rises. According to the Agricultural Outlook 2021–2030 report from the Organization for Economic Co-operation and Development (OECD) and the Food and Agriculture Organization (FAO) of the United Nations (UN), avocado is expected to become the second-most traded major tropical fruit by 2030, after bananas.[7] It will overtake the export volume of both pineapples and mangoes. The United States and the European Union (EU) are expected to remain the largest importers. According to the same OECD/FAO report, these regions will be responsible for 40% and 31% of global imports in 2030 despite the growing trade with other regions such as China and the Middle East.

PREPARING FOR SHIPMENT

In fact, keeping avocados from ripening until it reaches the shelves has become an art form. The fruit is picked before it has fully ripened and packed into crates and loaded onto pallets. As anyone who has accidentally bruised an avocado at home knows, the fruit is highly pressure sensitive, so it must be packed with care. This is part of the appeal of the Hass variety, which due to its thick skin is more resilient to bruising and therefore less likely to be damaged during transport, reducing the risk of spoilage.

The storage itself has been carefully designed to maximise efficiency. According to the World Avocado Organisation,

The avocado carton was developed in South Africa by the CSIR (Council for Scientific and Industrial Research) where the industry gave them the challenge to come up with a carton that fits a container perfectly. This they did. But it needed a special pallet. Most pallets are ISO pallets which are 1200 × 1000 mm in length and breadth. Instead, they came up with a carton that fits on a 1200 mm x 1110 mm pallet base. This is a very tight fit for a container and fills the space efficiently.

The industry standard holds that when shipping avocados at 8°, the fruit can last up to 28 days before reaching peak ripeness, but stored at 3° with humidity of 85% and an O_2 level of 2–5% and a CO_2 level of 3–10%, then the fruit can be stored for up to 6 weeks, making a transatlantic journey aboard a container ship possible.[8] However, controlling this environment, especially on the high seas can be challenging. Damp, either for rain, snow, or sea-spray, can spoil an entire shipment and so the cargo must be constantly protected from moisture.

JOURNEY OUT OF MEXICO

For avocados bound for the US market, they tend to be transported by rail or truck from the fields of Michoacán. A network of high-speed, tolled roads crisscross the nation and allow goods to flow northwards to the United States and beyond. A major highway runs from Michoacán to Ciudad Juarez and across the border to El Paso, TX. Another route, known as the NAFTA Highway, connects Mexico City with Nuevo León and the US ports of Corpus Christi and Galveston. Avocados flow out of Michoacán and into America via both routes. Today, these rail and road routes are efficient and cheap. However, this was not always the case. Until recently, it was three times more costly to transport food from Sinaloa to Mexico City via rail than shipping it from New Orleans via Veracruz on container ships. To tackle this infrastructure failure, the National Infrastructure Programme that was launched in 2007 under Mexican President Calderón and enabled trucks to move seamlessly between both highways. However, despite the significant economic gain associated with these highways, the creation of the Mexican federal highway system caused significant environmental damage due to the associated land-use change and impact to biodiversity, which will be discussed in Chapter 9. Trucks are also reliant on fossil fuels and are heavy emitters of CO_2. The transport sector accounts for approximately 50% of energy consumption in Mexico and 31% of total CO_2 emissions, of which 94% come from road transport.[9] There are also significant social costs associated with highway infrastructure, as highways can cut through indigenous land and disrupt communities.

While the majority of Mexican avocados are bound for the United States, some head to Europe. Lázaro Cárdenas is the deep-water seaport in

Michoacán that handles container, dry bulk, and liquid cargo. However, it is still limited in size. The port currently has one container terminal, which can handle a total capacity of 2.2 million containers a year.[10] As a comparable, the largest port in the world – Shanghai – can handle 43.5 million containers per year.[11] The Manzanillo Port is further north on the Pacific Coast in the Mexican state of Colima. It is significantly larger than Lázaro Cárdenas, with 41% greater capacity, meaning more avocados can flow out of the country.[12] However, mindful of the potential for growth, both ports are looking to expand their capabilities. Connected via rail to the United States, the Port Authority is also hoping to position itself to ease the congestion in Los Angeles and Long Beach. In preparation for the port's increased capacity, railway and highway infrastructure running north–south through the centre of Mexico has been upgraded in recent years to handle the anticipated increase in volume of goods bound for the United States using this transportation corridor. That said, as we will discuss in greater detail in a later chapter, these two ports are not only exporting fruit. They have also become major shipping points for narcotics, such as fentanyl flowing into Mexico from Asia or Mexican heroin being shipped north to the United States. Many of these illicit exports are hidden away inside shipments of legal goods, likely including avocados. One of the largest drug busts in Mexican history occurred when federal agents stormed La Esmeralda in Manzanillo harbour and discovered 23.5 metric tons of cocaine, hidden under the ship's floor. "Everything enters through Manzanillo, it's no secret, even things that shouldn't," said Griselda Martinez, the mayor of Manzanillo, who survived a murder attempt in 2019.[13] However, we will discuss the overlap with the avocado industry and the drug cartels later.

CHOKE POINTS

For avocados grown in Mexico and shipped to Europe from either Lázaro Cárdenas or Manzanillo, they will have to cross the Panama Canal. The Panama Canal is an 82-km channel that connects the Caribbean with the Pacific. Opened in 1914, it saves ships sailing around Cape Horn in the South of America. Critical from the moment it opened, today, roughly $270 billion worth of cargo crosses the canal each year. It serves more than 140 maritime routes to over 80 countries.[14] Annual transit of the Panama Canal has risen from about 1,000 ships in 1914 to 13,342 in 2021.[15] However, the global importance of the canal also makes it a vulnerability. Were it to be inaccessible, vessels would have to make a longer and more perilous journey around the bottom of Chile – extending the shipping time considerably, raising the risk that avocados would arrive in Europe too ripe to sell.

But the Panama Canal is not the only essential – if vulnerable – route for global shipping. There are a number of other choke points within our global shipping system. According to Chatham House, there are 14 major maritime, coastal, and inland choke points which global trade relies upon.[16] One choke point is the Strait of Malacca between Indonesia and Malaysia sees 25% of all global traded goods (including Indonesian avocados) pass through the passage that is less than 40-km wide.[17] Another is the combination of the Bosphorus and the Dardanelles that make up the Turkish Straits, connecting the Black Sea to the Aegean. Given the geopolitics of the region, particularly through the Ukrainian Crisis, the Straits are a volatile and tense region. Another, Gibraltar remains as critical as it has been through history, connecting the Mediterranean to the Atlantic. Still today, the United Kingdom maintains control of the 2.6-square mile territory, as it has since 1802, and refuses to return it to Spanish control. With the rise of avocado production across the Mediterranean basin, many containers of avocados pass through the Straits of Gibraltar on their way to the supermarkets of Northern and Western Europe.

However, the main one that mirrors the Panamanian waterway is the Suez Canal – critical for all avocados (and other produce) shipping from East Africa to Europe. The majority of South African avocados will make the 14- to 25-day voyage to Europe via Suez. The opening of the Suez Canal in 1869 immediately altered global trading patterns. Mediterranean countries immediately benefitted from the Canal since they were infinitely more connected to the world and their goods could travel to their destination much faster. However, as with every subsequent step towards globalisation, there were also losers. Many in Egypt saw little benefit of the Canal since the British held control of the Canal until 1956 when President Nasser acted to reclaim the benefits of the canal for the people of Egypt. He nationalised the Canal, leading to the Suez Crisis and, ultimately, the invasion of the Sinai by Israel. There has been a more recent Suez Crisis, however, that demonstrates the fragility of the system. In 2021, the Suez Canal was blocked by the container ship, the Ever Given. It took six days to unwedge the ship, impacting nearly $60 billion of trade.[18]

These key maritime choke points are critical to the functioning of the global shipping industry. When blocked, as the Suez Canal was in 2021, it causes significant disruption to the flow of goods around the world, includ-ing to food supply. This risk has created a weakness in the food system. According to a recent Chatham House report,

> Disruption to choke points has the potential to threaten food and nutrition security, drive market uncertainty, prompt distortive trade measures and push up global food prices. Even small-scale, localized disruptions can cascade through global supply chains and across sec-tors if these occur at locations of strategic importance to the continued flow of global trade. Yet international efforts to manage the risk of disruption to − or the degeneration of − these chokepoints remain largely lacking even as the risks increase.[19]

Authorities are working to minimise disruption to these routes. This includes creating international conventions to maintain access. For example, the 1888 Convention of Constantinople governed the Suez Canal and was interpreted as a guaranteed right of passage of all ships through the Suez Canal during war and peace.[20] However, in addition to the passages, the ships themselves also pose a vulnerability from a geopolitical perspective. Maritime analyst Cormac McGarry of Control Risks said,

> The broader concern with megaships is that we are pouring highly concentrated volumes of our critical supply chains into vulnerable positions, so we are losing the spread of risk. It leaves businesses more exposed to singular, isolated events. And it's not just wind that threatens to stop these ships.[21]

This vulnerability could be targeted and used strategically within a conflict. Iran and Israel seem to regularly engage in harming each other's vessels, and more recently, President Putin has weaponised the shipping of Ukrainian grain during the recent Ukrainian–Russia conflict.[22] However, nation states are not alone in seeing benefit from disrupting shipping routes. Pirates have long been a risk for vessels from the ancient Greeks through to today's industry. The IMB Piracy Reporting Centre received 132 incidents of piracy and armed robbery against ships in 2021, including 115 vessels boarded, 11 attempted attacks, 5 vessels fired upon, and 1 vessel hijacked – although this is a decline on previous years.[23] This mostly occurs in the Malacca Straits and off the coast of Somalia up to the Gulf of Aden – including vessels loaded down with avocados from Kenya. The current average length of a hijacking of vessel and her crew is over seven months, meaning any fresh produce aboard (avocados included) will have long since rotted, even in the unlikely event that the temperature-controlled environment can be maintained throughout the siege.[24]

With consumers in the Global North demanding constant and immediate access to fresh produce, in addition to other consumer goods, the need for increased capacity along shipping routes has been constant. Those in charge of these choke points have been working to increase their capacity. In Egypt, the government began widening the Suez channel in 2014, almost doubling the capacity of the Canal from 49 to 97 ships per day – at a total cost of approximately $9 billion.[25] In 2016, a new side channel was also added to accommodate berthing ships.[26] Panama has also worked to expand the capacity of their canal by building a new set of locks to allow for bigger vessels to cross the Gatún Lake.[27]

CLIMATE IMPACT

However, wider disruption to the shipping industry is not only likely but to be expected with the added pressure of climate change. As James Zhan of the UN Conference on Trade and Development wrote in a recent article, "The decade to 2030 is likely to prove a period of transformation for global value chains."[28] Climate poses one of the biggest (and increasing) risks. The Panama Canal is susceptible to El Niño, which is likely to become more extreme in the coming years due to the shifting climate. The dry weather caused by the phenomenon leads to water levels dropping in the Gatún and Miraflores lakes on either side of the Canal. In 2016, this resulted in depth restrictions on vessels transiting the canal.[29] Ultimately, it could affect half of all vessels using the Panama Canal – nullifying any benefit from the new locks. However, climate change might well also create new routes that help mitigate that risk. Opening the Bering Straits in the Arctic region to commercial traffic could pose an alternative to the Panama Canal in the long term. As the global temperature rises, the passage could be navigable for a number of months each summer. However, the passage through the Arctic would require significant investment for escort vessels (given the risky nature of the journey) and staging ports. The Canadian commercial marine transport industry does not anticipate that this route will be a viable alternative to the Panama Canal for at least another 10–20 years – and it seems a long and circuitous route for avocados to take.[30]

HUMAN IMPACT

Another potential weakness within the shipping industry is the human side. The labour practices on board are notoriously exploitative and dangerous, which is what keeps wages low and shipping inexpensive.[31] Sadly, human life at sea is cheap. While we will discuss the growing demand for Fairtrade and Organic certified avocados in Chapter 14, those assurance schemes do nothing to certify the transportation stage of the supply chain. The human rights and labour abuses that regularly occur on board sit outside the purview of these schemes. The International Labour Union has been working to improve conditions on board, but slavery still continues.[32] Were campaigns for decent wages and better working conditions to succeed, it is likely that shipping costs would increase as shipping companies adapted to the new regulations, and as a result, consumers would face higher prices at check-out as companies would likely pass the rising costs onto consumers. This could mean more expensive avocados. Ironically, labour costs are part of the reason why shipping avocados became so cheap in the first place. The move towards containerisation from the manual method of loading ships after the Second World War led to greater degree of automation in the industry. The army of dock workers were no longer required and thousands were laid-off. The cost of shipping declined, and the savings were passed onto consumers, enabling the global shipping industry that we have today.

GLOBALISATION

While the shipping industry has made this possible, the ubiquity of fresh produce imports, specifically in our case avocados, has also been facilitated by the rise in free trade agreements and the alleviation of tariffs. The impact of NAFTA and the subsequent USMCA has already been addressed in earlier chapters. However, many other markets have been opened up to avocados as a result of a push towards free trade. On 28 April 2020, the EU and Mexico concluded negotiations to modernise the 1997 EU-Mexico Economic Partnership, Political Coordination and Co-operation Agreement ("Global Agreement" or "GA"). The parties had already reached an "agreement in principle" on 21 April 2018 following two years of talks, but the final agreement on some technical details of the chapter on public procurement was still pending. The updated agreement removed tariffs and quotes for the majority of agricultural goods, including avocados. Unlike many other agricultural goods, there was little push back since the European production of avocados is limited, and therefore, there was no significant industry resistance to opening the market to cheaper imports.

Now that the United Kingdom (UK) has left the EU, the nation requires their own free trade agreement with Mexico in order to continue to benefit from access to tariff-free avocados. Prior to Brexit, the import of avocados into the United Kingdom would have been governed by the trade relationships determined by the EU. Currently, South Africa, Colombia, Peru, and Israel are the largest suppliers of UK avocados. But this could change. Post-Brexit, it is up to Westminster and the UK government's Department of International Trade to determine trade relations. Central to the future of avocados, the United Kingdom signed a Trade Continuity Agreement[33] with Mexico in 2021, which would ensure tariff-free avocados[34] (amongst other key considerations). This was required to maintain the trading relationship that the United Kingdom had with Mexico when part of the EU. However, this trade relationship is not set in stone. There was hope (and a stated objective) that this agreement would be the first step, with both countries committing to start negotiating a new and ambitious free trade agreement next year that would go much further towards removing trade barriers.[35] Secondly, the UK government has indicated a desire to join the Comprehensive and Progressive Agreement for Trans-Pacific Partnership (CPTPP). If successful, the CPTPP would bring the UK's trade relationships closer to the South American markets and increase trade. This move is part of the UK government's wider shift towards non-European markets. This could mean more avocados from Mexico, and other producers in the region. It could also potentially alter trading dynamics in avocados between the UK and other regions and could reduce the market share of Israeli or South African avocados within the UK market. The UK government also floated the idea of joining the successor to NAFTA, USMCA, but the other parties do not seem to be entertaining the idea.

The free trade agreement with Mexico and Europe means that avocados can flow into the EU without tariffs or quota, making them more affordable. As a result of this agreement, Mexico was the EU's second-largest trading partner for trade in goods in Central and South America after Brazil in 2021. The Mexicans certainly hope that the removal of these tariffs will entice the European consumers to increase their consumption. The average consumption in Europe is approximately 1.33 kg per capita, while in the United States, it is 3.8 kg, suggesting there is a lot more guacamole that Europeans could be eating if adequately primed.[36] However, increasing consumption requires more than just a new trade deal. Infrastructure is required to support it. The United Producers of Mexico, founded in 2016 to improve and increase Mexican agri-exports to the European market, has been lobbying for a direct shipping route from Mexico to Rotterdam (Europe's largest port) to speed up the delivery rate.[37] According to UPM's Managing Director, Lia Bijnsdorp,

> Ships from Peru, for example, take a week shorter than from Mexico, while Peruvian ports are further from Rotterdam. And, for fresh fruit, a week makes a big difference. It takes longer to ship Mexican products because the ships dock in the U.S. or Central America along the way, slowing them down enormously. Enough reason to make a strong case for shortening the shipping time, which also reduces quality and product loss.[38]

The shipping industry's reasoning for not having a dedicated route from Mexico to Rotterdam was that there was insufficient demand, but this is a catch-22 since without the route, it is difficult to boost exports. A test voyage was undertaken in 2020, and the journey took only 14 days, opposed to the average 28 with a US stopover. However, the Covid-19 pandemic and the associated impact on supply chains due to sickness and rolling lockdowns ended plans to expand it. That said, UPM are still determined in their efforts to expand exports of Mexican fresh produce, including avocados, into Europe via Rotterdam, with the ultimate goal of one fixed sailing from Mexico to Rotterdam every two weeks for the entire year.

IN CONCLUSION...

As this chapter relates, the growing of avocados is only a small part of the picture. Transporting the fruit safely and efficiently around the world is central to developing a global industry. Without container ships and the network of global shipping routes, it would have been next to impossible for fresh avocados to reach consumers in the Global North. The shipment of avocados relies on fine-tuned infrastructure that works seamlessly to deliver them just-in-time. However, the tight nature of these deliveries makes them vulnerable to disruption. The innate fragility of our globalised shipping industry is finally being acknowledged and efforts are being made to make it more resilient.

NOTES

1   *The Wall Street Journal*, "How a steel box changed the world: A brief history of shipping." *YouTube*, 2018, January 24.

2   Durisin, Megan, "Global food import bill Set for record, taking toll on poorest." *Bloomberg*, 2022, June 9.

3   Porter, John, "How reliant is the UK on imported food?" *The Caterer*, 2010, September 30.

4   Barrett, "How far does your food travel? 4 reason to choose local." *Natural Society*, 2013, December 17.

5   Walsh, Bryan, "Set sail for greener maritime cargo shipping." *Time*, 2013, August 7.

6   "United Kingdom food security report 2021: Theme 2: UK food supply sources." *Gov.uk*, 2021, December 22.

7   OECD/FAO, *OECD-FAO Agricultural Outlook 2021–2030*. OECD Publishing, Paris, 2021.

8   Cargo Handbook, "Avocados." https://www.cargohandbook.com/Avocados.

9   TRANSfer, "Mexico—Road freight transportation sector." *Federal Ministry for the Environment Nature Conservation, Building and Nuclear Safety*. http://www.transferproject.org/projects/t-nama-countries-iki/mexico/.

10 Secretaría de Comunicaciones y Transportes, "Informe Estadístico Mensual." *Coordinación General de Puertos y Marina Mercante*, January-December 2011–2012.

11 *World Shipping Council*, "The top 50 container ports." https://www.worldshipping.org/top-50-ports.

12 *iContainers*, "Top 5 ports in Mexico." 2018, June 12.

13 Diaz, Lizabeth, "Mexico's Wild West: Vigilante groups defy president to fight cartels." *Reuters*, 2019, September 13.

14 *International Finance Corporation*, "Panama canal expansion—Key to global trade." 2016, June.

15 Sekine, Hiroshi, "Panama canal data for current operations." *UKP&I*, 2021, September 17.

16 King, Richard, "Exploring the cascading impacts from climate shocks to chokepoints in global food trade." *Resource Trade Earth*, 2022, June 20.

17 Ibid.

18 Christian, Alex, "The untold story of the big boat that broke the world." *Wired*, 2021, June 22.

19 King, Richard, "Exploring the cascading impacts from climate shocks to chokepoints in global food trade." *Resource Trade Earth*, 2022, June 20.

20 Suez Canal Authority, "Constantinople convention." https://www.suezcanal.gov.eg/English/About/CanalTreatiesAndDecrees/pages/constantinopleconvention.aspx.

21 Braw, Elisabeth, "What the ever given taught the world." *Foreign Policy*, 2021, November 10.

22 Braw, Elisabeth, "Attacks on Gulf shipping leave the global economy vulnerable." *Politico*, 2021, August 5.

23 Intercargo, "Global piracy and armed robbery situation." *International Association of Dry Cargo Shipowners*, 2022, December 2.

24 "Best management practices or protection against Somalia based piracy." *Witherby Publishing Group*, 2011.

25 Hansen, Kathryn, "The new Suez canal." *NASA Earth Observatory*, August 2014–April 2016.

26 Ibid.

27 Bogdanich, Walt, Williams, Jacqueline, & Méndez, Ana Graciela, "The new Panama canal: A risky bet." *The New York Times*, 2016, June 22.

28 *The Economist*, "The structure of the world's supply chains is changing." 2022, June 16.

29 Reuters Staff, "Panama canal sets depth limit on ships due to drought." *Reuters*, 2016, March 21.

30 U.S. Arctic Research Commission, Arctic Marine Transport Workshop. *International Arctic Science Committee*, 2004, September 28–30.

31 Anti-Slavery, "Slavery in supply chains." *antislavery.org*.

32 International Labour Organization, "Shipping and inland waterways." https://www.ilo.org/global/industries-and-sectors/shipping-ports-fisheries-inland-waterways/shipping/lang--en/index.htm.

33 Gov.UK, "Trade with Mexico." *Department for International Trade*, 2020, December 31.

34 Gov.UK, "Product export information for 0804.40.00.10 from Mexico to the United Kingdom." 2023, February 28.

35 Gov.UK, "UK and Mexico sign trade deal." *Department for International Trade*, 2020, December 15.

36 CBI Ministry of Foreign Affairs, "The European market potential for avocados." *ICI Business*, 2023, January 23.

37 Bijnsdorp, Lia, "Direct Mexico—Rotterdam ocean route seems a sure thing." *Fresh Plaza*, 2022, March 22.

38 Ibid.

KEY READINGS

- King, Richard, "Exploring the cascading impacts from climate shocks to chokepoints in global food trade." *Resource Trade Earth*, 2022, June 20.
- *The Economist*, "The structure of the world's supply chains is changing." 2022, June 16.
- *The Wall Street Journal*, "How a steel box changed the world: A brief history of shipping." *YouTube*, 2018, January 24.
- TRANSfer, "Mexico—Road freight transportation sector." *Federal Ministry for the Environment Nature Conservation, Building and Nuclear Safety*. http://www.transferproject.org/projects/t-nama-countries-iki/mexico/.

9

GROWING ORCHARDS

LAND-USE CHANGE AND BIODIVERSITY LOSS FROM AVOCADO CULTIVATION

INTRODUCTION

The expansion of avocado production has been rapid. The significant profit that it offers to farmers, predominantly in the Global South, has made it an appealing crop. However, the rapid expansion in rural areas has led to land-use change since traditional mixed farms have been converted into monoculture plantations and the use of more agrochemicals to maintain and maximise the land's productivity. This has meant significant changes to the natural biodiversity and local ecosystems. More problematic than just cultivating avocados, these plantations often only cultivate one type of avocado. Cultivating only Hass avocados in an orchard creates a weak system since monocultures remove the resilience of genetic diversity from the system, threatening the natural ability to resist pests or diseases. Such was the case with the Gros Michel banana, which was the most popular variety until the 1950s, when a fungus known as "Panama disease" wiped out the entire line. A fate that could await the Hass.[1]

THE IMPACT OF MEXICAN PRODUCTION

The environmental impact of the avocado is not caused by the fruit itself. It is not inherently damaging. The real issue is the method of production and lack of regulation. This is particularly the case in Mexico. Due to the fruit's commercial value, they are increasingly grown in unsuitable locations, including formerly forested land, to maximise yield. At the same time

DOI: 10.4324/9781003371915-9

as the pressure to increase supply, the regions where they are grown are also becoming unsuitable due to changing climates. Avocados grow best in moderate temperatures and humidity. However, Central and South America are becoming increasingly arid with longer dry, hot seasons and reduced annual rainfall.[2] For five years straight, many regions in Central America, including Mexico, saw rainfall less than 80% of the rainy season average.[3] To sustain these avocado plantations, huge amounts of irrigation are required when before the region's agriculture relied on precipitation. The diversion of natural water bodies to supply irrigation on these farms can create widespread drought pressure that lead to wildfires, which destroy forested habitats.[4] If they can't afford irrigation, producers are forced to expand plantations into new areas with favourable climatic conditions, such as those at higher elevation, pushing plantations further up the hillside. These areas have often been uncultivated previously and contain pristine habitats and so can result in the destruction of incredible and irreplaceable biodiversity.

As has already been established elsewhere in this book, when considering avocado production in Mexico, we are not focusing on the entire nation but on one district – the western state of Michoacán. We have already discussed the vast quantity of avocados that Michoacán produces each year, but what has not yet been explored is its incredible biodiversity. In fact, it is one of the most ecologically important regions of the country. This creates an inherent and unavoidable tension. Due to the demand for agricultural land, an estimated 15,000–20,000 acres of forest are cut down each and replaced with commercial avocado plantations each year.[5] Yet, many areas of Michoacán have been classified as Key Biological/Biodiversity Areas (KBAs) – habitats or locations understood to be vital to the preservation of threatened and endangered species and hugely important for global biodiversity. Geospatial data shows that over 100,000 ha[6] of Michoacán's avocado plantations are in these KBAs, home to a number of endangered species,[7] including pumas, jaguars, and a host of exotic reptiles. Many native bird species rely on the canopies provided by the native forests, including the endangered yellow-headed parrot and a variety of macaw species.[8] These diverse forests of Michoacán are a key to the wider biodiversity of Mexico, which itself is the fourth most biodiverse country on Earth. The forests of Mexico account for 10% of global biodiversity.[9]

All of this might seem a bit academic. If one native tree is chopped down only to be replaced by an avocado sapling doesn't that negate the loss? An eye for an eye. A tree for a tree. Surely, one might exclaim, it's not as problematic as when the great trees of the Amazon are cut down for soy fields.

However, the deforestation of native forests and subsequent replacement with avocado trees has a knock-on effect on the landscapes and climate; avocado trees have a much less capacity to absorb carbon emissions compared to native tree species. A native pine in Michoacán captures 4 times more carbon dioxide per hectare than an avocado tree.[10] So, although to an extent the native trees are being replaced by trees (as opposed to traditional cropland), avocado trees do not offer the same environmental and climate benefits as the native pines. There are increasing programmes (one even sponsored by the Association of Avocado Exporting Producers and Packers of Mexico) to reforest the area with native pines, and these should be welcomed.[11] However, deforestation doesn't just impact trees. Thousands of species are dependent on native forests for their home and come under threat from land-use change. Forestation methods need to consider the wider ecosystem, not the trees alone. These habitats are fragile and complex, and the value of these ecosystems (and the services that they provide) is far harder to quantify. While attempts are being made to calculate the natural capital, much of the value remains unacknowledged, which in part is why many government officials view these areas as unused land, instead of vast natural resources.

POLLINATORS

One of the most iconic species that is impacted by the spread of avocados through Michoacán is the majestic monarch butterfly. The most well-recognised and well-studied butterfly, with their two pairs of brilliant orange-red wings, with black veins and white spots. Monarch butterflies are roughly categorised into Eastern and Western populations, depending on where they overwinter. The Eastern Monarch population breeds east of the Rocky Mountains and migrates to central Mexico in late summer and autumn. In contrast, the Western Monarch population breeds west of the Rocky Mountains, migrates to coastal southern California, where they spend the winter. As the agricultural borders shift and encroach into forests and marginal land, the Monarch breeding sites are being continually destroyed. Between 1996 and 2017, the total area of Michoacán forest where monarch butterflies could be found declined by 86%.[12] To try to combat this loss, the Monarch Butterfly Biosphere Reserve was established in 2006 and has been on the UNESCO World Heritage List since 2008. In addition to the butterflies, the Biosphere Reserve is home to a wide range of rare mammals and reptiles, including jaguars and pumas. Jaguars are currently listed as "near threatened" after concerted efforts to prevent them from going extinct due to habitat loss and illegal hunting.[13] They have long held a place as symbols of spirituality and strength in Central and South America. WWF has been working with the Mexican government and other local and national groups, going to significant lengths to restore and conserve monarch butterfly populations, as well as other key pollinators in the region, through the Monarch Butterfly Conservation Fund. To combat the economic incentives driving deforestation and land-use change, the conservation fund provides financial alternatives to deforestation of key habitats for monarch butterfly and pollinator populations. Luckily for monarch butterflies, their global recognition and public popularity has led to a significant government action to preserve them. In addition, the Mexican Hass Importers Association has sponsored a programme to help reforest the Biosphere Reserve.[14]

Butterflies aren't the only pollinator impacted by avocado production. Pollinators are critical to the healthy functioning of an ecosystem. Three quarters of global crops rely on pollinators to some extent, with one third entirely dependent on them.[15] Yet, across the globe, pollinator species are in decline.[16] This is true in Mexico where avocado plantations rely on the local bee populations to pollinate their crops. The Agricultural Research Council (ARC) recommends two to four bee colonies per hectare for effective avocado pollination.[17] Although widespread reporting and monitoring of bee populations in Latin America has only started in earnest in the past few years, conservation efforts are now underway. It was estimated that Mexican beekeepers have experienced losses of between 30% and 80% of their colonies.[18] While colony collapse is still little understood, correlations have been drawn to the expansion of industrial agriculture, in large part due to land-use change and intensive agriculture – specifically the use of pesticides and chemical inputs.[19] In Colombia, mass bee deaths have been attributed directly to avocado production.[20] Between 2014 and 2021, Colombia's avocado exports have boomed from 1,408 metric tons to 96,903 tons a year.[21] Simultaneously, there has been the collapse of, according to a report in *Nature*, over one third of Colombia's beehives collapsed between 2014 and 2017.[22] This mass increase in avocado production is dependent on intensive production practices, especially the use of highly hazardous pesticides. A neonicotinoid, fipronil, has been largely considered responsible for the impact on local bee populations.[23] Neonicotinoids, or "neonics," are very well documented as hugely detrimental to bee populations (as well as other pollinators) and have been banned in the EU since 2013.[24] While Colombia has now recognised the risk and passed a resolution in January 2023 to halt the use of fipronil, considerable damage had already been done and other highly toxic pesticides remain legal.[25] The impact of the pesticides on the pollinator populations is compounded by local deforestation. Research conducted in Colombia found that when farms are surrounded by high proportions of forested area, there is a buffer effect that allows local pollinator populations to withstand the impact of pesticide residues.[26] However, as the quantity of pesticides used grows, and the amount of local forested area declines, the pollinators are increasingly susceptible to population collapse. To address the lack of pollinators, farmers are turning to migratory beekeeping. The process by which beekeepers travelling with their hives to different farms and locations to aid pollination where the local pollinator populations are no longer sufficient is becoming an increasingly standard practice amongst global avocado producers.

COMMUNITY IMPACTS

While thoughts of a large evil corporation might be the first that jumps into mind when thinking of those deforesting land, the deforestation in Michoacán is often driven by small-scale farmers. Although large-scale corporations dominate the global avocado supply chain in Michoacán, they do not own much land. Instead, small-scale farmers sell their crop to middlemen that sell onto businesses with the size and infrastructure needed to access global consumers. This has led to many traditional subsistence farmers converting to avocado production since it is a far more lucrative crop than traditional subsistence farming. Those that do not make the switch, often end up being forced out onto marginal lands that are either unsuitable for cropping or are native areas, driving further deforestation. In these marginal lands, the climate and/or soil may often provide unfavourable conditions for the crops, so the farmers are forced to use more agrochemicals and irrigation in order to achieve comparable yields to those that would have been achievable on the fertile land now used for avocados. This has major environmental implications and economic consequences for the farmers, reducing their profits and creating greater income inequality.

It is worth pointing out that deforestation has been relatively commonplace in Mexican agriculture for a long time. Referred to as "Milpa," a small forested area would be cleared through slash and burn practices and then cropped for a few seasons, before moving on to create a new clearing, allowing the original to recover. Burning the land brings new fertility into the soil by breaking down plant matter into readily available nutrients with increased mineralisation rates, making it ripe for cultivation.[27] While this was sustainable on a small scale as subsistence land for local and indigenous communities, it is now being carried out at unsustainable rates by local producers trying to benefit from the large profits to be made from avocados. However, industry often cite milpa practices as a way to defend avocado plantations in deforested areas. They argue that slash and burn has always been present, particularly in Michoacán, where indigenous and local farmers have used it for centuries. They do not acknowledge the significant difference in scale or the long-term implications of agricultural pollution, water scarcity, and subsequent soil erosion. In a 2018 study[28] of the Mexico–US avocado supply chain, one industry actor was quoted as saying "A lot of deforestation took place before the avocado industry … started to blossom … There was barren land ready and the avocado industry kind of moved in," as a justification for not accepting the links between avocado industries growth and subsequent expansion of deforestation in Michoacán in particular.

TRANSPORT

Once the fruit is off the farm, the environmental impact does not end. As discussed in the last chapter, there are huge consequences from the transport of the fruit that need to be considered when weighing the environmental and social impacts. The land-use change extends beyond the farm gate, with huge processing facilities built in Michoacán as well as the expansion of transport routes, namely roads from these facilities, across the border to US distributors and food companies. As previously discussed, avocados require cold storage distribution to remain fresh for sale and are normally transported in refrigerated containers. It is also recommended that the fruit be pre-cooled right after they're harvested to maximise and prolong ripeness.[29] Both pre-cooling at packing facilities and transport in refrigerated containers are incredibly energy intensive and will contribute to greater greenhouse gas emissions throughout the supply chain. Mexican avocados are overwhelmingly transported by truck.[30] Mission Produce, a large-scale avocado producer in Michoacán, reports 20–22 truckloads produced and transported a day from their two major facilities in the region.[31] As discussed in the last chapter, while Mexico might have had a pre-existing network of roads, they were not sufficient to cope with the additional trucks on the road. These routes were expanded (with additional associated infrastructure such as rest-stops) under the National Infrastructure Programme. This requires more land to be converted and therefore puts further pressure on habitats. Expansion of the roads is also responsible for indirect influences on surrounding habitats, particularly noise and air pollution, which can disturb local wildlife and have a knock-on effect on local biodiversity beyond the physical boundaries of the road networks.[32] Many varieties of plants, particularly lichens, are negatively impacted by the air pollution created by road traffic.[33] Since Mexico is home to 20% of the world's lichenized fungi, the impact on global biodiversity is considerable.[34]

OUTSIDE MEXICO

Challenges around avocado production and land-use change are not limited to Mexico. As referenced with the decline of bees, Colombia has recently expanded into avocado production and has seen environmental degradation as a result. Historically, Colombia has been widely considered to produce the best coffee beans in the world. Yet, as discussed, coffee yields are declining globally due to climate change and many farmers are starting to switch to avocados. This has ultimately led to Colombia becoming the world's third largest avocado exporter.[35] Farmer Riobardo Zapata said in an interview, "All my life, my family, my grandparents, my parents, everyone grew coffee. But now, coffee is disappearing and avocado is taking its place."[36] While there are benefits to poverty alleviation and addressing the decline in coffee yields, the switch has caused concerns, especially since it's one of the most biodiverse areas. The rush to plant avocados has led to a surge in deforestation across the country and major losses of biodiversity.[37] At present, the estimated 58,312 known species are at risk of extinction in Colombia due to widespread habitat loss, driven by the booming avocado production.[38]

Unlike many other nations, Australia has found a way to produce avocados while minimising the damage to the environment. As previously discussed, Australia has a long history with avocados and a strong domestic industry that is still growing. Yet, despite that scale, avocado production in Australia is also mostly free from deforestation and habitat loss. This is in part due to the size of the country, its regulatory system (allowing for greater enforcement than in the Global South), and the vast amounts of suitable land available to grow crops, meaning that the Australian avocado plantations are grown at a much lower density than equivalent plantations in South America, putting less strain on the soil and local water sources.[39] That said, as anyone who has paid attention to the media in recent years will know, Australia is susceptible to drought (and the associated wildfires). This means that orchards in Australia still require irrigation or soil moistening to different degrees. The sustainability of Australian production is also partly because there is a suitable climate and appropriate growing conditions in many regions. Unlike in Mexico where avocados are only grown in one region, Australian avocados are grown across the entire territory. Each of these regions has their own climate, which means that there is a wide range of growing seasons across the country. Queensland produces the majority of Australian avocados, with 69% of production.[40] Western Australia produced the next largest share at 18% and then New South Wales with 9%.[41] While Western Australian fruit will be harvested in the summer, Queensland fruit will ripen in the winter. Each region grows their crops during the most suitable period of the year, minimising the need for irrigation and broader inputs. This means that demand can be met all year round in a way that is environmentally sensitive and without relying on agrochemicals that damage the land.

NATIONAL PROTECTIONS

Recent years have seen growing awareness of the environmental damage associated with wider food production and a greater focus in reducing that impact. Globally, there has been a shift to recognise the need to protect the biodiversity, and there have been moves across the world to restrict the expansion of productive land into native habitats. We have seen this in the campaigns to stop the Amazon from being cut down and from pleas to save the habitats of orangutans in Borneo. As has (hopefully) been made clear, the real issue is not with the fruit itself, but with the method of production. In Mexico, the sudden boom in avocado exports to North America and associated deforestation in recent decades has accelerated faster than government regulation and enforcement can keep up. The consequence is that the Mexican government has not been able to halt deforestation in Michoacán. Half-hearted attempts have been made to create regulations. Just prior to the creation of NAFTA, Mexico enacted the General Law of Ecological Equilibrium and Protection of the Environment and created the Environment and Natural Resources Secretariat following the signing. Incremental environmental changes were made subsequently, and Mexico's General Law of Sustainable Forestry Development was recently amended in 2021 to include the provision that any changes to land use of forest land must be subject to analysis of carbon storage capacity, and local indigenous communities must be consulted. Furthermore, Mexico has committed to achieving net-zero deforestation by 2030 as a Nationally Determined Contribution (NDC) under the Paris Agreement. Yet, there has been no clear enforcement of these laws and little resource put behind them. Although the blame for that cannot all be placed at the feet of Mexico City since the enforcement of any statute in Mexico is especially challenging due to the widespread presence of the drug cartels and associated corruption – an issue that will be addressed in Chapter 12.

However, in the absence of Mexican leadership on the issue of deforestation, activists are urging the US government to step up and show leadership. The international conservation community wrote to the Biden Administration in 2021, saying, "As one of the world's largest producers and consumers of agricultural commodities, the United States must play a key role in setting standards for trade and finance that promote good governance." In response, Senator Brian Schatz (D-HI) and Representatives Earl Blumenauer (D-OR) and Brian Fitzpatrick (R-PA) introduced the Fostering Overseas Rule of Law and Environmentally Sound Trade (FOREST) Act of 2021 to "deter commodity-driven illegal deforestation around the world" through a "risk-based framework to ensure transparent supply chains" that would aim to halt the import of products that resulted in deforestation.[42] However, this Bill has not yet progressed through Congress. Despite the cute acronym, whether the measure could have any significant impact is doubtful since enforcement and reporting along the Mexican portion of the supply chain would prove challenging. Similar efforts are being enacted in the EU and in the United Kingdom.

LOCAL RESPONSE

At a more local level, indigenous groups are pushing back and communities taking matters into their own hands in order to combat the rise of illegal deforestation. Michoacán's predominant indigenous community is P-urhépecha. The community has a long and proud history, having been a wealthy metallurgy economy, maintaining independence through the Aztec period and fighting against the Spanish colonialists. However, recent history has seen the population dwindle and the marginalisation of the community. Angahuan in Michoacán has established strong community rules to stop illegal logging with citizens patrolling 600 ha of woodland. Under the rules, tree clearing is forbidden, and people are allowed to collect wood only when it falls naturally to the ground.[43] The timber can be used only for community purposes, such as building schools. They are also committed to reforestation efforts as Gracia Bravo, a community leader and traditional healer in Anguahuan, explains,

> [Plantation owners] bring water to their avocado orchards, and for this reason, there is not enough for the community… My husband and brother have already planted 500 pine trees on the hills. They want to stop the avocado a bit, to do reforestation, and help to retain water.

Something similar happened in Cheran, 50 km to the west of Angahuan, where a small indigenous community[44] outlawed change in land usage, since roughly half[45] of Cheran's 59,000 acres of forest was illegally felled between 2008 and 2011. They see this as essential to protecting the future of their land and their community and have formed a volunteer anti-logging patrol unit.[46] David Ramos Guerrero, a member of Cheran's self-governing farmers' board, said, "The community is the one demanding and asking that we respect nature, just like our ancestors taught us. Taking care of nature, instead of destroying it, fortifying it through reforestation."[47] We will return to these communities when discussing water stress in the next chapter and also in Chapter 12 when we discuss the growing resistance to drug cartels in Michoacán.

IN CONCLUSION…

The avocado itself is not an environmentally damaging crop. If anything, a solitary avocado tree provides a home for insects, food for birds and small mammals, sequesters carbon, and improves soil organic matter. However, when planted in large monoculture plantations, the method of production can cause negative environmental impacts. As the land is switched over, biodiversity is displaced, and ecosystems are put under pressure, with a knock-on impact for communities. While Michoacán is the primary location of avocado production, all regions that engage in large-scale production of the fruit experience environmental and ecosystem changes.

NOTES

1 Handwerk, Brian, "Holy Guacamole: How the hass avocado conquered the world." *Smithsonian Magazine*, 2017, July 28.

2 *World Meteorological Organization*, "New report shows impacts of climate change and extreme weather in Latin America and Caribbean." 2021, August 17.

3 Masters, Jeff, "Fifth straight year of central American drought helping drive migration." *Scientific American*, 2019, December 23.

4 Shreeves, Robin, "The dark side of the trendy avocado." *Treehugger*, 2018, May 25.

5 Stevenson, Mark, "Mexico: Deforestation due to avocados, higher than calculated." *Associated Press*, 2016, October 31.

6 Cho, Kimin, "Environmental impacts of the U.S.-Mexico avocado supply chain." *The University of Michigan*, 2020.

7 Butler, Rhett, "Forests of Michoacan, Mexico disappearing." *Mongabay*, 2005, November 7.

8 Ibid.

9 Forest Legality Initiative, "Mexico." *World Resources Institute*, 2016, April.

10 Global Forrest Watch, "Forests falling fast to make way for Mexican avocado." *World Resource Institute*, 2019, 2019, March.

11 *Avocado Institute of Mexico*, "The initiative by APEAM to rehabilitate the forests of Michoacán." 2020.

12 *World Wildlife Fund*, "As monarch butterflies lose ground in Mexico, WWF seeks solutions in America's heartland." https://www.worldwildlife.org/stories/as-monarch-butterflies-lose-ground-in-mexico-wwf-seeks-solutions-in-america-s-heartland#.

13 Marin, Ganesh, & Koprowski, John, "Jaguars could return to the US Southwest—but only if they have pathways to move north." *The Conversation*, 2022, April 19.

14 *Avocado Institute of Mexico*, "Saving the monarch butterfly: The efforts by MHAIA to reforest Michoacán." https://avocadoinstitute.org/long-live-the-monarch.

15 Ritchie, Hannah, "How essential are pollinators for global food security?" *World Economic Forum*, 2021, August 9.

16 Millard, J., Outhwaite, C.L., Kinnersley, R. *et al.* Global effects of land-use intensity on local pollinator biodiversity. *Nature Communications* Vol. 12, Issue 2902, 2021.

17 Louw, Marinda, "How to farm avocados." *South Africa Online*. https://southafrica.co.za/how-to-farm-avocados.html.

18 Estrada, Laura Yaniz, "We have to talk about the bees." *Interamerican Association for Environmental Defense*, 2018, August 27.

19 Datz, Todd, "Use of common pesticide linked to bee colony collapse." *Harvard T.H. Chan School of Public Health*, 2012, April 5.

20 Sarmiento, Joaquin, "In Pictures: Is avocado boom to blame for bee deaths in Columbia?" *Aljazeera*, 2021, March 2.

21 Hemmes, Marieke, "Columbia's booming avocado industry." *Fresh Plaza*, 2022, June 1.

22 López-Cubillos, Sofia, Suárez-Castro, Felipe, McDonald-Madden, Eve, Biggs, Duan, Nates-Parra, Guiomar, Gutierrez-Chacón, Catalina, & Runting, Rebecca, Columbia short on political will to protect pollinators. *Nature*, 2019, September 10. https://pubmed.ncbi.nlm.nih.gov/31506628/.

23 *France 24*, "Columbia's apiarists say avocado buzz is killing bees." 2021, February 26.

24 *Safe Food Advocacy Europe*, "Fipronil." 2022, September 27.

25 Instituto Colombiano Agropecuario, Resolucion No 00000740, 2023, January 31.

26 Wight, Andrew, "How did this Colombian use drones to solve a bee mystery?" *Forbes*, 2020, August 9.

27 *Northern Arizona University*, "Fire effect on soil." https://www2.nau.edu/~gaud/bio300w/frsl.htm.

28 Cho, Kimin, *Environmental Impacts of the U.S.-Mexico Avocado Supply Chain.* The University of Michigan, 2020.

29 Bill, Malick, Sivakumar, Dharini, Thompson, Keith, & Korsten, Lise, *Avocado Fruit Quality Management During the Postharvest Supply Chain.* University of Pretoria, Tshwane University of Technology & Hamelmalo Agricultural College. https://www.tandfonline.com/doi/abs/10.1080/87559129.2014.907304.

30 Cross Border Freight, "Shipping avocados from Mexico to the United States." *Global Logistics*, 2019, August 15.

31 Mission, "A rich history of avocados." *Mission Produce.* https://missionproduce.com/our-avocados.

32 Rodrigue, Jean-Paul, "The geography of transport systems." *Hofstra University.* https://transportgeography.org/.

33 Coffey, Heather, & Fahrig, Lenore, Relative effects of vehicle pollution, moisture and colonization sources on urban lichens. *Journal of Applied Ecology*, Vol. 49, Issue 6, 2012, October 8.

34 Herrera-Campos, Maria, Pérez-Pérez, Rosa, & Nash, Thomas, *Lichens of Mexico.* Schweizerbart Science Publishers, 2016.

35 Hemmes, Marieke, 2022, "Columbia's booming avocado industry." *Fresh Plaza*, June 1.

36 Sarmiento, Joaquin, "In pictures: Is avocado boom to blame for bee deaths in Columbia?" *Aljazeera*, 2021, March 2.

37 Cheong, Keeven, & Tan, Remus, "Colombia's avocado boom." *SMU Economics Intelligence Club*, 2022, January 13.

38 Ibid.

39 Mitchell, Dudley, *High Density Avocado Production: Constructing an Integrated Management Model.* Nuffield Australia Farming Scholars, 2018.

40 Avocados Australia, "Facts at a Glance 2016/17 for the Australian avocado industry," *Hort Innovation*, 2017.

41 Ibid.

42 *Congress.Gov*, "Forest Act of 2021." 2021, June 10.

43 Pelliccia, Monica, "Indigenous agroforestry dying of thirst amid a sea of avocados in Mexico," Civil Eats, 2022, June 10.

44 Brown, Hannah, "This Mexican town declared independence to protect its forest from avocados." Euronews.green, 2022, February 2.

45 McDonnell, Patrick, "One Mexican town revolts against violence and corruption. Six years in, its experiment is working." Los Angeles Times, 2017, July 10.

46 Brown, Hannah, "This Mexican town declared independence to protect its forest from avocados." Euronews.green, 2022, February 2.

47 Ibid.

KEY READINGS

- *Avocado Institute of Mexico*, "Saving the monarch butterfly: The efforts by MHAIA to reforest Michoacán." https://avocadoinstitute.org/long-live-the-monarch.
- Global Forrest Watch, "Forests falling fast to make way for Mexican avocado." *World Resource Institute*, 2019, March 2019.
- López-Cubillos, Sofia, Suárez-Castro, Felipe, McDonald-Madden, Eve, Biggs, Duan, Nates-Parra, Guiomar, Gutierrez-Chacón, Catalina, & Runting, Rebecca, "Columbia short on political will to protect pollinators." *Nature*, 2019, September 10.
- McDonnell, Patrick, "One Mexican town revolts against violence and corruption. Six years in, its experiment is working." *Los Angeles Times*, 2017, July 10.
- Pelliccia, Monica, "Indigenous agroforestry dying of thirst amid a sea of avocados in Mexico. *Civil Eats*, 2022, June 10.
- Stevenson, Mark, "Mexico: Deforestation due to avocados, higher than calculated." Associated Press, 2016, October 31.

10

EMBEDDED WATER

HOW AVOCADOS IMPACT WATER AND THE POTENTIAL POLICY SOLUTIONS

INTRODUCTION

Asked to think of a grove of avocado trees, most people would probably imagine the soft rolling hills of Central America – maybe even with picturesque rain clouds hovering over the hillside. South and Central America became key producers of avocados for a number of reasons – including proximity to North America – but in particular because their natural climate and natural water sources were ideal for the avocado. The most prolific region for avocado production, Michoacán, was known for its consistent groundwater levels and adequate annual rainfall with an annual precipitation of 909 mm.[1] These favourable conditions suited the fruit since it is a thirsty crop. One kilo of avocados requires 283 L of water on average.[2] That is equivalent to about four full baths. In comparison to other fruit, this usage is substantial. It takes 110 L for a kilo of oranges and only 63 L for a kilo of tomatoes.[3] The World Avocado Organisation (WAO) admits that this water usage is high but points out that it "pales in comparison to the vast quantities needed for a range of other foods."[4] Figures compiled by the Institution for Mechanical Engineers and quoted by the WAO show that chocolate (17,196l), bananas (790l), and apples (822l) consume more water than avocados.[5] However, due to the climate crisis, rainfall has changed, Michoacán (along with the rest of the region) has become increasingly water stressed. This has

DOI: 10.4324/9781003371915-10

led to high levels of irrigation for the crops, diverting water away from communities and other crops.

Climate change is increasing Mexico's susceptibility to water stress; the warmer air temperatures, driven by increasing greenhouse gases in the atmosphere, lead to higher levels of evaporation from soils and water bodies. Compounding these atmospheric impacts, la Nina (periods of sea cooling, reducing rainfall) are becoming increasingly frequent and extreme compared to previous centuries – climate modelling for the Coupled Model Intercomparison Project identified a doubling in frequency, possibly increasing to every five years.[6] The true extent of the growing water crisis in Mexico was fully realised in the summer of 2022. Over half[7] of the country experienced drought, with Conagua, the national water authority, declaring a state of emergency[8] across four northern states. It was considered the worst water crisis in Mexico in the last 30 years.[9] Reservoirs supplying over 23 million people dried up, causing widespread unrest as both rich and poor had to decide between being able to wash or drink.

Even outside of the drought periods, this rising water stress has had a substantial impact on farmers and agricultural production. Agriculture is a major contributor to increased water stress in Mexico; 77% of the country's water is used for agricultural purposes, and as one of their major crops, avocados drink up a substantial portion of this.[10] Ideally, avocados should be grown seasonally and only in areas with suitable water supplies that can be accessed sustainably. In the main avocado growing belt in Mexico, centred around Michoacán, irrigation for avocado production consumes 120% of the surface and groundwater volumes that the government designates for agricultural use in dry years.[11] In Mexico, surface and groundwater fall under federal government jurisdiction. As a result, the rights to water volume, including agricultural and industrial rights, can be granted by the National Water Commissions, and these are not necessarily granted in equitable proportions, instead they may be adjusted by the Commissions in light of current pressures on water supply – with the potential for outside factors influence decision. Today, Mexico has the highest water scarcity footprint from avocado production, with 27% of the global total, with Chile in second place at 22%.[12] That said, within the region of Michoacán, there has been more precipitation in the last two decades, even while other regions are experiencing extended drought from 803 mm annually in 2000 to 819 mm in 2021.[13] However, while that might seem like a good thing, there is a note of caution. Climate change increases the frequency of extreme weather events, so it is feasible that this increase might come in the form of torrential downpours. Large volumes of rainfall over a short timespan are problematic as the ground cannot absorb and retain it, especially if the soil is not in a good condition, and can lead to flash flooding and landslides.

GREEN, BLUE, AND GREY

When we consider the water footprint of agricultural products, like avocados, we can distinguish between blue, green, and grey water. In simple terms, green water is rain that the trees will draw up from the soil through their roots. Blue water is that which is drawn from natural water bodies like rivers and aquifers. Grey water is water that has already been used by humans, such as for washing. Across the world, regions that were once water rich are now experiencing water stress and drought due to a combination of climate change (less rainfall and hotter, drier climates) and the unsustainable usage of natural water sources (blue water). For avocado production in Michoacán, blue and green water are the most pertinent. The fruit's production belt in Mexico relies on surface water and groundwater, directly depleting the wider availability of blue and green water. When considering the rise in water stress in Mexico, a lack of green water has been the direct and immediate cause of these droughts, but the lack of resilience has resulted in longer term overexploitation of blue water by companies. At a national level, many industries and companies contribute to this exploitation. There has been significant media coverage of the role of Coca-Cola and Heineken in Mexico who directly source blue water from public reservoirs around Monterrey for their products, extracting in total about 90 billion litres a year, with 50 billion directly from these public reservoirs, to the detriment of the local population.[14] Large-scale avocado producers are increasingly facing similar criticism for taking an excessive amount of water out of the local environment and Mexico has been ranked as one of the countries with the fastest increase in unsustainable water consumption in agriculture for export markets, since 2000.[15]

AQUIFERS AND NATURAL SYSTEMS

Historically, prior to modern irrigation, indigenous communities in Michoacán relied on traditional water management to hydrate their crops via the presence of underground aquifers – known locally as cenotes. Cenotes are sinkholes formed from water from underground rivers flowing through limestone bedrock; as exposed sources of groundwater, it is easy to access and extract the water.[16] They have supported societies since ancient times. In fact, due to their invaluable and society-supporting nature, the Mayans held the cenotes in high regard and made offerings in them – valuables, jewels, and sometimes even children.[17] These cenotes normally replenish themselves naturally by rain and have historically provided the water for the avocado trees. However, today, cenotes are being drained at an unsustainable rate. The expansion of avocado plantations and the decline in rainfall caused by the climate crisis has meant there is not sufficient natural rainfall to replace what is extracted, and these aquifers are now running dry. To make up the difference, water is often sourced by illegally diverting rivers, which can lead to water stress downstream and other ecological damage.

It is not just the removal of blue water that creates water stress, the water quality and production of grey water is also an issue. This is of particular concern in Michoacán's case due to the level of intensive avocado farming associated with the use of fertiliser, pesticides, and other agrochemicals. This leads to an excess of nutrients (nitrogen, potassium, and phosphorus) that run off and pollute existing water bodies and surrounding soil. Excess nitrogen in water systems can directly cause significant loss in aquatic wildlife through "algal blooms," which consume much of the oxygen present in the water. Over long periods of time, these algal blooms can create hypoxic dead zones.[18] Avocado plantations can be sources of fertiliser pollution, especially if planted too close to the groundwater drainage basins. If too much fertiliser is applied to the avocado plantations (or during a rainy period), then the excess fertiliser can run off the soil and pollute the drainage basin. High levels of nitrates from fertiliser run-off can impact human health if they enter the drinking water. It has been associated with colon cancer, thyroid disease, and cause birth defects.[19] A high concentration of pesticides in water can also pose serious health risks to people if the water body is also for drinking and sanitary supply. The health impacts can be acute (diarrhoea and sickness) as well as chronic (reproductive issues and various cancers).[20] It can also lead to developmental issues in young children. Local residents voiced concerns that the growers' use of chemicals caused breathing and stomach problems for their children.

EMBEDDED WATER

The role of embedded water is also key to understanding the impact of modern agriculture and global trade on water. Ultimately, the global trade of avocados is the trade of embedded water. Embedded water can be thought of as virtual water. As an avocado grows in Mexico, it absorbs water. By the time it reaches maturity, that individual fruit has absorbed 320 L of water. This water has been extracted from the Mexican landscape. That water is embedded within the fruit, and that embedded water is sent with the fruit when it is exported from Mexico to the Global North. Essentially, when you buy an avocado, you are also buying the water used to produce each avocado. This water has been taken out of a water-stressed environment and will not be returned. Such is the case with all exported crops but is particularly problematic with crops that have high levels of embedded water, such as avocados. Since the vast majority of avocados are exported, Mexico is, in essence, exporting their water alongside the crop.

INDIGENOUS COMMUNITIES

The heavy use of blue and green water in Mexico by agricultural industries (and the pollution of grey water from agrochemicals) has a detrimental impact on local indigenous communities that are already marginalised. The lack of ready access to water amplifies the inequalities that they face and can disrupt traditional lifestyles. As mentioned, the P-urhépecha are the main indigenous community in Michoacán, living in the highlands around the Lakes of Patzcuaro and Cuitzeo, and are traditionally fisherfolk. However, today, Lake Cuitzeo and surrounding reservoirs regularly run dry due to climate change and overconsumption of water for the avocado plantations. It was estimated in the 1990s that more than 5,000 tonnes of fish were annually taken from the lake, with around 19 different species. Now, fisherfolk barely catch 250 tonnes with only 6 species remaining, impacting both the local diet and economy. And it is not just the fisherfolk who are impacted by the decline in water levels. The traditional healers within this community have played a critical role for generations, growing their own medicinal plants. These plants, such as *Ruta graveolens*, *Brickellia cavanillesii*, and *Satureja macrostema*, are grown on a small scale in the healer's traditional patio gardens called *ekuarho*, an agricultural system that dates from the pre-Columbian era and are a key aspect of their cultural heritage.[21] However, this tradition has been significantly impacted by the lack of water. Many healers within the community are resorting to buying clean water to keep their medicinal crops alive. One of the healers, Juana, explained,

> I use only a bit because we have to avoid waste. We have running water only every three days for just an hour, normally from 8 to 9 a.m. I use recycled water [and still] we need to buy gallons in shops to prepare salves and essential oils.

This lack of access has a direct impact on both the indigenous community's health and cultural traditions. Rosendo Caro, director of the Forestry Commission of Michoacán State (COFOM), said of the situation,

> P'urhépecha women have a fundamental role in the richness of Indigenous territories' preservation. They are the custodians of the plant wisdom used for medicine, ritual, and food. Their legacy is endangered by avocado development in the region. This business consumes the water previously used for the ekuarho, deteriorates soils with agrochemicals, and has long-term consequences on water resources.[22]

For the communities in Michoacán, the lack of access to water is a problem of inequality as well as cultural identity. While the wealthy can insulate themselves from the risk of water stress, marginalised communities do not have the power or the resources to do so. As a result, the consequences of drought and limited access to safe water are disproportionately felt by poor and marginalised groups. Water is one of the most important elements in poverty reduction.[23] Communities without access to clean water face long odds of ever escaping poverty. Currently 2.2 billion people in the world still don't have access to safe water, causing nearly 10% of the global population to live in poverty.[24]

OUTSIDE OF MEXICO

The impact of avocado production on water supply is not just limited to Mexico. Other avocado-producing countries are similarly water stressed, and avocado production impacts them to differing degrees. For example, avocados from the Petorca Province in Chile require an average of 1,280 L (versus the average 283 L) of applied fresh water needed to produce 1 kg of avocados due to a less hospitable climate.[25] The litres required differ from region to region due to the specifics of the local climate and topography. In contrast to Petorca, avocados in South Africa have little impact on water stress despite South Africa being classified as "water short" and facing a significant drought from 2015 to 2018. These droughts were predominantly in the Western Cape and not in the avocado-growing areas of the country in the north-east. Chile ended 2021 with more than half of the 19 million population living in an area suffering from "severe water scarcity," following four years of drought that is predicted to continue. The dramatic shift to the monocropping of avocados in Chile has resulted in a dangerous water shortage for the people of the Petorca region and enforced water rationing. However, one avocado tree requires more water than the quota set aside for each resident.[26] In 2004, Petorca's Ligua river was declared dry, and in 2019, Chilean President Sebastián Piñera ordered the creation of a disaster zone in the area.[27] Today, many of the Petorca inhabitants rely on trucks that deliver water twice per week.[28] The water shortage has hit small-scale farmers particularly hard as larger commercial farmers have had more success getting access to water or have found workarounds to the problem by constructing illegal underground water pipes.[29] Many smaller scale farmers have had to sell their land and find work in other sectors (such as mining) as a result of water stress.[30] Currently, Chile's government is under pressure from the UN to prioritise its inhabitant's rights to health and water over avocado plantations and electricity generation.[31]

As discussed previously, Peru is a major avocado exporter for the UK market, sending with it embedded water from Peruvian communities. According to USAID,[32] "Peru has seen a sharp increase in major flooding, prolonged droughts and increasing water scarcity during dry seasons, negatively impacting agriculture, migration, conflict and economic growth" and is highly vulnerable to climate change, according to the UN.[33] Just like the restoration of the cenotes in Mexico, rural communities in Peru are working to restore traditional methods of irrigation. Communities in Nazca have revived local puquios (a series of aqueducts) that dates from 100 BC to bring water via deep trenches into lowland fields to feed the crops, easing irrigation and water stress.[34] However, other approaches to increasing water availability in Peru have had negative impacts. The Olmos Project (located in Lambayeque, Peru) irrigated 38,000 new hectares and 5,500 ha belonging to traditional communities, diverting water that would have run off the Andes into the Atlantic basin into the valley on the Pacific Coast instead.

The goal was to increase production of export crops, including avocados, to bring wealth into the region. However, local communities have challenged the equitability of the project. "Priority [has been] given to big businesses at the expense of local populations," said Manuel Paulet-Iturri, a specialist in soil and water management, who previously worked at the Inter-American Institute for Cooperation on Agriculture.[35] Fernando Eguren of Cepes, a group that advocates for small farmers, added, "It was a good idea, but in reality, the project has favoured agroindustry over the farmers in the region who dreamed of it for 100 years."[36]

Kenya is mindful of the lessons learned from declining coffee harvests due to climate change. They have demonstrated a commitment to the UN's Sustainable Development Goals (SDGs) – a list of 17 aspirations that UN have committed to delivering – where SDG6 is to "Ensure availability and sustainable management of water and sanitation for all."[37] Kenyan avocado producers have identified that avocado crops should not be grown in areas with competing water needs to avoid conflict of resources. Large-scale Kenyan producers also manage their water resources carefully, investing significantly in water storage, rainwater harvesting, and responsible irrigation. By carefully managing large areas of land as water catchments and constructing earth dams, avocado growers have been able to harvest rainwater during the long, wet seasons; rainwater from the five-month wet season is enough to irrigate 900 ha of Kakuzi's avocado orchards, alongside a further 400 ha of macadamia orchards. Sustainable water management is essential in these orchards in the semi-arid region of Makuyu. The farmers there explain that the orchards create a micro-climate, with the fallen, dried leaves help retain water in the soil, reducing evaporation by creating a layer of mulch. Similarly, the coffee producers in Ethiopia are also switching to avocados. US-company Nutiva sources avocados from Ethiopia, which are often intercropped with coffee[38] to reduce pest risk and provide crucial shade for the coffee plants.[39] Ethiopian avocados have long been grown for a local market but not exported since the dominant domestic variety has thin skin, bruises easily, and does not transport well.[40] As a result, Nutiva worked to process the fruit into avocado oil in-country before exporting it in liquid form to the United States.

While water stress in the Global South has thus far primarily been framed as an environmental issue, there is evidence to suggest that it is also a geo-political security question too. Many warn that water could spark the next resource war.[41] According to the Carnegie Endowment for International Peace, from the Great Ethiopian Renaissance Dam dispute to border skirmishes between India and China, and political unrest in the North Africa and the Middle East, it is clear that water-related competition only escalates in scale and intensity as climate change further restricts access to this ever-vital resource.[42]

Lake Chad is an example of the impact of water stress for at-risk communities. Water vulnerability has been directly linked to the rise in extremism and the recruitment into terror organisations, such as Boko Haram.[43] Disaffected youth cannot find employment in the traditional industries of fishing and agriculture and have turned to these groups for purpose and employment. Secondly, displacement caused by climate migration has bred resentment and hostility in communities already pressured and constrained. Similarly, Afghanistan has faced a 70% deficit in precipitation in 2018, resulting in two million food insecure people.[44] One farmer said, "I would do anything to save my son from hunger. I would join Daesh or the Taliban," which demonstrates the direct security impacts of water stress.[45]

WATER IN THE GLOBAL NORTH

Avocados are not purely grown in Global South nations. As discussed, countries in the Global North like Spain, Portugal, and Israel have similarly started to produce and export the fruit and similarly have issues with water. Israel experienced an unprecedented series of diminished annual rainfalls during the last decade. The extended drought cycle caused a dramatic decline in the country's freshwater supply. Currently, Israel's water resources yield 449 billion gallons each year, but annual consumption rose to 580 billion gallons, due to population growth and a general increase in the standard of living.[46] With an annual deficit of 131 billion gallons of water, Israel is over-consuming its water resources. Today, 60% of Israel's fresh water goes to the agricultural sector – down from 72% in 2003.[47] Current quotas have reduced agricultural consumption of water resources and ensured water access for the wider public, but they have also put many farmers out of business.

In the La Axarquía region of southern Spain, the rush to profit from global demand for avocados has led to poorly planned irrigation and diversion of natural water sources. This has led to growing water scarcity in the region in conjunction with increasingly high stress climate impacts.[48] Rivers and water courses in the region often become dry in the summer, but more recent use for irrigation in subtropical crops, including avocados, has led many of them to be permanently dry for years. Farmers and land managers are planting avocado trees without considering the carrying capacity of local water sources. Just across the border in Portugal, there is building tensions between the avocado growers and the municipalities with allegations that one large company tore up cork oak and prickly pear trees, laid water pipes, and sunk three deep wells (despite local bans on drilling new wells after many years of low rainfall and forest fires) while buying off local officials with the promise of economic growth.[49]

In areas like the Jordan Valley, the Algarve, and La Axarquía, there simply is not enough water available to meet irrigation needs for the vast avocado plantations. However, unlike countries in the Global South, the governments in these two countries have more resources to curtail water usage. In Portugal, avocado farmers find this frustrating. Célia Vences said,

> Right now there is a campaign against avocados, which is wrong. There are many more citrus fruits in the Algarve, around 18,000 hectares, and avocado trees don't reach 1,800 and, using the same kind of irrigation, the difference between avocados and citrus fruits water consumption is only nearly six%. Indeed, we have a water problem in the Algarve, it rains less and less, but avocados are not the problem. Tourism also consumes water and there is no reason to stop tourism.[50]

In Spain, the summer of 2022 saw the government restrict the growers of subtropical fruit to just half of their irrigation needs, the lowest allowance since 1990, in response to the worst drought the region has faced.[51] The Junta de Andalucía (regional government of Andalusia) labelled La Axarquía as a region with highly active desertification processes, leading to urgent action to prevent irreversible desertification, including rapid desalinisation efforts.[52] Researchers at the Institute of Subtropical and Mediterranean Horticulture are working with local farmers to challenge the approach of "plant now and ask for water later" (Inãki Hormaza, CSIC Research), trying to limit the cultivation of water-intensive crops including avocados. While in Israel, the government signed an agreement with Turkey to purchase 13.2 billion gallons of water annually, at a price that most countries in the Global South could not afford.[53] The Israeli government has also taken a longer-term vision to increase its water access. It has heavily increased R&D funding to support innovation within the recycled and desalinated water sector to make it more efficient and reduce the cost. Similarly, it has funded mega-infrastructure projects, such as reservoirs, to provide more consistent access.

The United States is similarly struggling with drought. In the avocado heartland of California, there has been consistent drought for the past three years. In 2021, over 350,000 Californians had to receive state help to address a lack of access to drinking water, through state-assisted funding of rising water and sewage bills. The 2020–2022 drought period was the driest on record since 1896. The Metropolitan Water District, wholesaler to 20 million Southern Californians, called for a 35% reduction in water use.[54] In response, the Los Angeles Department of Water and Power limits residents' water usage, while the California Water Resources Control Board has ordered many farmers and San Francisco Bay-area cities to stop diverting water from the San Joaquin River system. California's farmers are now looking to adapt their planting strategies and crops to move away from water-intensive crops in light of the persistent drought and lack of investment in improved water storage facilities in the region.

GOVERNMENT INTERVENTION

Governments around the world – in both the Global North and the Global South – have recognised the urgency to tackle water stress through policy intervention. Just like California, Israel, and Spain, countries around the world have taken action. Some of this has been actioned at a local level, while others have taken a national (or even transnational) approach. There are examples from the past that are worth considering when designing these laws that can help improve their effectiveness.

Bolivia was one of the earliest countries to act to protect water. The current Bolivian Water Law was passed in 1906 (*Ley general de aguas*), following the 1899 Federal Revolution.[55] This basis establishes water as a public good, meaning it must be provided without profit to all members of society, and names the Bolivian government as responsible for water management. This law was updated in Bolivia's 2009 Constitution, following a public referendum.[56] The Constitution requires the government to manage water resources sustainably and ensure equitable access to water for all residents. These provisions are increasingly essential since in November 2016, a national emergency was declared with water rationing in La Paz and El Alto.[57] This crisis was generated by the worst drought in 25 years with the main reservoir dropped under 1% capacity.[58] Bolivia's Vice Ministry of Civil Defense estimated that the drought had impacted 125,000 households and damaged 290,000 ha of agricultural land.[59]

Chile is also taking bold steps to protect its fresh water. Currently, control of water resources is largely based on the 1981 Water Code, which motivates resource management through water markets and tradable water permits.[60] This approach was inspired by the rise of free-market economic policies in Chile in the 1970s and 1980s, promoted by the economists known as the Chicago Boys. In 2005, the code was amended to protect social issues, notably allowing the president to exclude water resources from free-market policies if necessary for the public good. It also required consideration of environmental impacts in new policies.[61] In 2020, the Chilean assembly attempted to redraft the constitution to address the growing number of social and economic inequalities; however, the final draft was rejected. This has largely been put down to a significant lack of political experience amongst many of the independent assembly members, resulting in an unrealistic, vision for Chile's future, deemed to be too risky to implement.

However, water quantity is not the only issue that government policy has the remit to address. Water quality is also central. As discussed, pesticide and fertiliser run off from industrial agricultural fields and can detrimentally impact biodiversity and the public health of local communities. In order to tackle these impacts, governments around the world have acted to minimise the run-off and improve water quality. Centralised policymaking is key to Europe's water quality. The EU Water Framework Directive establishes a framework to protect inland surface waters, transitional waters, coastal waters, and groundwater. EU member states draw up their own river basin management plans based on their local geography as well as specific programmes to achieve the framework's objectives. This is a preemptive approach to maintaining water quality and preventing the formation and spread of dead zones. The EU also established Nitrate Vulnerable Zones to tackle fertiliser run-off and the associated environmental and public health damage. These are areas that have been identified as being particularly vulnerable to nitrate pollution in the waterways and therefore have additional restrictions in place to halt the pollution.

POSSIBLE FARM-LEVEL SOLUTIONS

While there is a critical role for governments to play in tackling water stress within agriculture and ensuring equal access to fresh water for all citizens, there is also a role for farmers to play in reducing usage and adopting less water-intensive measures. The World Avocado Association has offered examples of how they have taken steps to limit the impact, including combining efficient irrigation with precision farming methods. As Portuguese avocado farmer, Célia Vences points out,

> My father, when he was a farmer, used more water than I do today and he didn't have avocados. Do you know why? Because techniques are getting more and more efficient and people are now aware of the need to adopt more sustainable policies.[62]

She also pointed out that farmers have an incentive to save water, saying, "farmers are not interested in spending water, as water now costs a lot of money, electricity is very expensive, and people don't spend water just for the sake of it."

Known as drip irrigation, this type of micro-irrigation allows water to drip slowly to the roots of plants, either from above the soil surface or buried below the surface. The goal is to place water directly into the root zone and minimise evaporation. Drip irrigation can reduce water use by 30 to 70% compared to conventional sprinkler irrigation.[63] Increasingly, farm-level data is being used to identify exactly when to irrigate. Smart irrigation models are being designed and rolled out in fields across the world. These predictive models combine information about plant physiology, real-time soil conditions, and weather forecasts to make informed decisions about when and how much to irrigate. This could save 40% of the water consumed by more traditional methods, according to new research from Cornell University.[64] However, much of the technology needed for these innovative approaches to irrigation are expensive and out of reach to many farmers, even those in the more affluent Global North. Until there is competitive pricing or government subsidies, adoption will be slow.

IN CONCLUSION...

Avocados are an inherently thirsty crop and require consistent access to water to thrive. In large plantations, this voracity can require irrigation and can divert water from other areas to keep the trees fed. This can create tensions with local communities who can sometimes see their access to freshwater decline when it is routed to the plantations. This raises questions of social equity and power dynamics, particularly when these communities are marginalised indigenous people. Water access has become a greater concern in recent years with climate change. Avocados tend to do well in subtropical regions, but these are also the regions that are experiencing high levels of water stress due to rising global temperatures, exacerbating questions over water usage and whether it is fair for water supplies to be used to produce fruit for export when it is urgently needed for local communities. Concerns over water supplies and avocado production are pertinent in all avocado growing locations. However, there are more policy options available in the growing countries of the Global North since they can use resources to redress the water shortage while countries in the Global South have less opportunities for intervention. The avocado industry is mindful of the issue of high water usage and is employing methods to reduce irrigation and therefore minimise the water footprint. However, there might be a more dramatic shift in production towards agroecology that could help mitigate the environmental and social impacts, which will be discussed in Chapter 11.

NOTES

1 Sánenz-Romero, Cuauhtemoc, Rehfeldt, Gerald, Crookston, Nicholas, Duval, Pierre, & Beaulieu, Jean, "Spline models of contemporary, 2030, 2060 and 2090 climates for Michoacán State, México. Impacts on the vegetation." 2011, March 15.

2 Janetsky, Megan, "Columbia's avocado boom shows the hidden cost of 'green gold.'" *Aljazeera*, 2021, October 8.

3 *Hard Seltzer Served News*, "Served hard seltzer embraces 'Ugly Fruit' to save them from landfill." 2021, October 22.

4 Searle, Fred, "Avocados' nutritional value 'justifies water use'." *Fresh Produce Journal*, 2020, February 5. https://www.fruitnet.com/fresh-produce-journal/avocados-nutritional-value-justifies-water-use/180819.article

5 "The avocado's water consumption is proportional to its incomparable nutritional value." *The Fruit of Life*. https://avocadofruitoflife.com/wp-content/uploads/2020/12/The-avocado-water-consumption-is-proportional-to-its-incomprable-nutritional-value.pdf.

6 Cai, W., Wang, G., Santoso, A. *et al*. Increased frequency of extreme La Niña events under greenhouse warming. *Nature Clim Change*, Vol. 5, pp. 132–137, 2015.

7 James, Ian, "Western megadrought is worst in 1200 years, intensified by climate change, study finds." *LA Times*, 2022, February 14.

8 García, Jacobo, "El norte de México se seca." *El País*, 2022, July 18.

9 "'A Monterrey le llegó el día cero': La grave crisis de falta de agua en la segunda ciudad más poblada de México." *El Universal*, 2022, July 18.

10 Vélez, Enrique, & Saez, Enrique, "Water use for agriculture in Mexico, water resources in Mexico." 2011, January 1.

11 Ibid.

12 Sommaruga, Ruben, & Eldridge, Honor, Avocado production: Water footprint and socio-economic implication. *Wiley Online Library*, Vol. 20, Issue 2, 2020, December 13.

13 Gobjerno de Mexico, Consulta Tematica, "Precipitacion media historica por entidad federative." http://dgeiawf.semarnat.gob.mx:8080/ibi_apps/WFServlet?IBIF_ex=D3_AGUA01_01&IBIC_user=dgeia_mce&IBIC_pass=dgeia_mce&NOMBREENTIDAD=*&NOMBREANIO=*.

14 Comisión Nacional del Agua, "Gobierno de México exhorta a industriales y agricultores de Monterrey a ceder agua temporalmente para abasto a la población." *Gobierno de México*, 2022, June 28.

15 Hartman, Sarah, Chiarelli, Davide, Rulli, Maria, & D'Odorico, Paolo, "A growing produce bubble: United States produce tied to Mexico's unsustainable agricultural water use." *IOP Publishing*, 2021, October 5.

16 Britannica, "Cenote." 2023, January 18.

17 *The Botanical Journey*, "Cenotes, extinction & The Maya underworld." 2020, June 29.

18 *United States Environmental Protection Agency*, "The effects: Dead zones and harmful algal blooms." 2023, January 20.

19 Wisconsin Department of Health Services, "High levels of nitrate in drinking water can affect everyone." *Bureau of Environmental and Occupational Health*, 2019, December.

20 Syafrudin, Kristanti, Yuniarto, Hadibarata, Rhee, Al-onazi, Algarni, & Almarri, Al-Mohaimeed, Pesticides in drinking water – A review. *International Journal of Environmental Research and Public Health*, Vol. 18, Issue 2, p. 468, 2021, January 8.

21 Pelliccia, Monica, "Indigenous agroforestry dying of thirst amid a sea of avocados in Mexico." *Civil Eats*, 2022, June 10.

22 Ibid.

23 Bodine, Hayley, "Clean water: Pouring a foundation for social justice". *World Vision*, 2018, April 25.

24 Healing Waters Media, "Can access to safe water diminish poverty." *Healing Waters International*, 2020, October 18.

25 Voller, Louise, "How much water does it take to grow an avocado?" *Danwatch*, 2017, March 19.

26 Heller, Leo, "Chile must prioritise water and health rights over economic interests, says UN expert." *United Nations Human Rights Office of The High Commissioner*, 2020, August 20.

27 De Paiva, Rommana Patricia, "The avocado agribusiness and the water crisis in Petorca, Valparaiso Chile." *Environmental Justice Atlas*, 2021, November 11.

28 Ibid.

29 Milne, Nicky, "Chile's booming avocado business blamed for water shortages." *Global Citizen*, 2019, June 3.

30 De Paiva, Rommana Patricia, "The avocado agribusiness and the water crisis in Petorca, Valparaiso Chile." *Environmental Justice Atlas*, 2021, November 11.

31 Heller, Leo, "Chile must prioritise water and health rights over economic interests, says UN expert." *United Nations Human Rights Office of The High Commissioner*, 2020, August 20.

32 Thomas, Jene, "Climate adaptation, & water security." *USAID*, 2017–2020.

33 United Nations, "Climate change in Peru seen affecting the fishing, high Andes' livestock and agricultural sectors the most." *Economic Commission for Latin America and the Caribbean*, 2014, December 10.

34 iMedia, "Aqueduct built by the Nazca culture in the Peruvian desert 1500 years ago is still in use today." 2023, January 3.

35 Portillo, Zoraida, "Peru: Olmos irrigation project sparks development debate." *Farm Land Grab*, 2014, December 11.

36 Taj, Mitra, "Peru bores through Andes to water desert after century of dreams." *Reuters*, 2013, April 4.

37 United Nations, "Sustainable development goals report 2022." Department of Economic and Social Affairs, 2022.

38 Chhabra, Esha, "Why This food company is developing an avocado supply chain in Ethiopia." *Forbes*, 2021, July 30.

39 Govindappa, M., & Elavarasan, K., Shade cum fruit yielding avocado under coffee ecosystem. *International Letters of Natural Sciences*, Vol. 27, pp. 61-66, 2019.

40 Chhabra, Esha, "Why this food company is developing an avocado supply chain in Ethiopia." *Forbes*, 2021, July 30.

41 *Carnegie Endowment for International Peace*, "Water war: How a life sustaining resource goes geopolitical." 2022, March 22.

42 Ibid.

43 Frimpong, Osei Baffour, "Climate change and violent extremism in the lake Chad basin: Key issues and way forward." *Wilson Center*, 2020, July.

44 Frankopan, Osei Baffour, *The New Silk Roads*. Bloomsbury, 2018, November 5.

45 Ibid.
46 *Tech Sci Research*, "Israel Hydroponics Market to be supported by Growing Food demand through 2028." 2022, December.
47 Ibid.
48 Walker, Kira, "Avocados – farmers' green gold – push southern Spain toward water collapse." *The National*, 2019, June 27.
49 *DW Documentary*, "Portugal's avocados: Green god or ecological nightmare?" 2021, August 10.
50 Martins, Paula, "Avocados: an evil fruit?" *The Portugal News*, 2021, October 22.
51 Cabezas, Eugenio, "Axarquia farmers angry as the area faces summer with the least amount of water for irrigation in history." *SUR in English*, 2022, May 27.
52 *In Spain News*, "From popular avocado to desertification in southern Spain." 2021, August 17.
53 *The Washington Institute for New East Policy*. "Turkish Water to Israel." 2003, August 14.
54 Smith, Hayley, "Unprecedented water restrictions hit Southern California today: What they mean for you," *LA Times*, 2022, June 1.
55 USAID, Bolivia, *Land Links*, 2011, January.
56 Constitute Project, "Bolivia (Plurinational State of)'s Constitution of 2009." 2022, April 27.
57 Farthing, Linda, "'We are in shock': historic Bolivia drought hammers homes and crops." *The Guardian*, 2016, November 25.
58 Hecimovic, Arnel, "Bolivian water rationing – in pictures." *The Guardian*, 2016, November 23.
59 Reuters Staff, "Bolivia declares state of emergency due to drought, water shortage." *Reuters*, 2016, November 21.
60 Morán, Jose Ignacio, "Water legistlation in Chile: The need for reform." *Thomson Reuters Practical Law*, 2014, October 1.
61 Global Water Partnership, "Water and sustainable development: Lessons from Chile." 2006, June 14.
62 Martins, Paula, "Avocados: An evil fruit?" *The Portugal News*, 2021, October 22.
63 Larson, Ryan, "How drip irrigation helps conserve water." *Landscape Business*, 2016, February 25.
64 Lefkowitz, Melanie, "Smart irrigation model predicts rainfall to conserve water." *Cornell University*, 2019.

KEY READINGS

- Hartman, Sarah, Chiarelli, Davide, Rulli, Maria, & D'Odorico, Paolo, "A growing produce bubble: United States produce tied to Mexico's unsustainable agricultural water use." *IOP Publishing*, 2021, October 5.

- Heller Leo, "Chile must prioritise water and health rights over economic interests, says UN expert." *United Nations Human Rights Office of The High Commissioner*, 2020, August 20.
- Janetsky, Megan, "Columbia's avocado boom shows the hidden cost of 'green gold.'" *Aljazeera*, 2021, October 8.
- Pelliccia, Monica, "Indigenous agroforestry dying of thirst amid a sea of avocados in Mexico." *Civil Eats*, 2022, June 10.
- Sommaruga, Ruben, & Eldridge, Honor, Avocado production: Water footprint and socio-economic implication. *Wiley Online Library*, Vol. 20, Issue 2, 2020, December 13.
- Vélez, Enrique, & Saez, Enrique, "Water use for agriculture in Mexico, water resources in Mexico." 2011, January 1.

11

VIDA CAMPESINA

MEXICAN AGROECOLOGY AND FOOD SOVEREIGNTY

INTRODUCTION

Mexico has a long history of subsistence agriculture – avocado production is only one part of this deep culture. In 2010, recognising its complexity and cultural importance, UNESCO declared Mexican cuisine an "Intangible Heritage of Humanity."[1] Traditional foods have historically been grown in a way that is respectful of the natural world with indigenous people in North America commonly relying on "the three sisters" (corn, beans, and squash) to grow food in harmony with nature. These three crops form the staples of indigenous food and are frequently planted together since they support the growth of each other, in particular because the beans bring fertility into the soil naturally. Beans (and other legumes) are often used as a break crop to build fertility into the soil because they are able to fix nitrogen due to the rhizobia bacteria in their root nodules. The use of legumes to biologically fix nitrogen has been shown to increase soil organic matter, which can result in lower soil erosion and increased water retention.[2] This style of companion, light-impact farming is known in Mexico as Milpa farming, which we have previously discussed in relation to slash-and-burn practices. Avocados would have been grown in such a way – one or two trees of different landrace varieties, mixed into the wider farm system without the requirement of agrichemicals. Growing avocados in such a way would have produced a modest amount of fruit during a shorter growing season that could be consumed within the local community and would not have depleted natural resources.

DOI: 10.4324/9781003371915-11

MEXICAN AGROECOLOGY

However, the traditions of milpa farming came under attack with the arrival of the Green Revolution, which started in the 1960s in the Global North and took hold in the 1970s in Mexico. This shift in farming practices initiated the rise in monocultures and loss of traditional foodways, encouraging the development of hybrid plants, chemical controls, large-scale irrigation, and heavy mechanisation in agriculture around the world. Simultaneously, land was incorporated into larger and larger parcels as bigger businesses bought it up to increase efficiency. According to the data on land ownership in Mexico, larger, more successful export-oriented farmers represent only 3% of private farms but own 30% of private lands.[3] Adopting these modern methods resulted in a significant increase in yields and the decline of hunger around the world. The data shows[4] that the share of world population living in extreme poverty fell sharply during the years of the Green Revolution, and global hunger was reduced.[5] In Mexico, the Green Revolution and the arrival of industrial farming methods converted the country from a net importer to a net exporter of cereals and food products.[6] Along with advancing irrigation changes, the Mexican government (in partnership with the US-based Rockefeller Foundation) created the International Maize and Wheat Improvement Center to promote varieties that could survive the arid land of north-west Mexico and produce higher yields.[7]

However, the Green Revolution also meant a shift from maintaining long-term sustainability to focusing on immediate gains in yield, destroying resilience across much of Mexican agriculture. Avocado production did not escape this shift. The size of the avocado groves expanded, and farmers grew the fruit almost exclusively, with little space for other crops. In order to maximise yield and meet demand, the season was pushed to be longer and longer with agrochemicals being applied in order to increase productivity. However, this approach to production has led to environmental and social damage that we have discussed. Farmers in Mexico eventually began to recognise the damage that this new approach was having on their local communities and ecosystems. In recent years, a select number of small-scale Mexican farmers have returned to traditional methods and placed community at the heart of their production, rejecting the high-input approach of damaging monoculture.

Small-scale farmers returned to a mixed cropping approach that grew "the three sisters" in rotation with a few fruit trees scattered about and some livestock, bringing in natural fertility. This model of sustainable farming within the natural limits and with a strong community has progressively evolved to be known as agroecology. In addition to returning to the milpa methods of the past, farmers in Mexico embraced an explicitly political identity to combat the marginalisation of rural and indigenous producers. This political aim was to establish a more socially just food system at a global and local level, focused on creating fairer conditions for agricultural and food-production workers. This became a core tenant of agroecology. Debbie Barker, the international coordinator of the International Coalition on Climate and Agriculture that works to promote agroecology globally, says

> What makes agroecology so attractive to small-scale farmers in Mexico is that it can help to address both food production pressures, environmental degradation, as well as raising the living standards of the farmers and their communities by focusing on equity and social justice.

From what began as a few individual farmers returning to milpa methods, soon turned into a national movement. The growth was amplified by an increasing frustration amongst indigenous people and rural "peasant" Mexican communities, who felt exploited by the global food systems and wanted greater autonomy. The Mexican Congress of Agroecology was formed in 2019 to advance the cause of agroecology within the country.[8] The initial meeting saw 53 organisations from around the country come together to create a plan of action and founded the Mexican Society of Agroecology, which adopted the specific goal of delivering food sovereignty in Mexico (whereby communities control the way their food is produced, traded, and consumed) with education programmes and peer-to-peer exchange.[9] Additionally, there are a number of organisations working with Mexican smallholders to support sustainable farming practices amongst these communities. At the forefront is La Asociación de Empresas Comercializadoras de Productores del Campo (ANEC), formed in 1995 as a result of the NAFTA.[10]

What has helped to ensure agroecology's success in Mexico is the ongoing power of rural communities. Approximately 5.6 million people still live in rural agrarian communities in Mexico, and while farming practices intensified, the agrarian social structures and communities in Mexico remain largely unchanged.[11] Today, over half of Mexico's territory is still owned by small-scale producers – this is equivalent to over 104 million ha.[12] Many of these producers remain part of community-based farming groups, known as *ejidos* or peasant communities. The ejidos ownership structure is a remnant of the Mexican revolution in the early 20th century when large estates ("haciendas") were dismantled and given to a vast number of smaller producers. Ejidos act as bastions of traditional agricultural practices since they must be communally owned by Mexicans or the community itself must approve ownership by a single individual of Mexican nationality.[13] While that's not to say all *ejidos* embrace agroecology, there is an inherent belief within the ejidos structure that food should first meet the demands of the community, which has natural synergy with the agroecological movement. Secondly, unlike commercially owned agricultural land, the *ejidos* communities' livelihoods rely on the land remaining productive long into the future, so it is in their interest that it be run sustainably.

It is worth noting that not all countries are as lucky as Mexico to have a history of Ejidos to help build momentum behind the idea of agroecology. Globally, land ownership demonstrates two key trends that create challenges for agroecological adoption. Firstly, the consolidation of land with fewer and fewer landowners as large businesses (with little interest in agroecological production) buy up the smaller ones.[14] Secondly, at the other end of the scale, the fragmentation of land where there are a large numbers of smallholders who cannot benefit from the economies of scale afforded larger enterprises.[15] Cooperatives can help overcome this issue, but this requires buy-in. For example, Peruvian farmers are reluctant to form cooperatives due to the agricultural reforms that took place in the 1970s when corrupt cooperatives were forced upon them and failed to deliver the equity that was promised.[16]

AGROECOLOGY GOES GLOBAL

This more politically motivated understanding of milpa agriculture that functioned in harmony with nature spread progressively across Central and South America, most notably through the creation of the international agroecological organisation *La Via Campesina*. From there, it spread to the world. Today, agroecology has gone global and has been embraced by international organisations. The Intergovernmental Panel on Climate

Change (IPCC)[17] believes that agroecology will be central to achieving climate change mitigation, and the Food and Agriculture Organization of the United Nations (FAO) has established the Agroecology Hub to help spread the word and defines agroecology as,

> an integrated approach that simultaneously applies ecological and social concepts and principles to the design and management of food and agricultural systems," adding that "it seeks to optimize the interactions between plants, animals, humans and the environment while taking into consideration the social aspects that need to be addressed for a sustainable and fair food system.[18]

WHAT DOES AGROECOLOGY DELIVER GLOBALLY?

Considering the global rise of agroecology, it is perhaps interesting and important to focus on what the approach can deliver. Agroecology's main pillars focus on its ability to protect nature, maintain water quality, ensure soil health, and deliver for communities. As the planet faces the twin crises of climate and biodiversity, it is critical to consider how to lighten the environmental footprint of food production and increase resilience in farming, so that our food system can survive into the future. Let's consider each in turn and how they can help.

- **Biodiversity**
  As discussed in Chapter 9, pesticides have been repeatedly identified as a core driver of falling global biodiversity (flora and fauna loss), which is particularly prevalent across agricultural landscapes.[19] This also has a knock-on effect on food security, creating a negative feedback loop where beneficial insects and plants are wiped out as collateral, and no longer can provide a natural pest control for other more damaging insects. The alternative, agroecological approach is biological control, which can include the introduction of natural predators (birds and insects) and mixed cropping with plants that stop weeds from growing but do not impact crop yields. This is known as integrated pest management (IPM). Through careful planning and a good understanding of natural systems, IPM can be a successful approach – although there have been some notable failures such as the introduction of cane toads in Australia.

- **Water**

As previously explained, agrochemicals from avocado plantations can pollute natural water bodies, including groundwaters. Excess chemicals drain into rivers and lakes and groundwaters, washed away by rain or through poorly structured soil. Agroecology can help maintain cleaner waterways. Planting reed beds and buffer zones around waterways can help to filter out some of the agrochemical pollutants before they reach the waterway and therefore improve water quality downstream. It also helps regulate flow to stop flash flooding during the rainy seasons. Having healthy soils can also help with water retention and build resilience to extreme weather events. According to the USDA's Soil Health Division Director, Dr. Bianca Moebius-Clune, "With better soil structure, infiltration of water into the soil improves, which allows the entire soil profile to take in and hold more water when it rains."[20]

- **Soil**

The health of the soil is a key determinant of crop yields and can also be improved by agroecological soil management. By rotating crops and building in a fallow or fertility-building phase, farmers are able to prevent soil erosion and build soil health. Ultimately, this improves the long-term viability of the farm and reduces the burden on local water sources, especially in a changing climate. Intercropping with a mixed rotation can help to build soil health and increase the total annual yield of the land by taking advantage of multiple growing seasons, as well as stabilising existing crop yields.[21] Importantly, intercropping greatly limits the amount of water lost to run-off and evaporation. In the case of avocado production, reducing water loss through poor soil structure is crucial for achieving sustainable production. One study demonstrated that farmers with 2 ha or less saw their yields grow by 25% following a shift to agroecological farming.[22] At a global scale, a study on agroecology across 57 countries found increased crop yield of 79% on average.[23]

- **Communities**

The soil, water, and biodiversity benefits that agroecology offers are vital for the future livelihoods and well-being of rural and indigenous communities. This style of light-impact farming is well suited to small-scale subsistence farmers in the Global South given that they are low cost, diversify farm income, build resilience, and ensure a healthier long-term environment. Agroecology has already played an important role in protecting rural communities' incomes and reducing poverty in semi-arid regions of Brazil.[24] Looking beyond livelihoods, many of these communities rely on their crops as a key part of their diets. The improved reliability of crops grown through agroecology ensure the food security of these groups; intercropping and mixed cropping systems can further provide a greater range of nutrition and health benefits, vital for alleviating poverty and illness.

AGROECOLOGICAL AVOCADOS

Adopting agroecological avocado growing could go a long way to mitigating the negative environmental and social impacts of production that have been discussed in the previous chapters. Adopting agroecological approaches would involve shifting away from monoculture plantations of Hass avocados that increasingly rely on agrochemicals towards a more sustainable approach of smaller agroecological production with less inputs and more resilience.

The first step would be removing the application of pesticides. Unlike other industrialised field crops, avocados have been less intensively applied with pesticides, but this level could decrease further with the adoption of agroecological pest management. This technique would include leaving the leaf litter and weeds underneath the trees in place, in contrast to intensive producers that keep the understory clear believing that weeds underneath the trees compete for nutrients and water if they grow too sizeable. However, competitive weeds are less of a concern for avocado production. healthy, mature groves have thick mulch and a dense canopy that shades the ground and makes it difficult for weeds to grow. Understory weeds can also help combat waterlogged soils and the risk of root asphyxiation and provide a habitat for beneficial insects that can provide biological control to pests. The H. Lauri (avocado seed weevil) is the most significant pest of avocados in Mexico. Around 60% of Hass avocados in Mexico and Colombia are reported as damaged by these pests.[25] IPM has proved quite effective in addressing these weevils since sprays typically fall on the top of the leaves and fail to adequately kill the infestation while natural predators like spiders are better able to target them. Switching to biological alternatives would not only reduce the reliance on imported agrichemicals but also ensure that water is safer to drink since the use of pesticides on commercial avocado plantations can have severe consequences for natural water sources.

Switching to agroecological production of avocados would also help improve the water quantity in addition to the water quality by adopting sustainable water practices. While agroecology cannot undo the impact of climate change on existing water suppliers, it can help reduce the impact of drought and evaporation by improving soil health so that the ground is better able to hold the water it receives. Many Californian avocado producers have benefitted from legislation in place to incentivise sustainable farming practices. The Healthy Soils Program (HSP) Incentives Program provides grants to implement conservation practices that sequester carbon, reduce atmospheric greenhouse gases (GHGs), and improve soil health.[26] With less water loss resulting from healthier soil, the pressure on farmers to heavily irrigate their crops is substantially alleviated, helping to shift away from exploitation of natural water bodies. Farmers around the world (including those growing avocados) have also been addressing the increased water stress by reverting to the traditional practices of water conservation that were used by their ancestors. As discussed in Chapter 10, Mexicans are replenishing their cenotes while communities in Peru have revitalised the Cantalloc aqueduct to bring water into their fields in a sustainable way. This decentralised action is taking place across many of the more rural regions where they still use traditional farming practices.

Lastly, switching to agroecological avocado production would benefit local communities. In addition to having a healthy environment, switching to agroecological avocado production can help improve food sovereignty and economic outcomes. Where avocados have been grown through agroecological principles, like in San Miguel Suchixtepec in Oaxaca, farmers have seen the cost of establishing their trees fall by 59%, adopting the principles of a circular economy model with zero waste.[27] By diversifying their crops, producing organic fertilisers, and using terraced farming, they have relieved much of the pressure on the existing forest and soils. They have even gone as far as to reforest 187 ha around the village, helping to secure 14 substantial water sources supplying 2,500 people. As a result of these practices, now use 64% less water for irrigation.

MICHOACÁN AND AGROECOLOGY

Would these agroecological techniques work in the large-scale hub of Michoacán? Michoacán actually has very favourable conditions for sustainable crop cultivation; there is abundant sunlight, the land consists of rich volcanic soil, natural irrigation, and there are a range of altitudes and micro-climates ideal for avocado production. As a habitat, this is the ideal foundation for a strong agroecological avocado sector. However, there are significant challenges to adoption. Firstly, Michoacán production is almost exclusively geared towards the US market. Constant pressure from US consumers for an ever-increasing supply of avocados would make it difficult for producers to switch to agroecological production that focuses on community growing and more sustainable yields. Secondly, land ownership in Michoacán would present an obstacle; 75% of the avocado production area is private property and only 25% in the ejido or communal sector.[28] The limited power of the ejidos hinders the ability for agroecological methods to be adopted in the region since there is not the communal ownership required for food sovereignty to be a core driver of production. The reliance on the "empresario model" of avocado production (as discussed in Chapter 6) means that the majority of avocado plantation owners have bought the land as an investment and are geared towards large-scale production to maximise revenue. It would seem unlikely that they would be willing to forgo profit and switch to agroecological production without added incentive.

Perhaps however, there is a middle ground? In the last chapter, we discussed the potential benefits of new agritechnology like micro-irrigation to reduce the footprint of large-scale avocado production. Given the cost involved, investment in agritech is simply not a realistic solution for small-scale subsistence farmers. For those smaller enterprises, agroecology offers a more accessible and long-term solution. However, this technology would be available and accessible to the larger growers in Michoacán who have considerably more resources at their disposal. Furthermore, there could be agroecological practices that the large-scale Michoacán producers could adopt without abandoning all industrial farming techniques. For example, they might switch to organic fertilisers but supplement with synthetic fertilisers as and when needed. This would reduce the impact of synthetic fertiliser on the ecosystem and benefit the wider environment.

IN CONCLUSION...

While the Green Revolution reduced hunger and brought wealth, many farmers in Mexico resented and rejected the industrial farming model that focused on exporting food. In Mexico, this meant returning to the traditional food ways, known as milpa, that had existed prior. This method of farming happened in harmony with nature and respected the limits of the environment to ensure long-term resilience and soil fertility. However, milpa evolved into agroecology which also has a strong political element to it. It focuses on equity and the concept of food sovereignty where communities are in control of their own food systems and are empowered to make their own decisions about its management. This political side of agroecology flourished in Mexico due to the history of land ownership and the concept of *ejidos*. Today, more and more farmers across Mexico and the wider world are adopting agroecology, including many small-scale avocado producers who can see a benefit to the long-term resilience of their business and community by switching production away from the more intensive approach.

NOTES

1 Arzaba, Andrea, "Mexican cuisine declared intangible heritage of humanity by UNESCO." *Global Voices*, 2010, October 7.

2 Legume Futures, "Legume-supported cropping systems for Europe: General Project Report." *Legume Future Consortium*, 2014, December.

3 Hufbauer, Greg, & Schott, Jeffrey, assisted by Grieco & Wong, *NAFTA Revisited: Achievements and Challenges*. Peterson Institute for International Economics, 2005, October.

4 Mehta, Devang, The Green Revolution did not increase poverty and hunger for millions. *Nature Plants*, Vol. 4, p. 736, 2018, October 4.

5 John, Daisy, & Babu, Giridhara, Lessons from the aftermaths of green revolution on food system and health. *Frontiers*, Vol. 5, 2021, February 22.

6 Moreno-Brid, Juan Carlos, Valdivia, Juan Carlos Rivas, & Santamaría, Jesus, "Mexico: Economic growth exports and industrial performance after NAFTA." Economic Commission for Latin America and the Caribbean, 2005, December.

7 *International Maize and Wheat Improvement Center*, Our History. https://www.cimmyt.org/about/our-history/.

8 Gliessman, Stephen, Advancing agroecology in Mexico. *Agroecology and Sustainable Food Systems*, Vol. 43, Issue 10, 2019, September 30.

9 Ibid.

10 Varghese, Shiney, & VanGelder, Zoe, "Agroecological transition in Mexico: ANEC's journey to a better farm and food system." Food and Agriculture Organization, 2017.

11 *Scottish Land Commission*, "Mexico—Communal Agrarian Tenure (Ejido System)." https://www.landcommission.gov.scot/our-work/ownership/international-experience/mexico-communal-agrarian-tenure-ejido-system.

12 Toledo, Victor, & Barrera-Bassols, Narciso, "Political agroecology in Mexico: a path toward sustainability." *MDPI*, 2017, February.

13 *Scottish Land Commission*, "Review of international experience of community, communal and municipal ownership of land." 2020, April.

14 Karoll Finance, "What is land consolidation?" *Advance terrafund.* https://advanceter-rafund.bg/en/what-is-land-consolidation.

15 Schiller, Katharina, Klerkx, Laurens, Poortvliet, Marijn, & Godek, Wendy, Exploring barrier to the agroecological transition in Nicaragua: AA Technological Innovation Systems Approach. *Agroecology and Sustainable Food Systems*, Vol. 44, Issue 1, 2019, April 14.

16 Quispe, Madai, "The neglected sector: Agriculture in Peru." *ReVista: Harvard Review of Latin America*, 2021, September 3.

17 IPCC, *Climate Change 2022: Impacts, Adaptation, and Vulnerability.* Contribution of Working Group II to the Sixth Assessment Report of the Intergovernmental Panel on Climate Change [H.-O. Pörtner, D.C. Roberts, M. Tignor, E.S. Poloczanska, K. Mintenbeck, A. Alegría, M. Craig, S. Langsdorf, S. Löschke, V. Möller, A. Okem, B. Rama (eds.)]. Cambridge and New York: Cambridge University Press, 2022.

18 *Food and Agriculture Organization of the United Nations*, "The 10 elements of agroecology: Guiding the transition to sustainable food and agriculture systems.", 2018.

19 Brühl, Carsten, & Zaller, Johann, Biodiversity decline as a consequence of an inappropriate environmental risk assessment of pesticides. *Frontiers Environmental Science*, Vol. 7, 2019, October 31.

20 Nichols, Ron, "A hedge against drought: Why healthy soil is 'Water in the Bank'." U.S. Department of Agriculture, 2017, February 21.

21 Raseduzzaman, Md, & Jensen, Erik, Does intercropping enhance yield stability in arable crop production? A meta-analysis. *European Journal of Agronomy*, Vol. 91, 2017, November.

22 Aubert, Pierre-Marie, Schwoob, Marie-Helene, & Poux, Xavier, "Agroecology and carbon neutrality in Europe by 2050: What are the issues?" *IDDRI*, 2019, April.

23 The United Nations Office for the Coordination of Humanitarian Aid, "New report shows urgent need for agroecology revolution to cut emissions and boost productivity." *Christian Aid*, 2021, September 23.

24 *International Fund for Agricultural Development*, "How agroecology can respond to a changing climate and benefit farmers." 2019, December 18.

25 Hoddle, Mark, "Proactive IPM of the Big Avocado Seed Weevil." *Department of Entomology, UC Riverside*, 2020.

26 California Department of Food and Agriculture, "Healthy soils incentives program." *State of California.* https://www.cdfa.ca.gov/oefi/healthysoils/incentivesprogram.html.

27 World Wildlife Fund, "Building an agroecological revolution in Oaxaca—Alternativa Agricola Suchixtepec." https://wwf.panda.org/projects/nature_pays/nature_pays/nature_pays_mexico/.

28 Stanford, Lois, "Mexico's Empresario in export agriculture: Examining the avocado industry of Michoacan." Department of Sociology and Anthropology, New Mexico State University, 1998.

KEY READINGS

- Food and Agriculture Organization of the United Nations, "The 10 elements of agroecology: Guiding the transition to sustainable food and agriculture systems." 2018.
- Gliessman, Stephen, Advancing agroecology in Mexico. *Agroecology and Sustainable Food Systems*, Vol. 43, Issue 10, 2019, September 30.
- John, Daisy, & Babu, Giridhara, Lessons from the aftermaths of green revolution on food system and health. *Frontiers*, Vol. 5, 2021, February 22.
- Nichols, Ron, "A hedge against drought: Why healthy soil is 'Water in the Bank'." U.S. Department of Agriculture, 2017, February 21.
- Varghese, Shiney, & VanGelder, Zoe, "Agroecological transition in Mexico: ANEC's journey to a better farm and food system." Food and Agriculture Organization, 2017.

12

CARTEL CONTROL

NARCOTICS, CRIMINALITY, AND AVOCADOS

INTRODUCTION

Much recent media attention has focused on exposing the links between Mexican avocado production and the drug cartels. In the beginning of 2022, the US media went mad with coverage over the link between avocado production in Mexico and the cartels. An APHIS officer who was working for the USDA in Michoacán received a threatening phone call on February 11, presumably from a local cartel, after he questioned a shipment of the fruit and refused to sign it off. Local reports are more extreme, suggesting that the gang arrived at the facility and threatened to murder the inspector if he didn't sign off the shipment, stole a truck and attacked a group of agricultural technicians nearby.[1] In response, the USDA paused all avocado imports until the safety of inspectors could be guaranteed. The USDA has inspectors in-country to continually assess the production and ensure its safe for export into the US market. The Mexican government was understandably furious with the suspension, given the importance of the fruit to the economy. Hyperbolically, the Mexican president suggested that the US move was part of a conspiracy against Mexico for political and economic interests. President Andrés Manuel López Obrador dismissed the threat, saying "The truth is there is always something else behind it, an economic or commercial interest, or a political attitude.[2] They don't want Mexican avocados to get into the United States, right, because it would rule in the United States because of its quality." Regardless of the motivation, the impact was almost

DOI: 10.4324/9781003371915-12

immediate. Avocado prices hit $26.23 per 9-kg box in February 2022 in the US grocery store, up 100% from 2021. The price of a single avocado rose to as much as $2.50 at some supermarkets from just $0.99 in January 2021.

Ultimately, the ban only lasted a week. The USDA soon reached an agreement with Mexico's Plant Protection Organization and the Packers Exporters of Mexico. On February 18, the trade of avocados resumed. However, in a statement, the USDA highlighted that the incident was not isolated and that "in 2020, a USDA employee conducting detection and eradication activities supporting our fruit fly and citrus pest and disease programs in Northern Mexico was murdered."[3] This is due to the rising involvement of cartels in the fruit industry. A recent Verisk Maplecroft report into the industry found that:

> From cultivation through to transportation, violence and corruption now pervade Mexico's avocado supply chain – particularly in Michoacán, a long-standing hotbed for criminal violence. The similarities with conflict minerals are striking for companies that source avocados from the region. Association with killings, modern slavery, child labour and environmental degradation is becoming an increasing risk when dealing with Michoacán suppliers and growers, especially when establishing traceability is increasingly hard.[4]

The story of the threatened USDA agent was enticing and soon was splashed across the media, fuelled by the proximity to the Superbowl that was held on February 13th that year, which sees the highest consumption of avocados in one day in the United States. The *Daily Mail*, *New York Post*, and other tabloids ran sensationalist stories on the embargo. The *Netflix* show Rotten featured a whole episode of the involvement of the cartels in the avocado industry. While the incident is horrific, it's worth highlighting some of the sensationalism contained within these reports. It certainly makes for a sexy story and can generate great clickbait. Not that many other stories about fruit production involve guns, gangsters, and cocaine. In an era when media channels are fighting for eyeballs, juicy stories are hard to resist and can quickly get overblown, and it's worth deeper examination. What the media coverage missed in its reporting is the long history that the rural community in Michoacán has to the cartels and to drug production. Many farmers and workers abhor the violence and the intimidation, but others have been working within the cartels system for generations and see the money and power that the gang brings to the region as a positive. As with so many things, the reality is much more nuanced and complex than the headlines would suggest.

RISE OF THE CARTELS IN MEXICO AND BRIEF HISTORY OF THE DRUG TRADE

While this book is about avocados, it might be useful to do a quick review of the drug trade in Mexico since a brief understanding will help understand the cartel's evolving relationship with the fruit. In the last decade, the violence linked to the drug cartels in Mexico has exploded and infects every corner of the country. The federal forces with US involvement try to stamp it out, but the reality is that, according to Ioan Grillo, an expert in the narcotics trade, "the Mexican drug trade is so productive that it is one of the country's biggest industries. It rivals oil exports in helping to stabilize the peso. It directly provided thousands of jobs, many in poor rural areas that most need them. Its profits spill over into a number of other sectors."[5] Consequently, curtailing the cartels would dramatically damage the Mexican economy given that analysts estimate that wholesale earnings from illicit drug sales range from $13.6 to $49.4 billion annually.[6]

The predominant narcotics that Mexico produces are marijuana and heroin. Marijuana was brought to Mexico by the Spanish colonists in the 16th century, while the seeds of opium poppies arrived with Chinese workers in the 19th century. Cocaine is a more recent addition to the narcos portfolio. Initially, Mexican gangs tend to act only as transporters, trafficking it from South America (Colombia in particular) into the United States, although they took more control once the Colombian cartels were targeted by the US forces in the 1980s under President Reagan. Following the death of Pablo Escobar and the arrest of the Rodriguz Orejuela brothers, a power vacuum was left in the cocaine industry, into which the Mexican cartels stepped. Recent years have seen expansion into fentanyl and methamphetamines.

Almost all of the drug production in Mexico is driven by demand north of the border. Consequently, it was not until the 1960s when drug culture took off in the United States that narco gangs in Mexico professionalised and expanded into what we know today. This rising demand from the United States "transformed drug producers from a few Sinaloan peasants to a national industry in a dozen states," according to Ioan Grillo's book on the rise of the cartels.[7] However, at the beginning, the business model was quite different. Local farmers would grow poppies or weed on their small holding and then would sell it to representatives of the cartels in the local town plaza, who would then move it northward with the help of their compatriots. Bribes and corruption to local officials and local police kept the drugs flowing unhindered. That is not to say that there were not any concerted attempts to curtail the industry. US presidents increasingly pressured Mexico to tackle the flood of drugs across the border. Presidents Nixon and Reagan in particular made the war on drugs central to their administration's priorities. This included sending Drug Enforcement Administration (DEA) agents and other law enforcement representatives into Mexico to arrest, deny, and terminate the cartels. At times, the presence of US forces on the southern side of the border escalated violence while they tried to shut down the flow of drugs.

The dynamic changed dramatically after NAFTA. The violence and scale of the narcotic gangs in Mexico increased dramatically. According to Grillo, "As the 1990s went on, Mexican traffickers flourished, moving tons of narcotics north and pumping back billions of dollars amid a surge in free trade created by NAFTA." This is not necessarily surprising.[8] Strengthening the ties between the two economies and easing the cross-border trade to increase the trade was the goal of the agreement. This happened for illegal goods as much as for legal ones. Just like the avocado industry, NAFTA led to increased demand north of the border, and Mexican producers rose to meet it by increasing supply. The consistent willingness to hand over dollars for products that net huge profits for enterprising Mexicans will keep the flow steady. Just like avocados, the Mexican gangs bring the drugs into the United States wholesale and pass on the direct customer interaction to others. Just like with avocados, "the modern drug business was now about riding the explosion of globalised trade, gaining comparative advantage, securing warehouse facilities and refining transport logistics," according to Mexican historian Benjamin Smith.[9] Smith continues that drug production is "now a fully integrated agricultural operation, similar to the coffee or tropic fruit businesses" with agronomists advising how to maximise yield. However, rather than paying peasant farmers by the kilo as they used to do, the gangs have increasingly brought production in house with a vertically integrated approach. This professionalisation of the narcotics industry also created more tensions between gangs as they competed for territory and market share.

The mid-1990s also saw a plunging Mexican economy with the peso plummeting, as has already been discussed, and this led to increased gang activity and violence. Smith highlights that "by the mid-1990s, the state was markedly weaker.[10] The economy was tumbling even before the signing of

NAFTA. Real wages nearly halved over the decade," and so it was pragmatic for low-wage workers to look for more lucrative employment. Some, like the Pueblan avocado farmers, went onto the automotive assembly lines. Others became narcos. During the period, according to figures crunched by Smith, to earn the median annual Mexican wage, a dealer needed to only shift 700 g of marijuana, 18 g of heroin, or 66 g of cocaine, a year. A tiny amount that was achievable with one trip across the border. Consequently, recruitment into these gangs became easier with a plunging economy while trading into the United States became easier under NAFTA.

There was another substantial increase in the narcotics trade (and the associated violence) in the late 2000s. This shift was prompted by a shift in Mexican politics. For Grillo, "The Mexican Drug War is inextricably linked to the democratic transition." The old power bases shifted. The Institutional Revolutionary Party (or PRI) that was discussed in relation to NAFTA had been in power for generations since 1929. The PRI had dominated Mexican politics from the national to the local level. Many PRI politicians had close links to the cartels, accepting money for protection and smoothing their business dealings. This dynamic (while far from perfect) kept the violence down and the corruption meant that each actor understood where they fit within the hierarchy. However, that dynamic fundamentally changed when the PRI's power began to decline. This began slowly in the late 1990s, but in 2000, Vicente Fox from the National Action Party won the presidential election, beating PRI's Francisco Labastida. From then on, PRI quickly lost elections and influence across the country. This had a direct impact on the drug industry. According to Benjamin Smith, "corruption has shifted since the 1990s as increased drug profits and declining state power have upended the old protection rackets that kept violence down,"[11] while Anabel Hernandez adds more forcefully "all the old rules governing relations between the drug barons and the centers of economic and political power have broken down. The drug traffickers impose their own law."[12]

In office, Fox strengthened ties to America's President, George W. Bush – both of whom were keen to demonstrate strong hawkish policies. The United States under Bush's leadership pumped money and manpower into Mexico to fight the cartels and stop the flow of narcotics across the border. Fox's successor, Felipe Calderón, took over in 2006. Once in office, President Calderón made even greater efforts to purge corrupt police and launched operations against the cartels. This led to the high-level extraditions and the deaths of many in leadership positions, as the federal forces took over from the local and state police. The loss of so many key figures in the narco gangs in a short period of time did not have the desired effect. Instead of killing the cartel, the hydra merely grew new heads and sparked infighting as leaders battled for control. In response to this, the gangs profession-alised their violence, bringing in paramilitary tactics that dramatically and instantaneously raised the body count. One unit that became infamous for their brutality was the Zetas. They started out as part of the Gulf Cartel but quickly split off and formed their own organisation. Many were former fed-eral, state, and local police officers or former US Army personnel. Yet, many were directly recruited from the special forces in Guatemala. The Kaibiles in Guatemala were known to be brutal, violent, and sadistic, and they brought these facets with them to the Zetas, making them one of the most ruthless gangs in Mexico. The escalation in violence causes the other narcos to step up their tactics, and it creates a death spiral of assassinations, murder, rape, abductions, and all kinds of other sins.

GANGS IN MICHOACÁN

While Michoacán is not on the border and has not been as readily associated with narcos in the way that Sinola or Sonora has been, it still has a deep con-nection to the illegal trade. In fact so much so, that when President Calderón posed for photographers, dressed in combat fatigues, following the mass extradition of senior narcos, the photo op was staged in Michoacán, his home state. While the notoriety of narcos entering the avocado industry has only gained attention in the Global North in recent years, the connection of the Michoacán gangs with the fruit industry is lengthy, in part because of the state's century-old ties to both industries.

Armando Valencia Cornelio founded the now-defunct Milenio Cartel in Michoacán in the 1970s. When he was a young boy, he worked in the state's avocado orchards and invested in an avocado business. However, the profits and allure of the narcotics business were too great and as he grew older, he moved away from honest work. Yet, he didn't turn his back on avocados completely – he took his knowledge of the avocado industry with him. The cartel became renowned for disguising their criminal activities with the production and marketing of avocados. He posed as a successful avocado producer and cleaned the drug money through the orchards. This proved an effective strategy. During its heyday in the 1990s, the Milenio Cartel reached across the states of Jalisco, Colima, Nayarit, and Tamaulipas, and for a time, Valencia Cornelio was known as the King of Avocado (*Los Reyes del Aguacate*) as a result. However, eventually the gang's power waned, and they were taken over by the Gulf Cartel and the Zetas in the early 2000s.

As discussed previously, the Zetas were incredibly violent and quickly took over territory, including in Michoacán. Grillo's interview with an imprisoned former smuggler details the shift that the new group wrought on farming communities. The source said,

> There has never been fighting over marijuana in Teloloapan. If you wanted to grow mota [cannabis], you just grew it and sold it in the town to smugglers. That is the way it had always been since back in the 1960s when we first started growing. Then these Zetas appeared and said that anyone who grew marijuana had to pay them. People in my part of the mountains are rough, and a lot of them told these men to fuck themselves. And then bodies started appearing on the streets. And people started paying up.

This tactic of violence and intimidation was used against the avocado farmers in Michoacán who were pressured into paying protection money to the cartel. Benjamin Smith's interview in *The Dope* with a former lookout recalls two spikes in violence in Michoacán. The first when the Zetas arrived and the second when the federal forces tried to crack down since the government was almost just as brutal as the Zetas and "didn't care who they killed." Numerous accusations of murder, abduction, and rape have been levelled at the federal forces in Michoacán and has earned them a poor reputation for violence and corruption. In 2014, troops lined up and executed 22 civilians in Michoacán suspected of having gang links without proof or trial.[13] One year later, local police shot dead another 40 suspects.[14] Despite claims that the police were acting in self-defence, the dead were shot at point-blank range, execution style.

However, a new gang soon emerged. La Familia grew out of Tierra Caliente in southern Michoacán. This has long been an agricultural heartland, filled with lime orchards and agave farms, and consequently, many recruits were from farming families. All three of the gang's founding kingpins hail from peasant farming families. Ultimately, La Familia made an agreement with Los Zetas and took over the entire region. This partnership was only achievable since La Familia demonstrated their aptitude for extreme violence, enough to suggest that they would be as ruthless in the region as the Zetas had been. It's even been suggested that the ultra-violent Zetas trained

La Familia representatives in their more gruesome techniques. To this end, the gang made their emergence onto the wider narco stage in 2006 by rolling five human heads onto a disco dance floor.[15] Only three years later, they again demonstrated their reach by simultaneously attacking a dozen police stations across Michoacán and executing 15 officers in retribution for the arrest of one single La Familia lieutenant. The attack was only feasible due to the number of corrupt officers in their pockets that were willing to help stage the assault La Familia was considered to be exceptionally violent. The police released the interrogation video of La Familia capo, Miguel Ortiz, when he was captured. He happily and plainly outlined techniques cutting up bodies, mass executions, and assassinations. To ensure their recruits are competent in this more violent side of the business, they often recruit straight out of butchers and slaughterhouses. Although there are allegations that La Familia also relied heavily on the anesthetising effects of their own narcotics to control their recruits. This aptitude for violence, and the initial training from the Zetas, resulted in rising incidences across the state, not helped by the fact that La Familia decided to reject the partnership that they had with the Zetas and control the territory solo. Predictably, the Zetas pushed back. In one of the most violent incidents in all of narco history, not just Michoacán but across Mexico, the Zetas threw a series of grenades into an Independence Day parade in Morelos, Michoacán, in 2008 that was filled with families as punishment for La Familia's actions.

However, La Familia used a different tactic than violence with the local farming communities of Michoacán. Due to their own roots within the state, they embraced communities, although still retained the threat of violence just under the surface. According to Grillo, "La Familia also uses regional pride to rally farmers and small-town hoodlums. They claim to be good Michoacán men who have driven out Sinaloans and Zetas." The gang claims that any violence, particularly against federal forces, is only in response to the harassment of their families. They even offered a public truce to the local police if they were left alone – although one wonders if this was only public performance and not sincerely meant. While the gang happily kidnapped and ransomed in other states, they banned the practice in Michoacán and executed anyone who disobeyed that order, which helped to make locals feel safe. La Familia bosses also argued that they brought better-paying employment to Michoacán and acted as benevolent godfathers, handing Christmas presents to poor kids. This is reminiscent of many other kingpins, such as Pablo Escobar, who bought goodwill by investing in their communities.[16]

There has long been a connection between rural peasant farmers and the cartels. In fact, many rural folk position themselves on the side of the cartels, according to narco historian, Ioan Grillo, who notes that "Valientes or brave ones – the term mountain folk use for drug traffickers, the men who pulled the community out of poverty."[17] Many farmers have earned a living for decades growing marijuana and/or opium poppies for the cartels, earning good money doing it, for the most part, more than they would earn were they growing subsistence crops. Wages on a marijuana field averaged 30–50 pesos a day, ten times the official minimum wage.[18] Such a salary was appealing. Benjamin Smith highlights that "by the 1960: the rural economy was in decline; poverty was worsening. Increasing birth rates were annulling the benefits of revolutionary land distribution; local elites were struggling bitterly against any further allocation of their lands; the government was keeping prices for agricultural crops artificially low; and rural wages remained pitiful." He maintains that the money from narcotics "floated rural communities that were struggling because of the termination of farming subsidies enforced by NAFTA."

However, avocados changed that dynamic since the price that the fruit commands today is so high that it competes with marijuana and opium. That is even in Michoacán, where marijuana commanded a price premium since it was considered darker and stonier in flavour due to the local climate. Unlike marijuana, avocados do not come with the risk of the crop being seized or set alight by the police. Michoacán had already established the infrastructure for exporting avocados to the United States, and therefore, the transition was easy, quick, and lucrative for those farmers who switched from marijuana to avocados. Other states have not had the wherewithal, resources, or impetus to make comparable investments into export infrastructure, and so narcotics remain a more lucrative crop. The combination of this economic power and community influence led to a deep loyalty from citizens of Michoacán. There have even been rallies and marches to support the cartel with demonstrators carrying placards in support of the gang. This taps into a deep history of activism and revolution in Michoacán since it was the base of Mexico's Independence Army in the 1800s.

Unlike other cartels however, La Familia used another, more unusual, tactic to connect with local communities: religion. La Familia has "its own version of evangelical Christianity mixed with some peasant rebel politics."[19]

The gang has its own spiritual leader, Nazario Moreno, who is also known as the Maddest One (El Mas Loco). He has written his own bible (entitled Pensamientos) that is a mandatory reading assignment for the foot soldiers in the gang. According to Ioan Grillo, "the cult helps villains justify barbaric actions, at least in their own minds," adding "the spiritual aspects were useful in providing a glue and discipline for its organisation." The origin of Moreno's spiritual vision is rooted in the power of the wilderness and struggle of man to overcome it – a message that deeply resonates within farming communities – and owes much to John Eldredge's Christian text, Wild At Heart.[20] Converts to La Familia's faith are said to number over 9,000 today. This is not unusual – although La Familia takes it to the extreme – narco religion has been growing alongside the violence.[21] It has proved a way of expanding the power and influence of gangs. Narco religion resonates with many Mexicans who no longer feel that the traditional Catholic faith speaks to their blood-soaked lives and connects the violence to the divine. It centres on uncanonised saints who exemplify the experiences and desires of gang members, such as Santa Muerte and Jesus Malverde, to whom they pray for protection and good fortune, safe in the knowledge that these saints won't condemn them to Hell for the atrocities that they commit.

In recent years, however, La Familia has split into factions and the Knights Templar have taken over Michoacán. This gang did not have the same deep ties to the local community, nor the approach of keeping the violence out of Michoacán. Simultaneously, the Jalisco Cartel New Generation and the Los Viagras gang have tried to gain a foothold in the region. Consequently, many more businesses have been threatened by the cartels and required to pay for "protection." This has caused terror and resentment of the narcos across Michoacán.

AVOCADOS AND CARTELS

Just like the Milenio Cartel, La Familia, and Los Zetas before them, Knight Templar gained greater and greater hold over the region. The gang used their money, influence, and power to take over other industries, including avocados, running extortion and racketeering operations. They forced avocado producers to pay protection money per acre. However, seeing this as merely a shakedown misses the intensity of it. The reality is that, according to Grillo, "when a cartel controls a territory, it becomes a shadow local government, one that officials and businessmen have to answer to." Given the escalation of violence to control the fruit's production, some question whether avocados might be the next "conflict commodity" – there are reports of approximately a dozen rival gangs operating in Michoacán and trying to gain a greater slice of the avocado pie.

The cartel also demands payment from the Michoacán timber industry, often helping them to get around the environmental protections discussed in Chapter 9 to expand into native land. It's reasonable to assume that this deforestation also happens for the avocado plantations that they control. Just as with the timber industry, high profits create huge pressure to expand production of avocados to bring in more revenue. Analysis by Verisk Maplecroft has concluded that "criminal groups clear protected woodlands to make room for their avocado groves."[22] It is presumed that this was the motivation behind recent violence in the Biosphere Reserve visited in Chapter 9. The Biosphere Reserve in the Michoacán has become a flashpoint with cartels and producers looking to expand plantations into the protected land. Sometimes this involves bribery to the right official to look the other way. Other times, intimidation can quickly escalate into violence. One suspected instance of violence was seen with the death of Raúl Hernández, a guide of the Reserve and committed nature conservation activist, whose body, bearing signs of violence, was found in 2020 in Michoacán. This death was followed only days later by the death of Mr. Homero Gómez González, also an activist and manager at the Reserve. Both murders remain unsolved.

RESISTANCE TO THE TAKEOVER

The growing violence and the difference in the approach taken by Knights Templar versus La Familia has led to growing resistance for the local farming community against the cartels. People are increasingly sick and tired of the intimidation, threats, and violence.

Cheran, which we visited in Chapter 9 when discussing their anti-logging activities, is 50 km north of Uruapan, the centre of the region's avocado belt. It is an indigenous P'urhépecha community that has experienced violence and intimidation at the hands of the cartels with gangs seizing common land to convert into avocado plantations and extort local businesses.[23] "We realised that the only thing the avocado brings is violence and blood, at the expense of the Indigenous communities," says local farmer, David Ramos Guerrero.[24] In response to this growing threat, and the perception that local law enforcement were not adequately protecting the marginalised P'urhépecha people from the narcos, Cheran rose up in 2011 and formed their own self-ruling indigenous community. According to a *Los Angeles Times* article on the uprising:

> That was the year that residents, most of them indigenous and poor, waged an insurrection and declared self-rule in hopes of ridding themselves of the ills that plague so much of Mexico: raging violence, corrupt politicians, a toothless justice system and gangs that have expanded from drug smuggling to extortion, kidnapping and illegal logging.[25]

This was not a peaceful takeover. According to news reports, armed individuals blocked roads, attacked buses, took prisoners, and evicted local law enforcement.[26] The locals took to patrolling the roads themselves in pimped-out pickup trucks, armed with AR-15 rifles. Ultimately, in 2014, the national government recognised the municipality right to self-rule, which the Mexican Constitution permits for indigenous groups, and a High Council was elected.[27] Subsequently, there has been a significant drop in crime,[28] with no major crime reported in the first six years of independence.[29]

The action by Cheran led to other Purepecha communities similarly rising up. There is a growing auto defensa movement in the regions of Michoacán, particularly those with high indigenous populations. Angahuan, the indigenous P'urhépecha community in Michoacán that has been committed to fighting deforestation (as discussed in Chapter 9), declared their right to self-government under Michoachán state law.[30] Some of these auto defensa forces can number over 200 people, and the total is placed around 20,000 individuals being involved across the entire state.[31] These groups are well armed. While guns are technically illegal in Mexico and require registration, firearms flood across the border from the United States and have made it easy to access them for whomever wants them. While most of these groups directly challenge the cartels, some have struck deals with the narcos for protection. More concerningly, the Knights Templar accuse the vigilantes of siding with the Jalisco Cartel New Generation, using it as a justification to target the auto defensa groups. The government is less tolerant of these vigilante groups than they were of the independent leadership of Cheran – concerned that this might spark similar movements in other states. "The basic problem with the self-defence groups is that the Government cannot disarm them without handing control back to the Knights Templars, but it can't tolerate them either," says Alejandro Hope, a leading expert on Mexico's drug wars. In May 2014, the Mexican government created a "Rural Defense Force" to legitimise the self-defence militias.[32] However, they quickly changed their minds, and the RDF was dismantled in April 2016, returning vigilantes firmly outside the law. However, the groups insist that they are essential. One local leader said, "if we turn in our weapons, they will kill us" – whether he refers to the gangs or the federal forces is ambiguous – and there is concern that the groups might bed-in and create a standoff with federal forces if directly challenged.[33] One study into the impact has found that initially, homicides increased in vigilante areas due to confrontations, while kidnappings and extortions decreased, but in the longer term, murder rates decreased.[34] When the government quelled the vigilantes, homicides and kidnappings increased, since the government removal of vigilantes created a power vacuum.

INTERNATIONAL REACTION

The media coverage in the United States after the temporary ban on imports and the sensationalism surrounding the links between the avocado and drug industries have led many to reject the fruit in recent months. More and more noise is being made about the cartel control of the industry. Some suggest that a boycott would be the best way to challenge the cartels. Boycotts have been successful in the past. One prime example of recent years was the effective boycott of Nestlé that was organised by Greenpeace in 2010 to stop the company from using unsustainable palm oil in their chocolate.[35] However, the issue of cartel involvement in avocados is distinctly different and raises concerns. Firstly, it would likely have a negative impact on the farming communities that rely on the fruit for their livelihood. A boycott would devastate rural incomes and throw many into poverty. Secondly, it is not realistic to suggest that the cartels would merely acknowledge the shifting international demand and silently exit the industry. Instead, it would likely lead to greater pressure. Falko Ernst, International Crisis Group senior analyst for Mexico, highlighted that this is a false solution – a boycott would not necessarily provide the best outcome since "most likely prompt criminal groups to prey on civilians more aggressively yet to make up for lost avocado income."[36] Lastly, while consumers might have the intention of reducing cartel involvement in Michoacán avocado production, there would likely be a knock-on impact to other regions if consumers boycotted all avocados, as opposed to taking the time to identify the ones from Michoacán – something that is challenging to do from a supermarket label. Instead, Ernest suggested that, "What consumers can and should do is voice their expectations toward the companies they buy goods from, to not remain silent bystanders to human rights crises in many of the producing regions in the global south. Governments often ignore their citizens, but if the private sector, if investors, start budging, it's a whole different story." Consumers should put more pressure on their supermarkets to encourage them to work with suppliers and apply pressure on the Mexican government to tackle the infiltration of cartels into the avocado sector and the wider economy.

IN CONCLUSION...

While the sensationalism of the media coverage of the recent altercation between the cartels and the USDA in Michoacán has brought attention to the relationship between narcotics and avocados, this is not a new phenomenon. In fact, due to the prevalence of both the narcotic and avocado industries in Michoacán, and the critical role that both play in the rural economy, this interplay has a long history. Depending on which crop was more profitable and in greater demand in the US market, many farmers have switched between producing poppies, marijuana, or avocados. The cartels have benefitted (to differing degrees) from all three of these crops. That said, the dynamic between the farmers and the cartels has not remained constant. As the cartels in Michoacán specifically, and in Mexico more widely, has changed so has the relationship with the farming communities. At times, this relationship has been perceived almost positively. During periods, the cartels, La Familia in particular, created economic opportunities and ingratiated themselves with the local communities, helped by the fact that they had deep roots within Michoacán. However, more recent developments have seen violence and intimidation rise as gangs with little concern for local populations have taken over the region. This rise in the murder rate has led to uprisings and rejection of the cartels. Only time will tell what the next permutation of the cartel/ avocado relationship will be, but it is likely not going away while both the fruit and the drugs are profitable and while Michoacán holds a near monopoly of avocado production.

NOTES

1 Blog del Narco Mexico, "Carteles Unidos amenazo a un inspector Gringo en Uruapan; Michoacánn y Estados Unidos cancelo las importaciones de Aguacate hasta nuevo aviso." https://t.me/s/blogdelnarcosincensura?before=341.

2 Stevenson, Mark, *Mexico Says Conspiracy Behind Avocado Ban; Us Cites Violence.* Associated Press, 2022, February 14.

3 Martinez, MaryAnn, "US lifts ban on avocados from Mexico after drug cartel threat." *New York Post*, 2022, February 18.

4 Wagner, Christian, "Are Mexican avocados the next 'conflict commodity.'" *Verisk Maplecroft*, 2019, December 5.

5 Grillo, Ioan, *El Narco: Inside Mexico's Criminal Insurgency.* Bloomsbury Press, 2011, November 1.

6 Cook, Colleen, "CRS report for congress: Mexico's drug cartels." *Congressional Research Service*, 2007, October 16.

7 Grillo, Ioan, *El Narco: Inside Mexico's Criminal Insurgency.* Bloomsbury Press, 2011, November 1.

8 Ibid.

9 Smith, Benjamin, *The Dope: The Real History of the Mexican Drug Trade.* W. W. Norton & Company, 2021, August 10.

10 Ibid.

11 Ibid.

12 Hernandez, Anabel, *Narco Land: The Mexican Drug Lords and Their Godfathers.* Penguin Random House, 2014, September 9.

13 Slotkin, Jason, "Mexican Police murdered 22 and manipulated crime scene, review finds" *National Public Radio*, 2016, August 19.

14 *Human Rights Watch*, "Mexico: Police Killings in Michoacán." 2015, October 28.

15 BBC, "Human heads dumped in Mexico Bar." 2006, September 7.

16 Bowley, Jenna, *Robin Hood or Villain: The Social Construction of Pablo Escobar.* The University of Maine, 2013, May.

17 Grillo, Ioan, *El Narco: Inside Mexico's Criminal Insurgency.* Bloomsbury Press, 2011, November 1.

18 Smith, Benjamin, *The Dope: The Real History of the Mexican Drug Trade.* W. W. Norton & Company, 2021, August 10.

19 Grillo, Ioan, *El Narco: The Bloody Rise of Mexican Drug Cartels.* Bloomsbury Paperbacks, 2013, January 17.

20 Eldredge, John, *Wild at Heart: Discovering the Secret of a Man's Soul.* John Eldridge, 2011, April 19.

21 Baily, Lauren, *In What Ways Have Mexican Cartels Used Religion and Popular Culture for the Purpose of Legitimizing the Drug Trade?* University of Kent, 2018.

22 Wagner, Christian, "Are Mexican avocados the next 'conflict commodity.'" *Verisk Maplecroft*, 2019, December 5.

23 Pelliccia, Monica, "Indigenous agroforestry dying of thirst amid a sea of avocados in Mexico," *Civil Eats*, 2022, June 10.

24 Brown, Hannah, "This Mexican town declared independence to protect its forest from avocados." *euronews.green*, 2022, February 2.

25 McDonnell, Patrick, "One Mexican town revolts against violence and corruption. Six years in, its experiment is working." *Los Angeles Times*, 2017, July 10.

26 Ibid.

27 Knoll Soloff, Andalusia "After long fight for self-government, indigenous town of Cherán, Mexico ushers in new council." *NBC News*, 2018, September 4.

28 Agren, David, "The Mexican indigenous community that ran politicians out of town." *The Guardian*, 2018, April 3.

29 McDonnell, Patrick, "One Mexican town revolts against violence and corruption. Six year in, its experiment is working." *Los Angeles Times*, 2017, July 10.

30 Elorriaga, Ernesto, "Purépechas from Angahuan vote in favor of self-government." *LaJornada*, 2021, October 25.

31 Tuckman, Jo, "Mexican vigilantes who ousted Knights Templar cartel could bring new violence." *The Guardian*, 2014, March 19.

32 Ibid.

33 Diaz, Lizabeth, "Mexico's Wild West: vigilante groups defy president to fight cartels." *Reuters*, 2019, September 13.

34 Del Rio, Juan, Do Vigilante Groups Reduce Cartel-Related Violence? An Empirical Assessment of Crime Trends in Michoacán, Mexico. *Studies in Conflict & Terrorism*, Vol. 46, Issue 7, pp. 1216-1240, 2023.

35 Ionescu-Somers, Aileen, & Enders, Elbrecht, "How Nestle dealt with a social media campaign against it." *Financial Times*, 2012, December 3.

36 Kamali Dehghan, Saeed, "Are Mexican avocados the world's new conflict commodity?" *The Guardian*, 2019, December 30.

KEY READINGS

- Agren, David, "The Mexican indigenous community that ran politicians out of town." *The Guardian*, 2018, April 3.
- Brown, Hannah, "This Mexican town declared independence to protect its forest from avocados." *euronews.green*, 2022, February 2.
- Grillo, Ioan, *El Narco: Inside Mexico's Criminal Insurgency*. Bloomsbury Press, 2011, November 1.
- Kamali Dehghan, Saeed, "Are Mexican avocados the world's new conflict commodity?", *The Guardian*, 2019, 30 December.

- Smith, Benjamin, *The Dope: The Real History of the Mexican Drug Trade*. W. W. Norton & Company, 2021, August 10.
- Wagner, Christian, "Are Mexican avocados the next 'conflict commodity.'" *Verisk Maplecroft*, 2019, December 5.

13

ALTERNATIVE GUACAMOLE

SHIFTING CONSUMPTION PATTERNS

INTRODUCTION

With the popularity of avocados rising, the fruit has become a now-consistent presence in cafes across the world. Brunch menus are increasingly homogeneous; every one of them featuring avocado toast. As told by Dan Saladino in *Eating to Extinction*, "if it strikes you that everything is starting to taste the same wherever you are in the world, you're by no means alone."[1] Chefs making endless avocado toasts to satisfy brunching Millennials are starting to feel their culinary creativity stifled. Maybe they pimp the dish with poached eggs or bananas or smoked salmon, but overall, it remains depressingly consistent. Chef J.P. McMahon, one of Ireland's most prominent chefs and passionate advocate of wild, seasonal, and sustainable local ingredients, removed avocados from his three Galway restaurants in 2018. J.P. McMahon argued that avocados are often "a lazy chef's option," and there are valid local alternatives that (1) can offer an opportunity for chefs to experiment and innovate in order to fill the avocado-shaped gap in people's hearts and stomachs and (2) are more in line with the culinary tradition of those countries where avocados cannot be grown.[2]

SOCIALLY RESPONSIBLE CHEFS

However, the lack of culinary creativity is not the only reason why chefs are switching away from avocado toast. Chefs are also concerned about the environmental and social sustainability of avocado production. There is an

DOI: 10.4324/9781003371915-13

increasing role for them to play in educating the public about the impacts of their food choices. McMahon isn't alone in rejecting avocados in his kitchen. Other restaurants, chefs, and well-known social media influencers are also shying away from the green fruit.

In addition to the responsibilities that chefs now have to educate their customers, it also makes good business sense. Businesses thrive when their decisions and actions actively consider the core values of those who they serve. Today, with the increased spending power of Millennials and GenX, being a sustainable company and caring about people and the planet is a requirement to compete in the market; 75% of UK consumers want supermarkets to only supply sustainably and ethically sourced products.[3] Consumers, especially Gen Z, are becoming more and more aware of the dangers of the climate crisis and are looking to make positive shifts in their consumption patterns. According to a 2020 report by First Insight, 73% of Gen Z consumers surveyed were willing to pay more for sustainable products, more than every other generation.[4] Therefore, consumers are interested in supporting businesses who have the same values and care about the same things. With growing coverage of the environmental and social damage caused by the industrial production of avocados, this means that both businesses and consumers are moving away from the fruit.

Some chefs cite the social impact on communities as the major motivator to switch. Wildflower, a vegetarian restaurant in London, stopped serving avocados a few years ago because of its effects on the global market. Head chef, Joseph Ryan, noticed parallels between avocados and quinoa. In the early 2000s, the South American grain became so fashionable within the "clean eating" community (a group discussed in Chapter 3) that it ended up driving up demand for imports from South America. "There was such a spike in the price of quinoa that [it] became unaffordable for people in their own country, which I think is so wrong," the chef said.[5] With growing consumption in the Global North, the prices escalated, boosting farmers' income, on the one hand, but driving down consumption locally, on the other hand. What was once a subsistence product for certain communities was now considered a luxury.[6] Instead of this traditional grain, calories now have to come from cheaper imports like white rice and pasta, leading to an increasingly westernised and less nutritious diet and affecting both health and cultural heritage negatively. Whilst for many consumers in the Global North, avocado is a trendy superfood that looks good on the Instagram feed, for many it is a core part of their cuisine, culture, and identity in a similar manner to quinoa.

In addition to the ubiquitous nature of the fruit affecting the global market, chef Mahon also cites the involvement of drug gangs in the supply chain as a reason to switch away from avocados after he proclaimed them Mexico's "blood diamonds," due to their connection with violence.[7] As mentioned in the last chapter, this connection to the cartels was heavily publicised in the United States in 2022 following the USDA ban of avocado imports and led to public outrage. Many US chefs had to quickly source alternatives or remove the fruit from their menus altogether. The owner of a Mexican restaurant in Utah switched to a combination of zucchini, spinach, and cactus.[8] At the same time in Edinburgh, Cult Coffee removed avocados from its menu as a result of fruit's connection to the cartels. The cafe announced on social media that they could not, with a clear conscience, support Mexican farmers through their sustainable coffee sourcing, whilst endangering their livelihoods at the same time through purchasing avocados. However, the irony is that few avocados in the United Kingdom originate in Mexico since the majority, as discussed, are shipped from Chile, Peru, South Africa, and Israel. The avocados from these countries are not associated with the drug cartels. It is unlikely then that the avocados served at Cult would have originated from the Michoacán region and therefore were unlikely to have funded the cartels. It might have made a stronger argument were the cafe to have focused on the environmental sustainability of the fruit instead, which, as has been made clear, is a ubiquitous problem the world over.

LEGUME ALTERNATIVES

A more sustainable alternative to avocados might be peas and beans. In addition to having less food miles since they can be grown locally, they are environmentally more sensitive because they are part of a healthy rotational approach to crop production. Recognising this relationship between legumes and environmental health, chefs are switching from avocados to peas and beans. Thomasina Miers, co-founder of the popular UK Mexican restaurant chain Wahaca, has introduced the so-called 'Wahacamole' on the menu with fava beans as centre stage, flavoured with green chillies, lime, and coriander like in the traditional guacamole recipe. To create this, Miers worked with the British pulse grower Hodmedod's. Founded in 2012, Hodmedod's is a small independent business committed to supplying pulses and grains that are British grown. They work with local farms to source a range of top quality ingredients and are particularly interested in searching out and promoting less popular products, like black badger peas, which have been grown in Britain since the Iron Age but are now almost forgotten. Miers' use of locally produced fava beans (the fully matured, dried cousin of broad beans) in her restaurants is a prime example of how searching for alternatives can translate into supporting small producers in the local economy.[9] Similarly, Johan Scheepers, general manager of the Kimpton Clocktower Hotel in Manchester, replaced avocados with broad beans, using both fresh and frozen so that they can be enjoyed all year round. Writer Bettina Campolucci, who used to live in Spain and relied on locally sourced avocados, said, "A few years ago, I was quite well known for my use of avocados in my cooking – so much so that I dedicated a whole Instagram account (@avodaily) to my love for them." Since relocating to the United Kingdom, she has not been able to source avocados locally like she could in Spain, and so she is reaching for British peas instead.[10] When crushed and mixed with sour cream, garlic, lemon juice, salt, and pepper, they offer a tasty option to put on toast. She has also renamed her Instagram account to the less controversial, @bettinas_kitchen.

OTHER OPTIONS

Other chefs have turned to other options. J.P. McMahon has been using Jerusalem artichokes. Chef Aldo Camarena, born in Mexico and based in Toronto, proposed an alternative to guacamole made with pumpkin seeds.[11] These seeds are often thrown in the trash, so finding ways to use them can help to reduce food waste. London chef Santiago Lastra, owner of restaurant Kol, is on a mission to showcase Mexican cuisine produced using native ingredients to the United Kingdom instead of imports.

> We were looking not to recreate, but to produce a similar sensorial experience.[12] What does an avocado mean in terms of sight, texture, aroma and flavour? And how do we paint that with the tools we have?

Lastra said. He has found that pistachios can be a great alternative when treated the right way, due to their fattiness and nutty taste. Instead of guacamole, he is now serving a dip made from pistachios and fermented gooseberries as part of his menu.[13] While the intention is good, it could be argued that pistachios are not the solution to the problem. Firstly, the nuts are not native to the United Kingdom. According to the CBI, the largest supplier of pistachios to Europe is the United States, accounting for almost 77% of total supply, followed by Iran (22%) – Iran raising significant geopolitical questions and potentially at risk from trade sanctions.[14] Secondly, the nuts are quite water intensive in terms of their production. Pistachios use 11,363 m^3/ton of water versus 1,981 m^3/ton for avocados.[15]

There is a tinge of irony here. Avocado itself was considered a more sustainable substitute not long ago. According to Jeff Miller, in the 1970s, it was becoming more challenging to source fatty tuna (toro) and fatty tuna belly (otoro) for sushi rolls. One chef thought to try the buttery avocado flesh as a sustainable alternative to the rarer and more expensive fish.[16] It proved a massive success and ultimately led to the creation of the infamous California roll now featured on sushi restaurant menus across the world. Now it is the avocado's turn to be replaced in the name of sustainability.

REACTION AND OPPOSITION

However, not everyone is happy. Some customers expressed their disapproval of the removal of the avocado from their brunch menu. And perhaps it is too simplistic to focus on one fruit as being damaging, when every single ingredient has some sort of environmental or social impact. Xavier Equihua, the former head of the World Avocado Organisation, criticised British chefs for getting rid of avocados from their kitchens, while still using other ingredients that were, according to him, even worse for the planet.[17] In a letter[18] to *The Guardian* in response to the article "End of the Avocado" written by Claire Finney in 2021, he mentions that fava beans require roughly 5,000 L of water to produce a single kilo, whilst avocados take on average 600 L/kg.[19] For him, serving products like meat and dairy whilst fighting a war against avocados is hypocritical. To a certain degree, he is correct. Intensively produced animal products certainly have high carbon footprints, and their production causes significant environmental damage.[20] However, that environmental damage is not so clear cut when it comes to pasture-based livestock systems that are managed in harmony with nature. These systems can help to build soil fertility and sequester carbon and allow the restoration of species-rich grasslands, an important, but increasingly rare, habitat.[21] As with any food product, the method by which it has been produced is central to understanding the impact that it has. One cannot conflate the impact of an avocado grown in a home garden without irrigation or agrochemicals with one grown in an intensive monoculture orchard. Nor can one conflate beef from an intensive cattle lot on deforested land in Brazil with the impact of one from a cow grazed in England on a holistically managed, biodiversity-rich meadow.

The move away from the global obsession with avocados, however, is not limited to IRL. The repudiation of avocados and the skirmish over the alternatives has been dominated by social media. These social media controversies on avocados are not merely a sideshow. Given the influence of social media on the rise of the avocado toast, this shift of users away from the fruit is worth considering, especially given the high usage of Millennials (for which avocados are commonly emblematic) with social media platforms. Recipes for alternative ingredients to replace the green fruit are proliferating and becoming viral where the hashtag #noavocado currently has over 3.3k posts attached to it.[22] However, the social media defence of the fruit is also vocal. One famous consumer who bristled on Twitter at the idea of an alternative guacamole was President Obama.[23] He sparked controversy when he voiced some hesitation over a recipe published by the *New York Times* that included peas in the mix. In a tweet from 1 July 2015, the President said, "respect the nyt, but not buying peas in guac. onions, garlic, hot peppers. classic." A large portion of the US public appeared to agree with Obama's purist take, and his words were retweeted over 15,000 times and liked 19,000 times in just over a week. However, it must be acknowledged that this was years ago, and it wouldn't be too much of a stretch of imagination to think that Obama's views on the matter might be different today, given his leadership on addressing the climate crisis. Or that his followers might have been swayed into accepting an alternative in their guacamole.

TECH SOLUTIONS

As with most sectors today, the tech industry is stepping in to disruption. We will consider the role of gene modification and gene editing in the next chapter; however, other technologies are also offering solutions to the avocado's environmental and social challenges. Arina Shokouhi, a graduate from London's Central Saint Martins' with a master's in Material Futures, created an avocado alternative called Ecovado, which is meant to wean people off the popular fruit. "Ecovado is an alternative to avocado that employs design thinking to help consumers reduce the amount of avocado they eat by introducing them to unfamiliar, yet more diverse, ingredient combinations," said

Shokouhi.[24] Like nicotine gum helps people stop smoking without going cold turkey, the Ecovado is designed to gradually break people's dependence on avocados by offering something similar. The product resembles avocados in taste and overall appearance, but it is made with all local ingredients. She designed a product for the British market, made with broad beans, apples, hazelnuts, and rapeseed oil – achieving the subtle creamy and nutty flavour of avocados with all local and low-impact foods. For other countries, different ingredients could be used that could be sourced locally. The Ecovado also resembles an avocado in terms of looks. The flesh is encased in a fake skin made with wax and coloured with food colouring that is all biodegradable and compostable. As for the pit, whole nuts such as walnuts, hazelnuts, or chestnuts are used. The Ecovado has not been marketed yet, and it is difficult to know whether its production could be scaled up to become a truly viable alternative.[25] However, it shows incredible creativity and could be an option to reduce, rather than completely eliminate, the sheer quantity of avocados in our diets.

GENETIC DIVERSITY

Despite these innovative alternatives, switching to alternative crops might not be the only solution. Currently, the majority of the world consumes Hass avocados; 80% of the avocado market is dominated by this single variety.[26] Yet, there are hundreds of different alternative varieties out there. Which begs the question, do we need to give up eating avocados altogether? Or just stop eating Hass? But which Hass alternative to choose? It should be noted that some are better suited to consumer taste. As discussed in Chapter 2, the Fuerte was the most popular variety before the Hass took over since it was resistant to drops in temperature. It is worth considering whether the variety could still once again provide an alternative option, especially in Mexico where the average temperatures are progressively rising.[27] While the Hass remains the most popular in the Australian market, another variety occupies a significant portion. The Shepard accounts for 10–15% of Australia's supply.[28] This variety is well suited to slicing in salads and similar dishes, since its flesh is firmer. However, this makes it poorly suited for the most beloved brunch dish, the avocado toast, since the Shepherd does not smash very well. Another option that could gain in popularity as a more sustainable alternative would be the Reed avocado that "produces more pounds per acre than the Hass does with less water per acre."[29] As orchards become drier and water stress rises, it would be valuable to consider other varieties that might require less water. Whole Foods producer buyer, James Parker, has suggested that Reed might be the best variety to challenge the dominance of the Hass.[30] The Gem is another likely contender. It shares many characteristics with the Hass in terms of flavour and texture, although its green skin might be less familiar to consumers who recognise the bumpy dark skin of the Hass. However, that green skin might make it more appealing to some. Zac Bard, chair of the World Avocado Organisation, said, "I expect a renaissance of greenskins in the future, but more as a specialist niche product" as consumers become more aware of the environmental risks associated with relying exclusively on Hass. Plus the Gem doesn't brown as quickly when cut as the Hass, potentially reducing wastage and making it appealing to anyone who has eaten half an avocado only to return an hour later to a browned and unappealing second half. The Gem is also a good bet for farmers. It has a higher yield, stays on the tree for longer when ripe (as opposed to rotting and falling to the ground), and the canopy of the trees is more compact.

IN CONCLUSION...

It is right that chefs and consumers are raising questions about the impacts of avocados and considering alternatives – the hospitality industry has a major role to play in behavioural change. As a society, we need to be more aware as to where our food comes from and how it is produced. However, the issue is not with the fruit itself, but the way it is produced. More diversity and more alternatives are needed. Fava beans and peas can be good options for certain dishes, while switching to different varieties of the fruit for use when only an avocado will suffice can help diversify the supply chain. Technology might also offer a solution. Essentially, anything we can do to tackle the exclusive demand for Hass and diversify the demand will help to reduce the impacts associated with production and build resilience.

NOTES

1 Saladino, Dan, "Eating to extinction: The world's rarest foods and why we need to save them." *Farrar, Straus, and Giroux*, 2022, February 1.
2 Ngo, Hope, "Why some chefs are trying to cancel avocados." *Mashed*, 2021, November 2.
3 Kelly, Stuart, "UK Foods trends: A snapshot in time." *LRQA*, 2019, December 2.

4 Jahns, Katie, "The environment is Gen Z's No. 1 concern—and some companies are taking advantage of that." *CNBC*, 2021, August 10.

5 Lavelle, Daniel, "Should you stop eating 'blood avocados.'" *The Guardian*, 2018, December 10.

6 Philpott, Tom, "Quinoa: good, evil, or just really complicated?" *The Guardian*, 2013, January 25.

7 Shelton, Justin, "Why chefs are ditching avocado." *Sweetish Hill*, 2022, August 7.

8 Crombleholme, Hayley, "Rising avocado costs prompts Salt Lake City restaurants to get creative." *KJZZ15*, 2022, February 15.

9 Saltmarsh, Nick, "What are fava beans? Aren't they just broad beans?" *Hodmedod's*. https://hodmedods.co.uk/blogs/news/what-are-fava-beans-are-they-just-broad-beans.

10 Ngo, Hope, "Why some chefs are trying to cancel avocados" *Mashed*, 2021, November 2.

11 Ibid.

12 Finney, Clare, "End of the avocado: Why chefs are ditching the unsustainable fruit." *The Guardian*, 2021, November 1.

13 Krader, Kate, "At London's best Mexican restaurant, There's not avocado in the Guacamole." *Bloomberg*, 2022, August 3.

14 *CBI Ministry of Foreign Affairs*, "The European market potential for pistachios." 2020, April 7.

15 Mekonnen, MM, & Hoekstra, AY, "The green, blue, and grey water footprint of crops and derived crop products." Vol. 1: Main Report, Research Report Series No. 47, *UNESCO Institute for Water Education*, 2010, December.

16 Miller, Jeff, "Avocado: A global history". *Reaktion Books*, 2020, April 13.

17 Pearson-Jones, Birdie, "Dip wars! World Avocado Organisation blasts 'comical and hypocritical' restaurants for ditching guacamole for environmental reasons while serving meat - but expert says UK produce is the ONLY sustainable solution." *Daily Mail*, 2021, November 25.

18 Equihua, Xavier, "Letter to *The Guardian* of the UK in response to article 'End of the Avocado' by Claire Finney." *World Avocado Organization*. https://theproducenews.com/sites/default/files/2021-11/WAO%20-%20LoE%20-%20The%20Guardian.pdf.

19 Finney, Clare, "End of the avocado: Why chefs are ditching the unsustainable fruit." *The Guardian*, 2021, November 1.

20 Garnnett et al., Tara, Grazed and confused? "Tara, Grazed and confused?" *Food Climate Research Network*, 2017.

21 *Sustain*. "Delivering the UK's Nationally Determined Contribution (NDC) across farming and land use," 2021, October 21.

22 *Mexico Daily Post*, "Goodbye to Avocados? Some Euro Chefs ask not to eat it anymore for this reason." 2021, November 2021.

23 *NDTV Food*, "President Obama's view on Guacamole: Yes please, but hold the peas.," 2017, July 19.

24 Long, Molly, "Avocado alternative developed with British ingredients to tackle unsustainability of the fruit," *Food Matters Live*, 2022, July 18.

25 Lee, Chelsea, "Evocado could be a greener alternative to 'green gold.'" CNN, 2022, August 12.

26 Eldridge, Honor, "Why our love for avocados is not sustainable." *Sustainable Food Trust*, 2020, January 31.

27 Amerena, Rosi, "Climate change in Mexico." *Climate Portal*, 2020, January 16.

28 Pigram, Kelly, "Shepard avocados: How to tell if they're ripe and how to eat them." *Taste*. https://www.taste.com.au/articles/shepard-avocados-tell-if-theyre-ripe-eat-them/cd7igfhl.

29 Miller, Jeff, *Avocado: A Global History*. Reaktion Books, 2020, April 13.

30 Ibid.

KEY READINGS

- Finney, Clare, "End of the avocado: Why chefs are ditching the unsustainable fruit." *The Guardian*, 2021, November 1.
- Lee, Chelsea, "Evocado could be a greener alternative to 'green gold.'" CNN, 2022, August 12.
- Ngo, Hope, "Why Some chefs are trying to cancel avocados." *Mashed*, 2021, November 2.

14

ASSURANCE

CERTIFYING AVOCADOS AND THE ROLE OF TECHNOLOGY

INTRODUCTION

More and more consumers are searching out products that reflect their values, including trying to source more sustainable avocados. The British public increasingly demonstrate the desire for transparent information to better understand the origin of their products. However, this can be easier said than done. The shelves crawl with sustainability logos: more than 460 of them on food and beverage packages, and a third of them created over the last 15 years.[1] An avocado alone can have multiple stickers and badges to demonstrate its environmental credentials. Current labelling regulations are not up to the task to provide the transparency that consumers desire. With so many different assurance schemes currently being used on packages, consumers are often confused as to how to assess one against another. Since its founding, the Sustainable Food Trust has been working to increase transparency in the food chain. According to Adele Jones, their Executive Director, "for the majority of citizens, these labels are opaque, offering little immediate explanation as to what they represent." Sarah Compson, Associate Director of Soil Association and International Federation of Organic Agriculture Movements (IFOAM) Organics International World Board member agrees saying, "it's important to look behind the label and understand the standards underpinning a certification in order to get a sense of the real difference it makes."

DOI: 10.4324/9781003371915-14

ORGANIC

If a shopper wants to reduce their environmental footprint, one of the best ways is to buy organic. For products to be certified as organic, they must meet a series of standards that are set and audited by certification bodies (CBs). Farmers need to have annual inspections to demonstrate delivery against those standards, ranging from controlled pesticide usage to crop rotations and natural fertiliser usage. These practices have been proven to limit environmental damage and improve ecosystem health. As a shortcut for time-pressed shoppers, looking for a more sustainable option, spotting the organic stamp can be a winner. Unlike other certifications for food, the organic standard is enshrined in law. This means that violations can be enforced and held to account, improving authenticity and trust. As Compson says, "Unlike some eco-claims, in most regions the term organic is protected by law. Organic certification bodies are themselves regulated by accreditation bodies and more often than not, national governments."

While the traditional use of farming methods that promote soil health (and do not use agrochemicals) have been practised for millennia, the "organic movement" started in the 1940s when the Green Revolution started to take full force. This happened almost simultaneously across the world with a strong presence in Asia (notably Japan and Korea) and in India. The primary ethos that underpins organic is the idea of building soil health through regenerative means. The movement grew progressively across the post-war period with American ecologists Rachel Carson and Jerome Rodale leading the fight against the expansion of industrialised agriculture. In 1972, the IFOAM was founded to help grow collaboration globally.

More recently, organic has come to be defined by certification. Most readers would recognise the organic label on their supermarket avocado, but how many would be able to clearly explain what that meant? Organic grew dramatically in the 1990s when certification moved mainstream. This growth was due to rising affluence (consumers were willing to pay more for products) and growing environmental awareness, meaning more farmers could see the benefits of switching to organic production. It moved from a niche sector into mainstream production. Some farmers choose to be certified organic because of the environment. Others do it so they can charge a higher price and make more profit. For most, it is a combination of the two. According to Compson, "Organic certification provides a market mechanism for farmers to be rewarded and recognised for their positive efforts towards tackling the climate and ecological crisis." Today, shoppers in the United Kingdom spend £60 million a week on organic.[2]

Yet, there are concerns about organic certification. Firstly, each country sets their own organic standard. This can differ from nation to nation. For example, the United States will certify hydroponics as organic while the EU does not. These differences make it more complicated to classify imported goods as organic. Each importing nation must recognise and accept the organic certification of the exporting nation through a process called "equivalency." Agreeing on what is equivalent tends to happen during trade negotiations, which often raises controversies. Government trade negotiators are not always experts on sustainable agriculture and might not always comprehend the real-world impacts of nuanced differences in organic standards. Secondly, the negotiations on organic (or phytosanitary standards overall) tend to happen as part of the wider trade deal discussions, and therefore, compromises on food standards can be part of an overarching trade negotiation. One might think back to the way in which NAFTA was negotiated to see how power dynamics and compromise play central roles in any trade negotiation. For example, in a negotiation for an FTA between the United Kingdom and the United States, the UK trade negotiators might accept hydroponics as organic to win a concession on automotive standards. Compson acknowledges this saying, "Equivalency can be a challenge, particularly for principles-led movements like organic, because uncomfortable compromises can potentially be made for the sake of political expediency. But they're also an amazing tool to help foster trade between farmers and markets around the world," and she highlights the IFOAM Organic International Norms as a global benchmark. However, potential differences in imported organic vs. domestic organic are not clear to the consumer. The majority accept the organic label as proof of a production standard and do not interrogate beyond that. For the most part, that is a reasonable assumption. Any certified organic product will have a smaller environmental footprint than a non-certified product.

However, organic certification is not cheap. Farmers must undergo an expensive (and sometimes bureaucratic) certification process. Most certifications require producers to manage their land in line with organic principles for multiple years (two in the United Kingdom, three in the United States) before produce can be labelled as "organic."[3] This means that farmers have to employ farming techniques that can be more expensive and produce lower yields without benefiting from the price premium that the organic certification can bring. After that, they still need to pay annually to keep up their certified status and undergo an invasive on-farm audit. According to Patrick Holden who founded the Sustainable Food Trust and was previously the Director of the Soil Association,

> the organic audit, now enshrined within the EU regulatory frame-work, focuses, wrongly in my opinion on compliance, meaning whether the licensee cheated or not, as opposed to the impacts and outcomes of the system. This seems perverse to me. After all, conventional farmers are doing all the damage, so they should be audited to make sure that they are legally compliant, whereas organic producers should be measured to see how well we are doing.

For many small-scale farmers, particularly in the Global South, this process is out of reach. They might farm in an agroecological manner (as discussed in Chapter 11) that would mean that they meet the organic standards, but they cannot afford to undergo the process to have that legally recognised. As Jones says,

> One issue is the cost of certification to farmers, both in monetary and time terms – audits are often long, stressful and at the end, even if they have passed, don't necessarily give the farmer any constructive feedback on how they can be incrementally better each year.

The World Avocado Organization maintains that this is the case. They say that the majority of small-scale avocado farmers are farming in a way that is essentially organic but choose not to go through the certification process because of the cost and the bureaucracy. Compson has a solution to this challenge,

> If we want to see more farmers certified organic in order to provide for markets, either local or international, it's important that the process is de-risked as much as possible. For too long, farmers have borne both the responsibility for farming in a way that's better for the environment and also the financial risks associated with doing so. An enabling policy environment, fair trading terms and good returns are all important ways to encourage farmers to get certified.

FAIRTRADE

The organic certification is not a panacea for all the negatives caused by avocado production that are discussed in this book. It focuses almost exclusively on environmental concerns and barely touches the social ones. While Mexico does have fairly progressive labour laws, the enforcement is weak and often abuses are overlooked. As a result, child labour remains a pressing concern in Mexico. It is estimated that 4% of children under the age of 14 (the legal working age) are in illegal employment in Mexico, often in poor conditions without adequate health and safety.[4] Of these children, over 30% are working in rural areas within the agriculture sector.[5] To select a certification scheme that addresses labour, a consumer should search out a Fairtrade certification. Today, 93% of British shoppers recognise the Fairtrade mark and roughly $9bn worth of Fairtrade products were sold in 2017, their raw material sourced from 1.66 million farmers.[6]

While the Fairtrade movement had been growing for decades, the World Fair Trade Organisation (WFTO) was established in 1989 with the goal of increasing transparency over labour rights in the food sector. The initial spark was the ill-treatment of small-scale Mexican coffee producers. A priest working with smallholder coffee farmers in Mexico collaborated with a Dutch non-governmental organisation (NGO) to create the concept of a Fairtrade label. It was not until 1997 that the Fairtrade label that we know today was created with the establishment of Fairtrade Labelling International (FLO) – now Fairtrade International. Fairtrade primarily focused on imported goods from the Global South, typically tropical commodity crops that have higher risks of child or forced labour abuses associated with them.

The Fairtrade standards for fresh fruit (which would logically include avocados) places stipulation on pricing and labour. It maintains that the scheme delivers "stronger, well-managed, democratic organization for small producers and improved labour conditions with freedom of association for workers."[7] As discussed in Chapter 8 when discussing shipping, Fairtrade does not consider the labour conditions across the entire supply chain, only the labour conditions on the farm. There are environmental standards included, but they are not particularly stringent or high. These essentially focus on pesticide usage and land-use change. If herbicides are used in the production process, producers need to demonstrate that they have gained knowledge of the weeds that affect the productivity of the crop, understood where weeds arise, and attempted to stop the spread of the weeds by non-chemical means (labour, mechanical, or thermic means) or alternative control techniques (i.e. mulches or cover crops).

They do stipulate that herbicides aren't applied in buffer zones to protect rivers or watersheds. Not exactly stringent restrictions. The CB has also introduced recently limitations on farm size, specifically detailing hectarage for avocado plantations. The maximum plot of land for citrus fruit or avocados must be equal to or below 30 ha, but there is a caveat. The maximum size for citrus and avocados in Brazil can be equal to or below 200 ha. Quite a jump from 30 to 200!

Fairtrade has also been accused of just being a marketing exercise.[8] Other certification schemes have similarly been accused of merely greenwashing and failing to deliver the income equality and poverty alleviation that it promises.[9] Like organic, Fairtrade is critiqued for being elitist and out of range for low-income consumers, especially when the CB sets a "price floor" to ensure that Fairtrade products (for example, coffee) cannot be sold below a certain rate.[10] The profit is meant to be ploughed back into community projects to enhance the lives of the people working in the fields, but there have been accusations that the money is misspent. Of equal concern is that Fairtrade can't sell all the commodities it certifies.[11] According to a *Guardian* article in 2016, of all the coffee grown as Fairtrade, only 34% of it could be sold at the minimum price set for Fairtrade.[12] The rest had to be unloaded into the standard market at the lower prices but without the Fairtrade label, negating any benefit. For cocoa, the rate is a bit better, 47%. For tea, it's much worse, only 4.7%. The CB argues that as the market continues to grow and the public demands more and more ethical products, this question of surplus will resolve itself. Yet, that seems overly optimistic – especially when we are heading into a cost-of-living crisis that could see consumers cut back on unnecessary expenses.

CERTIFIED AVOCADOS

Outside of organic and Fairtrade, there are three other certifications that dominate the avocado industry.

- *Rainforest Alliance*
  The Rainforest Alliance logo of the little frog is one of the most recognisable and is commonly found on avocados. The organisation was founded in 1987 by an American environmentalist and now operates in 70 countries. The CB's website states, "The Rainforest Alliance seal promotes collective action for people and nature. It amplifies and reinforces the beneficial impacts of responsible choices, from farms and forests all the way to the supermarket check-out."[13] The CB highlights

the role they have played in alleviating poverty, specifically in one case study for those working in the fruit sector in Mexico.[14] However, this certification scheme is not without controversy. The merger between Rainforest Alliance and UTZ in January 2018 means that the certification now covers both environmental and labour concerns.[15] From a labour perspective, there are some issues. The new scheme is based on a "due diligence" rather than a prohibitive approach, meaning that technically nothing will be outlawed under the new criteria. This concerns campaigners who maintain this means that even if a company was found to use violence against forced labourers, it could continue to bear the logo if it responded to the critique by putting improved processes in place. They also highlight that it falls short of the International Labour Organisation's (ILO's) Conventions and Recommendations – a vital benchmark for fundamental workers' rights.[16] It also does not guarantee the price of a commodity like Fairtrade does, leaving producers to the whim of the market. While in the environmental standard, there is (shockingly) no clear definition of forest, limiting the ability to stop native land from being changed over to plantations.

- *Global Good Agriculture Practices (GAP)*
  Global GAP state their goal as "safe and sustainable agriculture production to benefit farmers, retailers and consumers throughout the world" and that their vision is "a world in which farms are recognized for their efforts to continuously produce enough safe food while safeguarding our environment and the welfare of farming communities." It's worth noting the emphasis on feeding the world, which is often missing from other certification schemes, but the standards seem considerably thinner than other certification schemes leading to allegations of greenwashing. Despite its principles being underpinned by the FAO definition of "good agriculture" (economic viability, environmental stability, social acceptability, and food safety and quality), the implementation is light-touch. That said, they have recently amended the criteria (to become mandatory in 2024) to increase their environmental standards. Yet, they serve the purpose of providing the distributors and retailers of Global GAP certified products with the endorsement, which provides them cover for their environmental, social, and governance (ESG) credentials. It's used across the world in more than 135 countries,

and there are currently around 9000 Global GAP-certified avocado producers, mostly located in Kenya, Spain, Colombia, and Peru.[17]

- *SMETA*
  SMETA (Sedex Members Ethical Trade Audit) is the most widely used social audit in the world. Over 40,000 SMETA audits are uploaded onto the Sedex platform every year.[18] It focuses exclusively on working conditions and aims at mitigating the use of child or forced labour in the supply chain. Any issues flagged in the audit as potential violations can be remedied, based on a Corrective Action Plan (CAPR) and do not deny the business from being certified. This raises questions over whether the scheme allows questionable standards to be overlooked with the halfhearted promise of "working to resolve them," or whether the scheme's more collaborative approach means that businesses are supported to raise their standards. The process is almost entirely digital with a Self-Assessment Questionnaire (SAQ), a risk assessment tool and a virtual audit. Again, this might mean that the integrity of the inspection is lower since there is not an independent auditor on site to dive into the nooks and crannies of the production site, or it might mean that remote facilities where it might be difficult to inspect in person can now be audited via technology.

PROTECTED GEOGRAPHIC INDICATOR (PGI)

Another way that producers can currently differentiate themselves in the market is through the globally recognised system of PGI or protected designation of origin (PDO). These are normally associated with foodstuffs that are traditionally linked to specific places, for example, champagne, Parma ham, or stilton. The difference between the two being that PGI is merely the geographic location, while PDO also includes the method of production. These designations are recognised at a WTO level and have been fought hard over in the international trade arena.

Does this certification scheme have a role to play in avocado production? The Cretans certainly seem to think so. The successful production of avocado on the island during the last few years has encouraged producers to seek recognition of the Cretan avocado as a Protected Geographical Indication (PGI) product. Giorgos Kornarakis from the Agricultural Cooperative of Chania told *Ambrosia* magazine,

… If and when Cretan avocado gets a PGI designation, this will mean that it has its own 'identity', that its production and/or processing phase must be performed in a certain territory.[19]

Greece has had a fair amount of success with the scheme in the past from manouri cheese to mastic gum, feta to retsina. Given that concerns over the involvement of the drug cartels in avocado production are exclusively limited to Michoacán, is it possible that using PGI could help producers from Crete to distinguish themselves in the marketplace as being drug free? Or will more labels merely confuse the consumer even more and instead just relying on country-of-origin labels would suffice?

BLOCKCHAIN

Given such long supply chains and reliance on humans who are prone to error, it is difficult to have confidence in the certification's validity. Can consumers have full trust in an inspection that happens a million miles away? Can CBs feel confident that the same rigorous review would be conducted on the other side of the world? With such distances and lack of oversight, there is a risk of corruption and corners being cut. Blockchain has been proposed as a method to help ensure that the data that sits behind the certification cannot be corrupted. According to Jones,

> Longer, more centralised supply chains make transparency more challenging, particularly when producing products with many different ingredients. However, blockchain technology is making this more possible. In the not-too-distant future, it should be possible to see exactly which farm individual ingredients have come from, and if that farm is certified or even better, measuring their impact, the sustainability of that product.

Primarily associated with cryptocurrencies, blockchain is a shared ledger that facilitates the process of recording transactions and tracking assets across a network. That asset can be tangible or intangible: in this instance, it is avocados. The unique thing about blockchain is that the data cannot be altered once it's entered into the ledger, meaning that you can have confidence in its accuracy. For long supply chains, this means that data can be added into the ledger at each stage along the route, and it cannot be corrupted at a later stage. For avocados, this means that you could enter farm data into the ledger about the use of pesticides, soil carbon levels, or what plot it was grown on and that could not be altered down the line to create a more sustainable product. At each stage, more data could be entered: the port it was loaded at, the miles it travelled, and the temperature it was stored at. The retailer, and even perhaps the consumer, would be able to know exactly how the fruit had been produced and its journey. However, it is worth noting that while the data cannot be altered, it must be entered correctly in the first place. If the data is falsified from the outset, it will remain so. Therefore, it still requires a certain level of trust that the data entered is accurate – although, there are more and more moves to digitise and automate that data entry process so that data is not susceptible to human error or manipulation.

It is therefore logical to see the argument that blockchain could help to build a stronger sense of provenance since the data would be unimpeachable. Could this ultimately build a deeper connection between the farmer in the Global South and the consumer in the Global North? The UK company, Provenance, hopes that it can do just that. They hope to use technology to solve this problem so that "one day every great product will come with Provenance: accessible, trustworthy information about origin, journey and impact." A shopper could scan a QR code and access the full journey of the avocado from field to fork and gain a much better sense of the impact, confident that the data is incorruptible. This is also the model for companies such as Crowd Farming that allow consumers to purchase directly from a specific farmer. However, Compson is quick to highlight that it is not a silver bullet,

the rise of digital technology such as blockchain and other digital fingerprinting tools can be a huge help. But they aren't the total answer. Getting closer to suppliers and finding meaningful ways to share risk and reward along the value chain are also really important.

RESPONSIBLE SUPERMARKETS

That all said, this is an enormous burden to put onto consumers who are already time-pressed and most lack a deep enough knowledge of our complex global food system to adequately weigh up all the competing concerns. It has taken a whole book to consider the various impacts of avocado production – imagine doing that for every item in your shopping basket! It could be that supermarkets fill this role by curating the choices available to their shoppers to ensure that all products stocked meet a certain standard. Whole Foods have provided a model for this and have built a brand on the idea that consumers can trust that everything in their stores have been selected on the basis of having a higher environmental and social standard. This market positioning reflects a consumer desire; 75% of UK consumers want supermarkets to only supply sustainably and ethically sourced products.[20]

But as anyone who has heard the moniker "Whole Paycheck" knows, Whole Foods has a reputation of being expensive and out of reach for most consumers. Could it be that other more competitively priced supermarkets could set their own minimum of environmental or social standards for their store and communicate this with the public? Certainly, supermarkets that are under greater pressure from their customers to deliver more sustainable and ethical products are turning away from the traditional CBs and taking it in house. In 2017, for example, Sainsbury's revealed that its in-house tea brands were abandoning Fairtrade. Instead, an executive said, it was piloting its own ethical label – and calling it "Fairly Traded." Similarly, the global confectionery giant Mondelēz created its own in-house certification scheme called "Cocoa Life."[21] These own-brand sustainability programmes, like "Fairly Traded" or "Cocoa Life," are using blockchain technology to demonstrate the journey and the impact of the food from farm to fork. Doing this independently from the CBs is increasingly popular, although the CBs argue that allowing companies to set their own standards risks a watering down of what is expected.

IN CONCLUSION...

The market is increasingly demanding a more sustainable and ethical product. The consumer wants to ensure that the avocados that they buy in the supermarket are not causing damage. There is a role for CBs to play in this process since the consumers recognise and trust the label. However, with so many different types of labels and certification schemes functioning in the marketplace, it is difficult for the consumer to differentiate between them. Furthermore, it is nearly impossible for the public to unpick what standards and processes sit behind the scheme. Many schemes have inherent flaws that can be used to mislead the consumer into thinking that the product is more sustainable or ethical than it actually is. While organic and Fairtrade both have problems that need to be resolved, they each, respectively, remain the gold standard for certifying environmental and ethical production. However, this might change with blockchain. There is huge potential for the technology to disrupt the certification process and increase transparency. Only time will tell how this innovation will alter the certification space.

NOTES

1 *Ecolabel Index*, "All ecolabels." https://www.ecolabelindex.com/ecolabels/?st= country,gb.

2 *Soil Association*, "Organic Market Report 2022 reveals exceptional resilience throughout 2021." 2022, February 9.

3 *U.S. Department of Agriculture*, "About the Organic Standards." https://www.ams.usda. gov/grades-standards/organic-standards#.

4 "U.S. Department of Labor, Child Labor and Forced Labor Reports." *Bureau of International Labor Affairs*, 2021.

5 Ibid.

6 Subramanian, Samanth, "Is fair trade finished?" *The Guardian*, 2019, July 23.

7 Fairtrade International, "Fairtrade standard for small-scall producer organizations," 2019.

8 L.P., "Not so fair trade." *The Economist*, 2014, May 19.

9 Vidal, John, & Provost, Claire, "Fairtrade accused of failing to deliver benefits to African farmworkers." *The Guardian*, 2014, May 24.

10 Graham, Vernae, "Fair trade certified coffee partners update commitments ahead of sustainable coffee challenge and international coffee day." *Fairtrade Certified*, 2022, September 26.

11 Subramanian, Samanth, "Is fair trade finished?" *The Guardian*, 2019, July 23.

12 Ibid.

13 *Rainforest Alliance*, "What does 'Rainforest Alliance Certified' mean?" 2020, October 28.

14 *Rainforest Alliance*, "Project profile: Improving livelihoods of farmers and workers across the fruit sector in Latin America." 2022, February 25.

15 Carlile, Clare, "Open letter to rainforest alliance and UTZ." *Ethical Consumer*, 2018, October 15.

16 Carlile, Clare, "Questions about rainforest alliance." *Ethical Consumer*, 2019, April 29.

17 *QAssurance B.V.*, "What is GlobalGap (good agricultural practices)?" 2022, February.

18 SMETA, "SEDEX, the world's leading audit." https://www.sedex.com/solutions/ smeta-audit/.

19 Ambrosia: Fine food and Drinks of Greece, "Cretan avocado: Applying for PGI status." 2019, September 18.

20 Kelly, Stuart, "UK foods trends: A snapshot in time." *LRQA*, 2019, December 2.

21 Smithers, Rebeca, "Green & Black's new UK chocolate bar will be neither organic nor Fairtrade." *The Guardian*, 2017, August 3.

KEY READINGS

• Carlile, Clare, "Questions about rainforest alliance." *Ethical Consumer*, 2019, April 29.

• Subramanian, Samanth, "Is fair trade finished?" *The Guardian*, 2019, July 23.

15

A NEW GENERATION

GENETICS AND NOVEL BREEDING OF AVOCADOS

INTRODUCTION

Given the risks of monoculture and the vulnerability created by depending solely on one type of avocado, creating new cultivars of avocado is necessary to increase resilience in the production of the fruit. It also makes economic sense since researchers might be able to produce a fruit that is higher yielding, more efficient, or able to be bred year-round. This would give market advantage to the growers of those cultivars and allow them to outperform other growers. As discussed in Chapter 2, this is what happened with the Fuerte and the Hass that both gained popularity because of their beneficial attributes. Thus far, the Hass still remains the most appealing option. But the pressure is on. Climate change is presenting new challenges. In the immediate future, the risk of disease has been increased by rising temperatures. Laurel wilt now presents a real threat to avocado growers in California. The disease is spread by an invasive beetle that has felled vast stands of redbay trees, which share the Persea genus with avocados and is gradually spreading west from Georgia to Texas. If it reaches California, it might wipe out the entire industry – just as the Gros Michel banana was wiped out of Central America by the arrival of the Panama disease in the 1950s. Climate change is also altering the growing conditions in key areas of cultivation. Finding varieties that are more resilient to drought conditions or more salinity could be critical for the future of the industry.

DOI: 10.4324/9781003371915-15

RIVERSIDE BREEDING PROGRAMME

Universities and research institutes around the world are trying to develop new cultivars of avocado. One of the leading ones is in California. Mary Lu Arpaia oversees the avocado breeding programme at UC Riverside, a programme that has been running for 70 years and is funded by the California Avocado Commission. Each year the researchers plant three varieties at the research site in the San Joaquin Valley and three other locations. While the programme has a long history, it's still quite new for fruit breeding. "We're probably 20 years behind the apple industry at this point," says Arpaia.[1] But she envisions a time when the avocado will be more like an apple, with unique varieties harvested in different seasons and across an expanded geography.[2] The star of the programme so far has been the Gem, mentioned in Chapter 13. It has the same dark knobbly skin and the flesh has a similar texture and taste to the Hass, plus its high yielding and easy to transport.

MAPPING THE GENOME

Breeding is also made more difficult since avocados are highly heterozygous. As discussed earlier, it makes for unpredictable progeny and led to the popularity of grafting. Marker-assisted selection (MAS) breeding might provide a way to generate more predictable offspring. MAS breeding is a technique that can be used in plants and animals to select desirable qualities. It is considered a conventional breeding approach and uses DNA markers associated with desirable traits to select a plant or animal for inclusion in a breeding programme. This approach dramatically reduces the time required to identify varieties or breeds with positive attributes.

MAS breeding is only possible once the genome has been mapped. This has only recently happened. In 2019, researchers at the National Laboratory of Genomics for Biodiversity (LANGEBIO) in Mexico, Texas Tech University, and the University at Buffalo published their findings of the genetic sequence of the fruit[3] – the same project that finally discovered the genetic secrets of the Hass. Mindful of the importance of the avocado to their agriculture sector, the Mexican government funded the initial stage of the research.[4] Luis Herrera-Estrella, Ph.D., President's Distinguished Professor of Plant Genomics at Texas Tech University, said, "we needed to sequence the avocado genome to make the species accessible to modern genomic-assisted breeding efforts," adding "the long life cycle of avocado makes breeding programs difficult, so genomic tools will make it possible to create faster and more effective breeding programs for the improvement of this increasingly popular fruit."[5] The project also cited the risk of climate change to the crop as a reason why mapping was essential. To sequence the genome, the researchers isolated the DNA from avocado leaves and used several computers simultaneously to gather data on the avocado that they then analysed in comparison to other plants.

GENETICALLY MODIFIED AVOCADOS

Does the mapping of the avocado genome mean that genetic modification (GM) avocados are coming to a supermarket near you? GM is the process by which scientists change the traits of plants and animals by directly manipulating their DNA in the laboratory. Established techniques involve inserting whole genes that can be sourced from the same species or from a completely unrelated organism. Newer GM techniques often referred to as gene editing focus on making highly specific changes in the DNA sequence of a living organism, often by deleting or rearranging parts of the organism's existing genome. Gene editing uses enzymes, particularly nucleases, to break apart the target organism's DNA strands where it finds a particular sequence of nucleotides. A range of techniques are then used to encourage the cells to repair the DNA break in a way that achieves the desired result. This may involve the removal of existing DNA and/or the insertion of replacement DNA. Some commentators regard any differentiation between gene editing and GM as redundant since science is still manipulating the genes of a living entity to serve societal goals. "Genome editing is GM with better PR and, just like more established GM techniques, it needs to be treated with extreme caution," according to Liz O'Neill, the Director of GM Freeze, the UK umbrella campaign for a responsible, fair, and sustainable food system.

The mapped genome takes a step towards that future. Victor Albert, Ph.D., Empire Innovation Professor of Biological Sciences in the UB College of Arts and Sciences, and co-leader of the genome mapping study, said in a statement:

> If you have an interesting tree that looks like it's good at resisting fungus, you can go in and look for genes that are particularly active in this avocado. If you can identify the genes that control resistance, and if you know where they are in the genome, you can try to change

their regulation. There's major interest in developing disease-resistant rootstock on which elite cultivars are grafted.[6]

While for Herrera-Estrella, adaption to climate change would be the primary goal: "If we can identify genes that confer heat tolerance and drought tolerance, then we can engineer the avocados for the future."[7]

Others point to a more practical and market-based problem that GM might be able to solve – the browning of avocados. How many of us have chucked out an avocado that has gone brown once opened? Or discarded a pot of guacamole that sat on the table for too long? Cutting an avocado exposes the cells to oxygen, which allows the PPO enzymes to rapidly oxidise the phenolic compounds in the fruit's tissues into ortho-quinones (o-quinones). GM might offer a solution to this and help reduce the associated food waste. Such an intervention has been successful in other products. The Arctic Apple was developed so as not to brown after it had been sliced. The producers claimed that it would encourage kids to eat more fruit since the apple slices in their lunchboxes would remain appealing, as opposed to oxidising. The same could be said for non-browning avocados.

Supporters of the technology also point to the fact that the production of GM avocados would provide consistent income to farmers that embrace the technology. The troughs of production (such as in a drought year) can be debilitating for growers, especially in the Global South where margins are minimal. These inconsistencies are likely to increase with climate change. The technology aims to alleviate these concerns so that annual harvests are more reliable, which would mean that low-income farmers would be able to better plan for the future and avoid a boom and bust cycle that could wipe out their business.

CHALLENGES TO GM

However, not everyone is excited by the prospect of an evergreen guac. The negative impacts of GM or GE that activists cite are multiple. According to O'Neil,

The genome of even the simplest organism is more like an ecosystem than a code book. Our understanding of the complex interactions that take place between genes themselves and between the genome and the external environment has been transformed in the past few decades but there is no reason to think that we are done learning. With DNA, what you see is not necessarily what you get and that's why we need to bring some humility to the conversation about what should – and what should not – be released into the environment.

Historically, there might have been questions over the safety of eating them, but those arguments have more recently faded into the background. Instead, objections focus on the fact GMOs tend to be associated with monocultures and high pesticide use. This book has already discussed the serious environmental and social impacts that this type of industrial agriculture can bring. GM avocados would certainly further the expansion of monoculture plantations over agroecological ones. An example of GM technology leading to more industrial practices can be seen in the production of GM soya in the United States. This GM variety is known as "Roundup Ready" meaning that it can be sprayed with the herbicide, Roundup, without damaging the crop. This type of production (i.e. relying on high applications of herbicide) has led to a 7% increase in pesticide use,[8] which has a correlating impact on local biodiversity.[9] The pesticide residue is also a factor when such high levels of agrochemicals are used. Environmentalists and health campaigners highlight the negative impacts that residues can have, despite being heavily monitored by food safety agencies around the world.[10] However, this is less of an issue for avocados since (a) the application of pesticides is low in comparison to other crops and (b) the hard skin, particularly of the Hass, makes it difficult for the chemicals to get into the flesh of the fruit. As a result, the Environmental Working Group that publishes a list of the fruit with the highest and lowest pesticide residue each year placed the avocado at the top of the Clean Fifteen in 2022.[11]

Many suggest that GM avocados could bring wealth and prosperity into Global South communities. Despite the claims by industry, the introduction of GM is not a reliable tool for addressing poverty. Bt cotton was introduced in Burkina Faso with disastrous results. A GM variety of cotton that produced Bt toxins to kill bollworm pests was created by Monsanto. In 2008, it was approved for planting in Burkina Faso with the promise that it would help with poverty alleviation and raise rural livelihoods in a country where the per capita GDP is a paltry $918.[12] However, within only eight years, the project had been abandoned. The quality of the cotton produced with GM was inferior – it had shorter-fibre lint and ginning machines extracted proportionally less lint from harvested cotton bolls. The yields were lower. Ultimately, it cost Burkinabè cotton companies $76 million in losses.[13]

Thirdly, GM crops lead to more corporate control of the food system. Because the technology is patentable, GMO can be owned by a company. Open-source GM technologies are promised but have yet to appear so farmers must pay for the privilege of using the technology. This can become increasingly expensive over the years, and if there is a dip in the market price of the product, it can bankrupt farmers who are legally committed to purchasing from the company thanks to restrictive contracts. Given the prevalence of smallholder farmers in the avocado industry, this could have serious impacts on the economic viability of their businesses. This vicious circle of indebting farmers to corporations[14] has occurred in India, leading to accusations from many – ranging from then-Prince, now-King Charles to environmental leader Vandana Shiva – that there has been an epidemic of farmer suicides in rural India that they directly attribute to the crippling expense of GM seed.[15]

Next, it's difficult to contain the genetically modified material in the wild. Since avocados are open-pollinated, it is feasible that pollen from a GMO tree might pollinate a wild landrace variety. The offspring from that pollination would carry the GM material. It would be impossible to undo that spread were it to occur and would lead to many landrace avocados being lost. This presents a threat to the diversity of wild avocados and could impact the agroecological farmers who grow them. This happened with trials of GM wheat in the United States. There is no genetically engineered (genetically modified or GM) wheat approved for commercialisation anywhere in the world.[16] Yet, there have been four incidents where GM wheat has escaped from field trials in the United States – in 2019, 2016, 2014, and 2013 – and one reported in Canada in 2018.

Lastly, there would be trade implications. While the United States is accepting GMO fruit, other countries are not. It would be unlikely that the EU would accept the sale of GM avocados, and China has been opposed to GM imports in the past. Consequently, it could potentially segment the industry into countries willing to grow and countries willing to buy GM avocados versus those that are not. That might not be an issue for some territories, but for others, it could create tension. Mexico, for example, has been attempting to curtail the cultivation of GM within its borders in recent years, enacting a controversial presidential decree that seeks to ban genetically modified corn in 2024 and phase out the herbicide glyphosate, found in Roundup and associated with GM production.[17] For context, Mexico is the second-largest global corn importer, behind China. Mexico is also the destination for 24% of the US corn exports, so a ban on GM corn could have significant impacts on US corn producers and the United States has challenged the legality of the ban.[18] Depending on the outcome of the challenge, Mexico might be forced into adopting a more welcoming approach to GM, and by consequence, Mexican producers might feel additional pressure to switch over to GM avocados given the US market's friendly approach to GM products.

IN CONCLUSION...

The dominance of the Hass in the avocado industry has created a vulnerability. There is a growing risk of pests or diseases attacking the Hass avocado and resulting in the industry being decimated. As a result, plant breeders are trying to come up with alternative varieties that might prove popular with the consumer. This has been aided by technology and our ability to map the genome of the avocado in order to make breeding desirable traits easier. However, this technology also makes it possible to genetically modify or edited avocados, which remains a controversial proposition. While GM avocados have not yet made it onto the supermarket shelves, the technology now exists to make it happen. The next question is whether society wants them.

NOTES

1 Barber, Gregory, "The long, lonely quest to breed the ultimate avocado." *Wired*, 2017, January 5.

2 Ibid.

3 Rendón-Anaya, Martha, et al., The avocado genome informs deep angiosperm phylogeny, highlights introgressive hybridization, and reveals pathogen-influenced gene space adaptation. *PNAS*, 2019, August 6.

4 Yaffe-Bellany, David, "Avocado toast, meet Gene editing." *The New York Times*, 2019, September 27.

5 Karlis, Nicole, "Hass Avocados have been genetically sequenced, but is that a good thing?" *Salon*, 2019, August 7.

6 University at Buffalo, "Guacamole lovers, rejoice! The avocado genome has been sequenced." *ScienceDaily*, 2019, August 6.

7 Yaffe-Bellany, "Avocado Toast, Meet Gene Editing.".

8 Sirinathsinghji, Eva, "Study confirms GM crops lead to increased pesticide use." *Science in Society Archive*, 2012, August 11.

9 The Non-GMO Project, "How do GMOs affect biodiversity." 2022.

10 World Health Organization, "Food safety: Pesticide residue." 2016, May 16.

11 Environmental Working Group, "Clean 15: EWG's 2022 shoppers guide to pesticides in produce." 2022.

12 The World Bank, "GDP per capita (current US$) –Burkina Faso." https://data.worldbank.org/indicator/NY.GDP.PCAP.CD?locations=BF.

13 Luna, Jessie, & Dowd-Uribe, Brian, "Power and GM cotton in Burkina Faso." Ecologist, 2020, September 2.

14 Laird, Lynda, "India's farmer suicides: Are deaths linked to GM cotton? – In pictures." The Guardian, 2014, May 4.

15 Malone, Andrew, "The GM genocide: Thousands of Indian farmers are committing suicide after using genetically modified crops." Daily Mail, 2008, November 2.

16 Canadian Biotechnology Action Network, "Wheat." https://cban.ca/gmos/products/not-on-the-market/wheat/.

17 Garrison, Cassandra, & Barrera, Adriana, "EXCLUSIVE Mexico to proceed with GMO corn ban, seeks international grain deals -official." Reuters, 2022, October 27.

18 Reuters, "U.S. threatens legal steps over Mexico's planned GMO corn ban." 2022, November.

KEY READINGS

• Barber, Gregory, "The long, lonely quest to breed the ultimate avocado." Wired, 2017, January 5.

• Environmental Working Group, "Clean 15: EWG's 2022 Shoppers Guide to Pesticides in Produce." 2022.

• Karlis, Nicole, "Hass Avocados have been Genetically Sequenced, but is that a Good Thing?" Salon, 2019, August 7.

• Yaffe-Bellany, David, "Avocado toast, meet gene editing." The New York Times, 2019, September 27.

EPILOGUE

The goal of this book has been to highlight that, when it comes to food choices, everything is a trade-off. In our modern food system, there are no simple answers, and the avocado is a perfect symbol of this interplay. Hopefully, after reading each chapter, the reader has progressively gained more and more insight into the complexity that underlies the skin of this fruit.

The place it has come to occupy on our supermarket shelves is not accidental. The fruit's journey from the gullets of megafauna in Puebla in the Pleistocene to a brunch staple of Bondi beach was a result of carefully orchestrated decisions that turned the avocado into the commodity crop that we know today. That journey began in the colonial period when Europeans first discovered the fruit and escalated when they realised that its high-density fatty flesh could be used to efficiently feed enslaved workers across the world. Its reputation continued to be transformed from those initial European perceptions, and it has come to occupy a high-profile position in our culture due to the coordinated actions of Californian growers that cultivated its image and positioned it for a bright (and lucrative) future. The continuous investment in its marketing has successfully pivoted it towards affluent white shoppers, starting in the 1920s when racism was rife and its associations with Latino culture was a turn-off for American housewives. This journey continues today in the pages of women's magazines and social media platforms where it is presented as a "superfood," on the menus of trendy Millennial brunch spots where it is shown as a "clean eating miracle" and on Super Bowl Sunday as thousands crunch on guacamole and chips. Given this global reputation and growing fame, it's only logical that farmers across the world are trying to get into the green gold that avocados can bring and the profit that can be made from their production.

In addition to its history, The Avocado Debate also considered the challenges that the avocado faces today, conveying the complexity of the fruit's production. The impact that irrigation, fertiliser, and pesticides have on the ecosystem can be significant and can cause wide ranging damage to both nature and local communities. Fisherfolk and community healers are no longer able to practise their profession as freshwater dries up, having knock-on impacts on local traditions and livelihoods. Similarly, the change in land use as native land is converted into avocado orchards can result in biodiversity loss and can permanently alter natural systems. The hillsides of Michoacán can testify to the decline in native pines due to the rise of avocado orchards, and the associated loss of keystone species like pumas, and jaguars, and the eye-catching monarch butterflies, not to mention the less photogenic insects. While there is increasing awareness of the damage caused by intensive monoculture production, the adoption of agroecological measures that might present solutions has not been as rapid as they could have been. In part, this is because of market dynamics, driven by a globalised food system that demands fruit all year round, delivered by shipping containers endlessly crisscrossing the oceans.

Buy an avocado from Mexico and you might be supporting the activities of a drug cartel. Choose one from Chile and you might be furthering the extraction of much-needed freshwater while a Colombian one might be associated with high pesticide usage and pollinator decline. Yet, those avocados might have less negative impacts than other food choices. If it's the decision between topping your salad with an industrially produced chicken breast from a factory farm, a scattering of Iranian pistachios, or a Peruvian avocado, then the avocado might be the better option for both public and environmental health outcomes. That said, a handful of locally grown beans might be the best option.

Furthermore, one can question the equity of avocados in a globalised world when the fruit's production can be associated with land grabs and structural inequalities. Fruit grown in the Global South on behalf of the Global North sees local farms transformed into monoculture fields for export and denying communities the right to decide what is best for themselves.

But, on the other side, one could argue that investment into large-scale export agriculture brings much-needed money into a poor community that would otherwise suffer from a lack of opportunity. And if they aren't to be grown in the Global South, what happens when farmers try to grow them in the Global North? Growing them in Spain or Portugal that might be more "local" to their final point of sale also creates significant environmental impacts, particularly with a changing climate. Nor does buying a Fairtrade or Organic provide a perfect solution either, even if you can stomach the added expense. The certification schemes are not without their loopholes and flaws, and they do not offer a panacea to the ills of production that have been examined. Urging people to simply buy more expensive certified options is simplistic and reductive. While they provide some reassurance over the method of production and can be a useful tool, they are not a "get out of jail free" card for your avocado conundrum. Moreover, the prohibitive price acts as a barrier to the poorest in our society that have the greatest need for fresh produce.

The Avocado Debate focused on providing more information with which to weigh the impact of each food choice so that each individual reader can consider what is the right decision for them. In the most immediate, this might mean whether to buy avocados at all! Or it might mean deciding which ones to buy. That decision is personal and depends on each individual's priorities. Is the carbon footprint the primary concern? Or is it just one factor amongst many? How does the water stress of avocado production to a wider region measure up against the economic opportunity that it brings to one individual farmer? After reading this book, each reader should be better able to consider these questions – even if you don't yet have the answers.

More than that, while this conversation has focused on just one individual fruit, it will help to inform about every food choice, not just the avocado. Our food system is unendingly complicated. We might first think of how it impacts the communities that grow it and the people that consume it, but in reality, it will impact everyone along the supply chain from those that invest in the farm, to the truckers, to the cold-storage packers to the chefs who prepare the final dish. It's connected to our economic and social history. Food comes to us with layers of cultural context fostered upon it: some intentionally, some unintentionally. It has direct consequences for our planet, driving both the Climate and Ecological Emergencies, but also in adopting more regenerative practices that help the world to heal.

And so, *The Avocado Debate* closes without resolution, which might be frustrating to readers who wanted to get a clear answer as to whether they should eat avocado toast or not. The debate will continue. More importantly, the debate should continue. We should continue to question our food choices and weigh the impact that they have on the world around us. We need to stop mindlessly throwing things into a shopping basket. Instead, we need to make informed choices where we consider the consequences, whether good or bad. Hopefully, this book has provided some food for thought, and now, every time you order a bowl of guacamole, or add a Hass to your weekly online shop, you will pause and recall how multifaceted a journey it has had to reach you.

INDEX